A RACE FOR MADMEN

A RACE FOR MADMEN

THE EXTRAORDINARY HISTORY OF THE TOUR DE FRANCE

Chris Sidwells

Collins

First published in 2010 by Collins
an imprint of HarperCollins*Publishers*
77–85 Fulham Palace Road
London W6 8JB

www.harpercollins.co.uk

1 3 5 7 9 10 8 6 4 2

A catalogue record for this book
is available from the British Library

ISBN: 978-0-00-732141-4

Printed and bound in Great Britain by
Clays Ltd, St Ives plc

Mixed Sources
Product group from well-managed
forests and other controlled sources
www.fsc.org Cert no. SW-COC-001806
© 1996 Forest Stewardship Council
FSC

FSC is a non-profit international organisation established to promote the
responsible management of the world's forests. Products carrying the FSC
label are independently certified to assure consumers that they come
from forests that are managed to meet the social, economic and
ecological needs of present and future generations.

Find out more about HarperCollins and the environment at
www.harpercollins.co.uk/green

CONTENTS

1. A TOUR IS BORN

The noise of a racer's feet scrapes out of the darkness as he drags his bike to a halt outside Fougères in eastern Brittany. It's September 1891, the racer is Charles Terront, one of 206 pedalling pioneers who set out from Paris nearly two days ago. They are racing non-stop from the French capital to Brest, the Atlantic port at the tip of the Breton peninsula, and back to Paris again, a distance of 1,200 kilometres.

Fougères is a control town. Terront must stop at a lamp-lit huddle of officials, have his race card marked with the official stamp, then hurtle off into the night again. Six hours will pass before his nearest rival, Jacques Jiel-Laval, arrives here, and Terront will be even further ahead by the time he reaches Paris, where he will win in a time of 71 hours and 22 minutes.

Paris–Brest–Paris was the turning point in the early history of the bicycle. A steerable wooden-framed, two-wheeled vehicle was invented in 1817, but it was scooted along the road by the rider's feet. In 1861 a Parisian coach-builder, Pierre Michaux, attached pedals to the front wheel of one of these hobby-horses and called his invention the *vélocipède*.

That was the first bicycle, and it was quickly followed by the first bicycle race. The place was the Parc St Cloud, Paris, the date was 31 May 1868 and the winner was an Englishman called James Moore. Later the same year Moore won the first race on the open road, 120 kilometres from Paris to Rouen. More road races followed and banked tracks called *vélodromes* were built for racing in front of huge crowds.

Bike racing became very popular, but cycling itself was less so. Then came Paris–Brest–Paris, and it finally underlined the possibilities of this new machine. The 'safety cycle' had been launched in England by James Starley in 1885. It was a chain-driven bike, made from metal with a double-triangle frame, not so dissimilar to bikes today. Terront used a safety cycle to win this great race.

The race organiser, Pierre Giffard, was a committed cyclist who was evangelic in promoting cycling and the editor of one of the first bicycle publications, which was called *Le Vélo*. He fervently believed in the bike as a form of recreation and transport, and was determined to make others see the potential of a machine that could be ridden such vast distances.

Ninety-nine riders finished Paris–Brest–Paris behind Terront, the slowest only just beating the cut-off time of ten days, but that wasn't the point. The important thing for Giffard was that they all came through unscathed, confounding prevailing medical opinion that human beings trying to cover such huge distances by their own power would damage themselves and maybe even die.

After the race Giffard wrote in the editorial of his magazine: 'For the first time we saw a new mode of travel, a new road to adventure, a new vista of pleasure. Even the slowest of these cyclists averaged 130 kilometres a day for ten days, yet they arrived fresh and healthy. The most skilful and gallant horseman could not do better. Aren't we on the threshold of a new and wonderful world?'

Actually, we were. Young, upper-class men had already taken to the bicycle, showing off their skills on the road and racing on flat cinder tracks all over Europe, similar to the ones they used for running races. They rode 'ordinary' bikes, or penny-farthings, clumsy great things with one huge wheel in front and a tiny balancing one behind it. Penny-farthings were difficult to ride because the pedals were fixed directly to the giant front wheel. One pedal turn equalled one turn of the wheel, so to go faster the wheels had to get bigger. Not everyone could ride a penny-farthing.

The safety cycle changed that. Chain drive to the rear wheel meant gearing, so the rear wheel revolved several times for each revolution of the pedals. With this set-up wheels could be of equal sizes and the rider wasn't perched high up in the sky. He or she could stop, still seated in the saddle, and place both feet on the ground.

Anyone could ride one of these bikes and, because they were much cheaper than a horse, the bicycle became the first truly accessible mode of transport for working people. Before the bike most members of the working class were born, grew up and died without straying far from their village or part of town. Steam trains opened up the possibility of excursions, but these were expensive and had to be saved for and planned, and even then you could only go where the train went.

The bicycle meant freedom. Working people had never experienced anything like it. Bikes gave them mobility, and as the twentieth century approached, a huge market began to grow. To tap into it, manufacturers needed to show that their bikes were the best, the most durable, and long-distance bike races were the best place to do it. Bike racing had only just found its feet as an amateur sport; now it was going professional.

Those early pros were a tough breed, not that they are softies now. Off their bikes modern pro racers will whinge and grumble about not being on form, or having this pain or that ache, but on their bikes they are a different breed. Pro bike racing is a hard, uncompromising, uncomfortable, often brutal calling. Even the best lose more often than they win. All of them will crash or suffer hardships, but they keep coming back for more. It's always been the same, but today no one ever endures what the first professionals faced in every race.

Paris–Brest–Paris was the longest road race in this new sport, so long that after the first one they didn't organise another for ten years, but by the late 1890s there were several other long-distance races: Bordeaux–Paris was nearly 600 kilometres. Plus there were 24-hour races on velodromes, and some that lasted six days. No rest was ever officially set aside in these races – the clock kept running. If a rider wanted to sleep he did so in his own time, as the race went on around him.

Anyone who could stay awake and keep going had a significant advantage over the rest, a fact that led some riders to experiment. The 1896 Bordeaux–Paris was won by a Welshman, Arthur Linton. At Tours, just over half-way through the race, an eyewitness described Linton coming through the control point 'with glassy eyes and tottering limbs and in a high state of nervous excitement'. The eyewitness, whose name has been lost, was working as an assistant to a man hired by Linton called 'Choppy' Warburton.

Warburton, a former professional runner, now earned his living as a trainer of professional runners and cyclists. It was a lucrative business. Linton was of Welsh mining stock and cycling was his path out of the pits. When Linton won he earned money. Warburton's training produced results, so Linton paid him a percentage of his winnings. The higher Linton finished in a race, the more they both earned. But training didn't just mean proscribing a number of miles to be ridden at such and such a pace; Warburton advised his clients on what to eat and looked after them when they raced and trained in other ways too.

The eyewitness in Bordeaux–Paris says that Linton staggered on, just about maintaining his lead, but later, at Orleans, he stopped again. The Welshman was in a really bad way and on the verge of collapse. Warburton delved into the big black bag he always carried with him and administered various substances to Linton. From that moment the racer was renewed. He rallied, gained 18 minutes more on the second-placed rider and won the race. However, Linton died a few months later, the cause of death given as typhoid. He was 24.

Even young people as fit and strong as Linton did die of typhoid in those days, so his death can't be laid unequivocally at Warburton's door although people have tried to do so. However, the story suggests that Choppy's black bag contained things a lot stronger than smelling salts and mineral water. Long-distance pro cycling, where races require almost superhuman exertion but their outcome can affect hundreds of people working for a business, was a sport made for doping, and the two would walk hand in hand down through the ages.

But don't put this book down in disgust. Professional sport is also made for double deals, Machiavellian schemes and straightforward cheating; all of which have touched the Tour de France, just as they have other sports. But the Tour has something else, something more. It has a beauty and sense of theatre that captures you and drags you in. Its reason for being has always been the cold hard sell, but the Tour de France throws up heroes, and its spectacle can take your breath away.

Bike racing is like that. It might be fuelled by sponsorship, but passion keeps it alive. It would not have grown without capturing people's hearts and minds, which brings us to the real reason that the Tour de France was created. The early races provoked a thirst for news, and at the turn of the twentieth century the only way that thirst could be quenched was through specialist sports newspapers. It was a battle between two of these newspapers that gave birth to the Tour de France.

Cycling had its biggest following in France, where Pierre Giffard's *Le Vélo* was the leading magazine. A lot of this was due to the fact that Giffard had managed to wrest a stifling advantage over his rivals by becoming the official voice of the governing body of French cycling. So as well as extensive and flowery race reports, and grainy black and white pictures of tough-looking men battling along dusty country roads clad in tight-fitting clothes, *Le Vélo* published the locations and times when races started and finished. If you were into cycling you had to buy *Le Vélo*.

With that in his pocket things were ticking along quite nicely for Giffard, but then he became involved in the Dreyfus affair. This was a case that shook France to its core, as it flagged up prejudice that was occurring in Europe every day. A Jewish army officer, Alfred Dreyfus, was framed by a section of the French military for treason. The case sent shock waves through society, setting people against one another, but eventually it changed the way France thought. And while that was happening it inadvertently led to the birth of the Tour de France.

Captain Dreyfus was convicted in 1895 and sent to the French penal colony, Devil's Island. His Jewish heritage and the fact that he was born in Mulhouse in Alsace, which at the time was part of Germany having been taken during the Franco-Prussian war of 1870, was enough evidence to convict him of passing artillery secrets to the Germans.

However, even some members of the French army weren't convinced, and one of them, Lieutenant-Colonel Picquart, came up with some credible evidence that the real traitor was a Major Ferdinand Esterhazy. At first the French high command wouldn't listen and Picquart was transferred to Tunisia to keep him quiet, but the problem wouldn't go away and reports of a cover-up were leaked to the press.

A campaign led by artists and intellectuals, including the novelist Emile Zola, succeeded in gaining a pardon for Dreyfus in 1899, but the case stirred deep emotions and nearly ripped the country apart. Families, businesses, the arts – nothing was immune from the passions and opinions the affair generated. Everyone talked about it, and most people were firmly on one side or the other.

One of *Le Vélo*'s financial backers, the Count de Dion, an aristocratic and anti-semitic firebrand, was arrested for demonstrating against the campaign to pardon Dreyfus. Giffard, though, was pro-Dreyfus and a man of principle. So, caring little for his career, he criticised De Dion in an article he wrote for the highbrow publication *Le Petit Journal*. De Dion was outraged, and even though he was imprisoned at the time, promptly withdrew all his money from *Le Vélo*.

Unfortunately for Giffard, he then upset a number of advertisers in *Le Vélo* by charging higher and higher rates, and most of them were friends of De Dion. So when he was released, De Dion formed his own sports newspaper, *L'Auto-Vélo*, funded by his engine manufacturing business and by his disgruntled friends, who included Edouard Michelin, the biggest tyre manufacturer in France.

Their new venture needed an editor, and since their plan was to teach Giffard a lesson and steal his readership, they needed someone young and ambitious who knew about sport, but especially knew about cycling. They approached a 35-year-old former racer who had worked in advertising but then ran the biggest velodrome in Paris, the Parc des Princes. His name was Henri Desgrange.

Desgrange had a law degree but he wasn't cut out for the staid world of the Paris courts. When he started work he was a racer first and a lawyer second, and one day a client of the firm he worked for saw Desgrange pedalling furiously through a Paris park. The client complained to Desgrange's boss, pointing out that this was very unseemly behaviour for a man of the law, especially since Desgrange was wearing three-quarter-length breeches that exposed his calves. The firm agreed and Desgrange was sacked.

But they say you can't keep a good man down and Desgrange, showing the survival instincts that would see him through many a future struggle, switched careers, quickly becoming the head of advertising for the tyre manufacturer, Clément et Cie. And all the while he continued racing, setting a world record for the furthest distance ridden in one hour in 1895.

The hour record would later become a measure of cycling greatness, and setting it was definitely the height of Desgrange's racing career, even if his record was soon eclipsed. But what Desgrange lacked in the legs he made up for with business acumen, and with his power as a writer. While working in advertising he wrote articles on cycling for various newspapers, including *Le Vélo*, and he wrote a best-selling book on training called *The Head and the Legs*.

By the time Desgrange left advertising to take over managing the Parc de Princes he had a big following in French cycling, and he had made a lot of influential friends. De Dion was very shrewd when he asked him to head up his new project. It was 1900, the beginning of a new century, but starting a new publication, no matter how right it is for its age, has never been easy. Giffard was in a strong position: he had the backing of the French Cycling Federation, and he still had a lot of advertisers behind him because he'd only pushed up the rates for De Dion's associates. He also held the moral high ground because of his stand over Dreyfus. Then he won a very important battle in the courts by forcing *L'Auto-Vélo* to drop the word *Vélo* from their title.

At the time of what was then *L'Auto-Vélo*'s launch, bikes had to be registered for tax in France. Official figures put ownership at one million, but officials cannot be everywhere and probably twice that amount were being ridden around the countryside without being recorded. The bike market was huge, but Desgrange was now trying to tap into it with a magazine called *L'Auto*, meaning 'The Car'. His newspaper covered both motor racing and cycling, plus some other outdoor pursuits, but bikes had the mass market and so provoked the most interest. A publication created to tap into cycling but called 'The Car' was going to have a bleak future, unless its editor could think of something.

He tried to clarify the situation by printing the words motoring and cycling underneath the *L'Auto* masthead. He also listed the other adventurous pursuits *L'Auto* covered underneath the title, but it was still clumsy.

Desgrange was losing. Cycling was growing, but his circulation was static and advertisers started to complain. Then Giffard made it personal, he began to goad Desgrange. It never pays to gloat. The ex-bike rider's competitive spirit was stirred. He knew the magazine needed something slick, maybe a publicity stunt, that would attract people's attention beyond its title. Desgrange called a meeting of his staff and told them. 'We need to do something big, a big promotion. Something that will nail Giffard's beak shut.'

L'Auto had had a young cycling reporter called Geo Lefèvre, who was poached by Desgrange from *Le Vélo*. Lefèvre left because he believed in Desgrange and in what he was doing, but now his precarious position set him thinking. Lefèvre was really into cycling; he knew the pro riders and their fans. He raced as an amateur and he watched the pros whenever he could. Lefèvre knew it was long-distance road racers who had the biggest following, and the only way to switch their fans' attention to *L'Auto* was to promote the longest road race there was.

There was something noble about the fortitude of bike racers battling through heat and rain for kilometre after endless kilometre that struck a chord with the French. Some social scientists say it's because, up until mid-way through the twentieth century, France was an agricultural country. People who worked on the land day in and day out appreciated raw competition spiced with a battle against the elements and unyielding nature. It's as good an explanation as any, but what is certain in that the

French love of long-distance bike racing was real, so one day Lefèvre plucked up the courage to tell Desgrange that he had an idea and wanted to talk it over with him.

It was a big idea, and if successful would put *L'Auto* firmly at the centre of French cycling. Lefèvre wanted *L'Auto* to promote and organise a race, but not just any old race: it would be the longest bike race there had ever been. He discussed it with his editor one day over lunch. Lefèvre first told Desgrange that his race would last more than six days, the longest bike races so far having been six-day races on the track. Then came the bombshell. He wanted his race to be a circuit of France, internally replicating the hexagonal shape of the country. And it would start and finish in Paris.

The idea was huge and scary. At first, as often happened in the Tour's early story, Desgrange was sceptical, put off even. 'What you are suggesting, my little Geo, is a Tour de France,' he told his young colleague. But then Desgrange considered those words: Tour de France. The two spoke no more about it over their lunch, or in the office, but as the words rolled around in his head, Desgrange began to think.

A Tour de France already existed, and it had been a big part of French rural life for years. It was a rite of passage for apprentices. A tradition that began in Provence and the Languedoc region whereby a boy who wanted to learn a trade would be sent by that trade's guild on a journey between towns, roughly in a hexagon around the outside of the Massif-Central.

In each town he learned the skills and lore of his chosen craft and was looked after by a network of guild mothers. The boys gave up their names, each being referred to by his region, and when he left a town to move on to the next, a noisy procession of drums and fiddles led him into the surrounding countryside.

Every boy's Tour lasted four or five years, by which time he was a man and had become a 'Compagnon du Tour de France'. His regional name would have also taken on a quality that had been noted by his guild as he passed from place to place. One man's experiences of this Tour are recorded by Agricol Perdigeur, a cabinet maker from Avignon whose guild name was Avignonnais-le-Vertu, in a book called *Les Mémoires d'un Compagnon* (Memoirs of a Companion), published in 1854.

If it sounds idyllic, it wasn't. Life on the road was tough for these youngsters, and the 'mothers' they passed between were in it for the money. Also, there was a fierce rivalry between guilds, and boys were often involved in bloody battles when they met rival trades on the road. Even well into the twentieth century rural France was a tough place with tough values, fierce local pride and a very narrow, parochial view of things. Those values and views would badly affect the first cycling Tours de France.

Left to mull it over at his own pace, Desgrange slowly warmed to the Tour de France idea. Lefèvre backed off, sat on his hands and tried not to let his enthusiasm get the better of him. As he would prove time and again Lefèvre, and the rest of *L'Auto*'s staff, knew exactly how to handle Desgrange to get the decision they wanted out of him.

Finally, in late January 1903, Desgrange had decided, and after further talks with Lefèvre and his staff he made this announcement in the pages of *L'Auto*: 'We intend to run the greatest cycling trial in the entire world. A race more than a month long; from Paris to Lyon, then to Marseille, Toulouse, Bordeaux, Nantes and back to Paris.'

The race was initially scheduled to run for five weeks, from the end of May until 5 July, but as the summer approached it became obvious that the length of time an entrant had to commit to the race was attracting a limited field of top professionals. That wouldn't do; Desgrange needed a spectacle. He wanted a big field with a big story, but lots of smaller ones besides, so he cut the duration, although not the distance, to just under three weeks.

He also put back the dates so that the Tour de France would run at the same time as something that was becoming a feature of French life, their annual two-week holiday. That was a masterstroke and one of the keys to the Tour's success. To French people the Tour de France heralds the coming of summer, the holidays and happy memories. As much as anything that happy association has helped the Tour weather its bad times.

The first Tour de France was 2,428 kilometres long, split into six stages with between two and four days of rest between each one. You don't have to be a mathematician to work out that 2,428 divided by six means a lot of kilometres per stage: the shortest was 268 kilometres and the longest 471. Two or three days between stages were not only needed for the top men to recover, but for the stragglers to finish. The last man on the first stage was on the road for ten hours short of two days!

And no wonder. The riders had to make over 480 kilometres on highways of hammered stone chips, or country roads rutted by cart wheels and pock-marked by livestock. If it was hot, the roads were iron hard and covered with choking dust. If it rained, they became a sea of mud.

Then there were the bikes. Steel frames and handlebars, wooden wheel rims and big balloon tyres. Brakes worked by pulling a lever so a steel rod pushed a leather pad directly on to the tyre tread. The bikes were heavy, 15 kilograms or more, and they had just one gear. Well, they had two, but the rider had to stop and remove the rear wheel to place the chain on the other sprocket.

It would be tough. The 78 men who finally signed up for the whole Tour – a few extra riders elected to ride a single stage that was local to them – were racing into the unknown. They were a mix of racing stars and have-a-go heroes. A few raced under pseudonyms because the pro riders were a rough breed of mercenaries and some participants, who maybe came from posh families, didn't want their real names to be known. The one that stands out most on the start list was a Belgian who called himself Samson.

In the end 60 entrants came to the start outside a café called Au Reveil Matin in Montgeron, which is now part of Paris but was then a small satellite town. It was three o'clock in the afternoon on 1 July 1903. The café is still there, on the Rue Jean-Jaurès, and a plaque outside it records the first Tour. There have been changes during the intervening 106 years, but it is still a working café and restaurant. The surprise, though, is that there are no souvenirs from the first Tour de France – they have all been stolen.

The favourites were Joseph Fischer of Germany and two Frenchmen: Hippolyte Aucouturier and Maurice Garin, who was marginally the best rider so was given race number one. Garin was 1.60 metres tall, weighed 60 kilos, and he was a successful full-time pro racer who had taken up cycling at the age of 21 after a tough start in life.

He was born in the Aosta valley in the Italian Alps, so close to the French border that his native language was French. A legend grew up that Garin was swapped by his father for a wheel of cheese when he was quite young. A lot of children were traded in the poorer areas of France. Even babies, who were collected by unscrupulous entrepreneurs, stuffed into tube-like saddle bags and flung across the backs of ponies for the march to Paris. The noisy ones were drugged with wine, and a lot of them didn't make it.

The true tale of Garin's family is much more caring. Maurice was the eldest of nine children, but their father struggled to feed them in the remote Alps. Jobs were plentiful in the industrial north of France, so Monsieur Garin decided to move his whole family there. However, special permission was required for such a move, which Garin couldn't get. He decided to go ahead anyway, but taking the whole family in one go would attract attention, so Garin's father decided to move his kids in ones and twos.

Boys from the Alps were fearless climbers who made good chimney-sweeps, and one of the trades in children was a steady stream of young males from the mountains to Paris and other French cities to work in the smoke and soot. The children were met by gang masters from their own regions and put to work. When he was 15 Maurice did work for a while in the chimneys of Rheims, but he soon moved to join a brother who was already living with a relation near the Belgian border, and one by one the family joined him.

Being sold as a chimney-sweep for a piece of cheese was just a cover, but the idea of the diminutive Tour de France winner starting his working life scrabbling in the dark and covered with soot was too romantic to ignore, so the 'Little Sweep' nickname stuck for the rest of Garin's life.

Once he became established as a bike racer Garin made his name in 24-hour races, where the winner was the rider who covered the most distance in a day. He quickly graduated to long road races, like the Paris–Roubaix, which he won in 1897. Then in 1901 he dominated the longest race of all, Paris–Brest–Paris. The Tour de France was made for Garin.

He won the first stage, 467 kilometres from Paris to Lyon, in 17 hours 45 minutes and 13 seconds. It's a tiring drive, especially in summer, even if you do it on the A6 Autoroute, but Garin averaged 26 kilometres per hour, beating his closest rival, Emile Pagie by under a minute. The rest were spread out behind them, with the last rider, Eugène Brange, taking more than 38 hours to reach Lyon.

But even Brange did better than many. Twenty-two riders didn't get to Lyon, casualties of unfortunate mishaps or just too tired to continue. The spread of abilities in the first Tour was incredible: some were full-time pros but others had hardly ridden a bike at all. Jean Dargassies, a blacksmith from Toulouse, only completed his first-ever bike ride two months before the Tour, but he must have been a natural because he was 23rd on the first stage, just six and a quarter hours behind Garin, and he improved as the Tour went on.

The big news of the first stage was the retirement of Hippolyte Aucouturier. Hippolyte – the name must be the French equivalent of Cuthbert because you don't get many Hippolytes in France today – suffered stomach cramps, but was allowed to contest the next stage, although he was removed from the overall standings.

And Aucouturier won stage two. Riding out of Lyon the riders climbed the Col de la République, not a big mountain – they would come later – but still a long pull over the Pilat chain just south of St Etienne. Aucouturier broke away with Léon Georget to win the 374-kilometre leg to Marseilles, while Garin did enough to preserve his lead. Stage one runner-up Pagie dropped out, and Brange, the tail-end Charlie, finished third. It was already a mad race.

Not that Desgrange described it that way. He was the master of his own invention, and of one that French cycling journalists still aspire to: writing flowery prose in which sports contestants are portrayed as superheroes who right wrongs and fight the twin ogres of adverse conditions and hard luck. To this heady mix they sprinkle in a little brotherly rivalry to spice things up. 'With the broad and powerful swing of the hand which Zola in *The Earth* gave to his ploughman, *L'Auto*, newspaper of ideas and action, is going to fling across France today those reckless and uncouth sowers of energy who are the great professional riders of the road,' is how Desgrange introduced the first stage of the Tour in his editorial of 1 July 1903. And it is how he carried on writing as the Tour de France grew.

Maurice Garin won two more stages before ending up the winner of the first Tour de France and 6,000 gold francs, a sum equivalent to what a manual worker from the town of Lens, where Garin lived, would earn in nine years. The French tax rate in 1903 was less than ten per cent. As an established pro racer Garin wasn't badly off before the Tour de France, but now he was rich.

But if the Tour de France made Garin rich, it was nothing to what it did for Desgrange and *L'Auto*. The paper's circulation had been bumping along between 20,000 and 30,000 copies a day, but it grew to 65,000 copies during the Tour. Ten years later its average circulation was 120,000 a day, rising to a quarter of a million when the race was on. Big numbers by today's standards, although not so big when compared with the million a day then printed by papers with a broader spread of news. Newsprint was as big a deal at the turn of the twentieth century as the internet is now.

When the Tour arrived in Paris, there were 20,000 people waiting in the Parc des Princes Velodrome to welcome the 21 riders who had survived every stage. Even more thronged the city streets outside to goggle as the first riders weaved their way through the capital. Garin won the final stage in just over 18 hours, but not many spectators stayed on to see Pierre Desvages finish 12 and a half hours after him.

It had been a big adventure, not only for the riders but also for the organisers. After the racers were flagged away from the start of each stage, Fernand Mercier of *L'Auto* would set off in his car to drive to the finish, where he would liaise with the paper's local correspondent to find accommodation for the riders who made it through and wanted to continue. At the same time Geo Lefèvre would join in with the riders on his own bike to get on-the-spot reports from the top men as they raced. Lefèvre would slowly drop through the field, doing interviews as he did so, until he arrived at the first major town with a train service to the stage finish. The idea was that he could then jump ahead of the race and help Mercier check everyone in.

However, neither Mercier nor Lefèvre made it through to Lyon on the first stage before Garin did, so they had to rely on him to provide his own finishing time. Route finding was also largely down to the riders, which is why only main roads were used in the first Tours and the stages were in more or less a straight line between towns.

Still, Desgrange was very happy. Between them, Lefèvre, Mercier, his local correspondents and the riders got themselves around France without too much incident, except sporting ones of course, about which he could wax lyrical in *L'Auto*, and he was selling a lot more newspapers. He decided that the race would go ahead again in 1904. However, Desgrange hadn't taken into account the passions his race had aroused around the country. They would be difficult to tame in 1904.

2. GROWING PAINS

The first Tour de France was a success, but the second was nearly the last as the interest and passions it aroused grew out of control. The fans were one problem that would beset the 1904 Tour; the other was the win-at-all-costs ambition of those who took part.

France at the turn of the twentieth century was still a quite wild place. Most of the country was given over to agriculture, with just a few areas, most notably in the north, dominated by industry. Life was tough in the cities, mining villages and steel mills, but it was tougher in the countryside, where everything was magnified by a sense of local identity, or what the French call 'pays'. Suspicion was rife, and anyone you didn't know was an enemy who had come to do you down.

The route in 1904 was the same as before, but this time the fans were ready. Each set wanted the men from their own region to do well, and for some that actually meant delaying or even beating up their rivals. Aucouturier was the first to be hit. Once the bunch thinned out south of Paris, the first few riders were allowed through a lonely stretch of road, but Aucouturier raced on to a carpet of tin tacks spread across it. He punctured, fitted a new tyre and carried on, only to find another patch of tacks and pick up another puncture. He ended up two and a half hours behind the stage winner.

Later, close to Lyon, Garin and Lucien Pothier were well ahead of the rest, but they weren't from the area, so a bunch of locals tried to run them off the road in a car. They survived, but then the first evidence of riders cheating hit the race. Garin was getting food outside of the stipulated feeding zones, and he was getting it from the Tour organisation, having threatened to pull out if they didn't co-operate. There were reports of other riders getting lifts in cars, even taking the train, and one who was towed by a car using a cord that he held between his teeth. And this was just the first day.

Next day the riders climbed the Col de la République. At the start a racer from St Etienne, Antoine Fauré, was lying in tenth place, so some locals decided that everyone ahead of him should be slowed down and stopped if possible. A group of them hid in the pine woods on the climb, waiting for the riders. Garin was first through with an Italian, Giovanni Gerbi, and when the Fauré supporters saw them they jumped out into the road and set about them with sticks. Race officials weren't too far behind and tried to help, but it took Desgrange firing pistol shots into the air to disperse the mob. Garin carried on, but Gerbi suffered broken fingers and had to quit the race.

The next stage passed through Nimes, close to the home of another rider, Ferdinand Payan, and it all kicked off again. Men from Payan's village barricaded the street once their man had gone through town, and Desgrange had to get his gun out again. The Tour was totally out of control. The race staggered on to Paris, the organisers frequently having to enlist the police to help it do so. Passions were running so high that it was frightening.

The organisation had another problem. They had documented evidence of wholesale cheating by the riders that was enough to disqualify the first four overall in Paris, plus many others, but they were too frightened to use it. Instead they secretly presented a case to French cycling's governing body, who backed up the Tour organiser's decision to disqualify, but decided to delay the announcement until December 1904. Every one of the riders had probably cut some of the route. The stages were so long and in places so remote that they were difficult to police, but Garin, Pothier, Garin's brother César and Hippolyte Aucouturier, the first four, plus others, were all deemed to have cheated beyond any tolerable level.

They were all disqualified, and 20-year-old Henri Cornet was declared the winner. He is still the youngest winner of the Tour de France. Garin was outraged, as were the others. None of them would admit what they'd done, at least not straightaway. Garin stuck it out until he was quite old. By then he was running a garage in Lens, and he would laugh about it with friends: 'Of course I took the train, everyone did. I was young, the Tour was different. It didn't matter as much as it does now,' he would say.

The cheating riders were suspended from racing for two years, and you could almost taste Desgrange's despair as he wrote in *L'Auto*, 'The Tour de France is over. I very much fear that its second edition will have been its last. It has been killed by its own success.' It was a sham. He'd already set about organising Tour de France number three. He never missed an opportunity to milk public sympathy.

This Tour was different, a little longer but with shorter and therefore more stages. Desgrange decided that stages would start and finish outside of towns, and divert around as many other big places of population as possible, so if angry mobs wanted to get involved they'd have to travel and it would be easier for the authorities to monitor them. A car load of peasants carrying big sticks would stand out to even the sleepiest rural policeman. The Tour would also be decided by points – one for winning a stage, two for second and so on. It was felt that shorter stages would be easier to control, and that deciding it on points rather than time would prevent fans trying to delay the riders. It didn't entirely work; the organisation estimated that 125 kilograms of nails were spread around the route in 1905.

The biggest innovation, however, came from one of Desgrange's staff, Alphonse Steines. This young man loved the mountains, and he thought that including them in the race would add to its spectacle. Desgrange wasn't sure, predicting that even the best riders wouldn't be able to ride all the way up a mountain road, which in those days were stagecoach tracks at best, and goat tracks for the rest. On top of that, some of the less fit might get hurt, if not by their efforts then by wild animals such as wolves and bears, which were still a real threat in remote regions.

Most of the official records of the Tour de France, minutes of meetings and so on, were lost during the German occupation of France in 1940 when the Tour moved its offices, but it's thought that Steines wanted to really go for it with the mountains and head for the Pyrenees in 1905. Of course with that ambitious sugges- tion he may have just been using a tactic that all his junior staff used with Desgrange: have a project in mind, show him something along the same lines only bigger, then he'd go for the one you wanted in the first place.

This is conjecture, but what's certain is that Steines got his wish and the second stage would climb a genuine mountain, the Ballon d'Alsace in the Vosges. The stage went from Nancy to Besançon, and before it began Desgrange whipped himself up into another nervous frenzy. He predicted that no rider would make it all the way up the climb without walking. As usual he was wrong. Although he is called the 'father of the Tour', in many respects Desgrange was just the man who signed the papers; it was the likes of Geo Lefèvre and Alphonse Steines who had the ideas and vision.

Anyway, it was René Pottier who proved him wrong. Not only did he ride every metre of the Ballon, he over-took Desgrange in his official car at the head of the race. He suffered for it later in the stage and had to drop out, but everybody got safely over the climb, and mountains were in the Tour de France for good.

A couple of days later the racers tackled the Col de Laffrey and Col de Bayard on a stage from Grenoble to Toulon, right down on the Mediterranean coast. This attracted huge interest because the first part, from Grenoble to Gap, the bit that included the two climbs, was a stagecoach route. Everyone wanted to see how bike racers would compare with horses over these two climbs in the foothills of the Alps. It took a coach pulled by six horses, plus four extra ones for the climbs, 12 hours to cover the 103 kilometres. Julien Maitron and Hippolyte Aucouturier did it in four, then pressed on for another 245 kilometres to Toulon, where Aucouturier won the stage.

This feat really caught the public's imagination. The mountains had a mythology about them. Here were men, skinny men at that in knitted shorts and tops, riding their funny little bicycles where Hannibal had marched his elephants, where the Romans had come to conquer an empire, and they were three times faster than a coach and six horses. By taming the mountains, cyclists became heroes, and Louis Trousselier proved to be the biggest of all when he won the Tour in 1905.

The following year René Pottier made up for his collapse after the Ballon d'Alsace in 1905 by winning the 1906 Tour with ease. The first true mountain climber of the race, or *grimpeur* as the French call them, Pottier used the hilly first half of the race to win four consecutive stages and build an unassailable lead. But despite his success Pottier always looked sad, and no wonder. It was confirmed the following winter that his wife was having an affair, and in January 1907 Pottier hanged himself from the hook where he hung his bike in his sponsor Peugeot's workshop. There is a memorial to Pottier on the Ballon d'Alsace, the first of many mountain memorials to the racers of the Tour de France.

The Tour was now three years old, but it was still difficult to control. Desgrange had a small staff and they were all needed at each stage start. They then faced a race to the stage finish to get set up there, and were often in the hands of *L'Auto*'s local correspondent, not all of whom could be described as efficient. Some staff were also needed at control points along the way, to ensure the riders did the full route. It really was wing and a prayer stuff, and always made more difficult by seeking out more spectacular countryside to race through. Desgrange's response to the problem was a draconian rule book, and it was the rule book that decided the Tour in 1907.

By half-way Emile Georget had won five out of seven stages, but then on stage nine he crashed, badly damaging his bike, and swapped it with a team-mate. This allowed him to finish, but it had all been done under the noses of race officials and it was strictly against the rules, which said that a rider had to start and finish each stage on the same bike. If it broke he had to repair it, by himself too. He could swap a part if it was broken beyond repair, but then he had to carry the part to the finish to prove that such was the case.

What happened next would happen many more times in the Tour de France. Until quite recently race directors, who are the big bosses of the Tour de France, behaved like dictators. There have only been six in all of the Tour's history, all of them men. They wrote the rules and they enforced them. They could also interpret them in any way they wished, and there was no court of appeal. Barry Hoban, a British racer who won eight stages of the Tour in the sixties and seventies, tells a great story to illustrate this. He was given a sanction by the then director Félix Lévitan and appealed vociferously – and Hoban does vociferous really well. He ended by telling Lévitan that he had no right to do what he'd done. To which Lévitan politely and simply replied, 'Dear Barry, I have every right, I am the director of the Tour de France,' and with that he turned his back and walked away.

The rule book said that Georget should be thrown off the Tour, but he was a popular rider with a big following, so Desgrange, fearing the effect that disqualification might have on L'Auto's circulation, added just enough points to Georget's total score to drop him from first to third over-all.

This gave Lucien Petit-Breton the lead, and he ran out winner of the 1907 Tour. Petit-Breton was a pseudonym for Lucien Mazan. Mazan came from Brittany but his family emigrated to Argentina when he was young and they did quite well there. As a well-to-do businessman, Mazan's father thought bike racing was too rough for his son to get involved with, so when he took up the sport in South America, where track racing was quite big, Lucien took the name Petit-Breton so his dad wouldn't find out. He ended up in France because as a French citizen still he was drafted by the army in 1902. After he served his time Petit-Breton decided to stay in France to compete in the lucrative long-distance track races there. Then he started racing on the road.

Petit-Breton won the Tour again in 1908 as part of the powerful team sponsored by Peugeot, the car and bike manufacturer. Sponsored teams were something else Desgrange didn't like. He felt they went against the individual endeavour that was the spirit of the Tour de France, and he did everything to reduce their influence on his race. In 1908 he made every rider take part on a bike supplied by the Tour. They were all identical, but Peugeot riders still won, and the manufacturer wasn't happy with Desgrange. Battle lines were drawn. Firms like Peugeot put a lot of money into cycling throughout the whole year, because by now there was a full calendar of races in Europe, but they needed publicity from the Tour de France as well.

At first Desgrange didn't listen. He suspected the pro teams. He didn't allow riders to help each other anyway, even within a team, but he also suspected the teams of fixing the results. He had more Corinthian ideas about sport, and there's no better evidence of that than the admiration Desgrange had for the privateers, or 'isolés', who raced in the early Tours. They paid their own entry fee but got a small daily allowance for their board in stage towns, which they had to find for themselves after each stage finished. The race fed them during the stages, but everything else was down to them. These men ranged from good riders who were in the race to attract the attention of a team, to total amateurs, the most notable of which was Baron Henri Pépin de Gontaud.

Baron Pépin had money. He lived in a castle near Toulouse, and he had his enthusiasms. One of them was the Tour de France. He loved reading about it, and in 1907 decided to take part himself. He was into sport, kept himself in reasonable shape, but he knew he'd be no match for the tough, working-class racers who took part in the Tour, so he decided to hire a couple of them to help him. That's how two Tour veterans, Jean Dargassies and Henri Gaubin, found themselves invited to Pépin's castle one day.

At first Dargassies and Gaubin were unconvinced. Pépin said himself that he wouldn't be able to keep up, and if they stayed with him it would cost them a fortune in lost prize money. It would also hold them up to ridicule from their fellow pros, but Pépin offered them far more than they could hope to win, and that convinced them. Anyway a couple of weeks pedalling in the sun with this eccentric aristocrat, who promised to book the best hotels and that they would eat like kings each night, wouldn't be so bad.

And so they set off from Paris on the first stage to Roubaix, taking their time at the back of the field, with the Baron waving to spectators and raising his cap to any pretty women who caught his eye. Next day, when the race went into German-occupied Alasace-Lorraine, the first excursion into a foreign country, the trio enjoyed themselves so much that they finished more than 12 hours behind the stage winner. This began to stretch the organisation's patience. They did not then have the rule they have now which allows them to disqualify anyone outside a certain percentage of the stage winner's time, and the timekeeper had to hang around for ages waiting for Pépin and his crew.

On another stage this League of Extraordinary Gentlemen found a racer lying in a ditch, exhausted by his efforts to keep up with the leaders. The organisers knew about his collapse and had simply left him there to recover, but nobility obliged Pépin to stop and offer assistance. They got the man to his feet, then on to his bike, and pushed him to the nearest inn, where Pépin ordered a four-course dinner and plenty of wine. The man they helped was so thankful that he became the fourth member of their happy band.

Sadly, the mountains proved Pépin's undoing. Stage five went into the Chartreuse, a range of pre-Alpine climbs just outside Grenoble. When he saw the fearsome Col de Port, the Baron knew that he was staring at his own limitations, so he called a halt. The four friends rode to the nearest railway station, where the Baron told the professionals that he intended to return to Toulouse. He thanked them for their help and friendship, and gave each a bundle of money that was well in excess of the 5,000 francs the Tour winner received that year.

By the time the Tour de France neared the end of the first decade of the twentieth century it was the biggest race in cycling. The field was still predominantly French, but Swiss, Italians, Germans and Belgians had also taken part. The entry list in 1909 went from 162 to 256, and Desgrange had to give way to the inevitable and allow the sponsored teams to list their riders together. But he would be watching them closely.

There were 12 teams, ranging from the Italian outfit Legnano, with six riders, down to Le Globe and Buguet-Dunlop, with just two. Added to them were 154 *isolés* from France, Switzerland, Italy and Belgium, and it was Belgium who provided the first stage winner in Cyrile Van Hauwaert.

He was the first of a breed of hard-riding professionals from Flanders, who through cycling have put their region on the map. The French used to call them Flahutes, after the long cloth bags into which itinerant labourers of northern France put their baguette loaves. They slung these on to their backs where they were secured by two shoulder loops, rather as rucksacks are today. Then they cycled from town to town looking for work in the farms and factories, sustained by taking bites out of the bread.

They were tough men, and the Flemish were tough racers. They still are, and they remain very aware of a long tradition in which the best of them are referred to as the Lions of Flanders. The name is a combination of brave imagery and a salute to the Flemish regional flag, a black lion with red tongue and claws on a yellow background. Many Flemish people still hope that one day this will be their national flag.

Van Hauwaert was the first in this long line of champions. He was the son of a brick-maker from Moorslede, in West Flanders, and he started to ride an old bike he found in a farmyard to explore his region. Years after his racing career ended Van Hauwaert wrote his autobiography, and it contains a passage that will resonate with anyone who has discovered the joy and freedom of exploring on a bike. He recalls setting off to Turhout and then going on to Bruges when he was in his mid teens. He'd been to the old Flemish city before, but this time he carried on west into an area he didn't know. 'Then the road climbed and from the top of a small hill I saw ahead of me the vast green plain of the sea, which merges far in the distance into the blurred line of the horizon. Neighbours had told me about the sea when they returned from excursions by rail, but I was so proud that my little bike had carried me to see this magical site.' Van Hauwaert might have had the heart of a lion, but he also had the soul of a poet.

Van Hauwaert didn't win the 1909 Tour. Victory fell to a man who must be the heaviest rider ever to win the Tour de France, François Faber. Cyclists, even those who are described as big, aren't by the standards of the general population; 82 kilograms is about as heavy as you will find in a modern Tour. François Faber was a giant, weighing ten kilograms more than that, and he simply steam-rollered the course. The route, admittedly, was nowhere near as hilly as it is today, but again included the Vosges and the edges of the Alps.

Racers who weigh 92 kilograms are rare. One who raced in recent Tours, a Swedish pro called Magnus Backstedt, once told me, 'Any hill is too steep when you are my size.' Backstedt wasn't fat; neither was Faber, but climbing hills on a bike depends on power to weight ratio. A big rider like Backstedt can crank out 1,000 watts for a minute or so, but on long climbs like there are in the Alps and Pyrenees even this kind of bike-bending power cannot overcome the weight handicap. Backstedt was good on the flat though, which is why he won the Paris–Roubaix Classic and a flat stage of the 1998 Tour de France.

Backstedt was also very durable and could ride hard for extended periods of time, especially in bad weather, which doesn't affect big riders as much as smaller ones. That is how François Faber won in 1909. The summer was terrible that year, with most of the stages run off in cold rain and wind. Faber didn't seem affected and won stages two to six, then stage ten out of the 14 days' racing.

But 1909 was the end for big riders like Faber. Never again would they get the chance to win the Tour de France, because the following year the race would go into the mountains. Really big mountains this time, with peaks well over 1,800 metres, and the Tour would begin to take the shape that it has today.

3. INTO THE HILLS

Alphonse Steines, remember him? He was the adventurous young man who worked as a journalist for *L'Auto* and who nagged Desgrange into sending the Tour de France over the Ballon d'Alsace. It was a success, so successful that his boss allowed more adventures into more mountains – in the Jura and the Chartreuse. From there you can see the Alps, which stack up behind the smaller ranges and dwarf them, and Steines longed to see if the mad men of the Tour de France could race over them.

Then there were the Pyrenees. Steines had heard tell of their majesty, of names like the Tourmalet, Aspin and Peyresourde. He saw their pale grey silhouettes in the distance when he worked on the Tour's southern stages. Within them were wild and mysterious passes known only to locals. They were also high, far in excess of what any racer had tackled so far. That's where Steines decided he wanted to send the Tour next. It was too soon for the Alps, because his boss had seen them and would laugh at the suggestion, but Steines had quizzed Desgrange and found that he knew nothing of the Pyrenees, other than their distant profile in the hazy southern sun.

Still, at first Desgrange wouldn't entertain it, and so, as all the staff of *L'Auto* did when turned down by their boss, Steines dug in and tactfully, artfully and literally harassed the life out of him. Eventually he gave in and let Steines write about the possibility of the Tour racing in the Pyrenees, just to see what the public response would be.

Desgrange got more of a response than he bargained for. People who knew the region said the suggestion was mad, that the mountain roads Steines talked about were blocked by snow most of the year, and when they weren't they were just goat tracks and impossible to pedal over.

Desgrange spent his life in two minds. In one mind he liked that response. He liked the fact that people were outraged at what *L'Auto* was suggesting – outrage sells papers. In his other mind, though, Desgrange had to act responsibly. He couldn't wilfully endanger the racers. That would spell disaster. Desgrange can come over as an old fuddy-duddy worrying about the ideas of his much more adventurous staff, but if he had got it wrong in those early races there would be no Tour de France today. However, he did have an eye for spectacle, which pushed him to experiment. That's why he told Steines to go to the Pyrenees and check out a route.

And what an adventure that was. Steines drove his own car from Paris to Pau, one of the gateway towns to the high Pyrenees and seated almost at the foot of their highest pass, the Col de Tourmalet. When the locals found out what he was planning they laughed and told Steines about a Mercedes racing car that someone had just turned over while testing it on the climb. They were used to outsiders coming to the mountains to pit their strength against them. The mountains always won, they told him.

Undaunted, Steines put his plan to the superintendant of roads in the region, a man called Blanchet, who also laughed in his face. It was impossible. Maybe some of the roads over the passes could take the occasional car, but a whole entourage of support vehicles and 250 men on bicycles? Impossible. Not only were the roads steep, they were in a terrible condition. So Steines told him that he could do nothing about the steepness – that was the challenge for his racers – but he could do something about the road conditions. He could pull strings and get state help to repair them, state help that was beyond Blanchet's wildest dreams. 'Where the Tour de France is concerned nothing is impossible,' Steines told him. Cannily, Blanchet asked for 5,000 francs. Steines called Desgrange, who phoned back within minutes offering 3,000. Blanchet took it. The roads would be fine by July, he assured his sudden benefactor.

With that sorted, Steines headed for the hills. Next day, and with some difficulty, he negotiated the Col d'Aspin then stopped in Ste Marie de Campan, at the foot of the Tourmalet, to ask local opinion on driving over the giant climb. It was May and the consensus was no, it was impossible. Come back in a month, Steines was told. But then one gnarly old man, who had been a guide to toffs like Steines on walking tours, shook his head, disagreed with the villagers and said that maybe it was possible. The old man said that he would have to drive Steines's car, and Steines would need to be handy with a shovel and at laying sacking down under their wheels when they got stuck.

Unfortunately Steines's guide was more talk than substance, and after slipping and sliding their way for six kilometres up the pass, the car got stuck in a snowdrift and the driver wanted to turn back. It was six o'clock, getting dark and there was a long way to go to the summit, and even further down to the next place of habitation. He also told Steines about the local bear population. There are still a few native bears in the area, and a few more imported Slovenian ones, but at the turn of the twentieth century they were a common sheep killer, and weren't shy to attack humans if they felt threatened.

Steines wasn't deterred. Although wearing city clothes he pressed on alone. He walked until darkness fell, then began to panic. At this point a shepherd found him and Steines paid the man to take him to the summit. Once there his guide told him to just keep walking downwards; as long as he could hear the Bastan stream close by him, he would eventually arrive in Barrèges at the end of the descent. Only it wasn't as simple as that. Steines set off a small avalanche, fell over a precipice, and was eventually buried in a snowdrift. That was where he was found, hours later, by a bunch of concerned locals who'd heard that a mad Parisian was tramping around their mountain in darkness and had gone to look for him. By now it was three in the morning and Steines was almost dead with cold. Next morning, however, having thawed out, eaten and slept, he sent a telegram to Desgrange which read: 'No trouble crossing the Tourmalet. Roads satisfactory. No problem for cyclists. Steines.'

That was it. Next day Desgrange announced in *L'Auto* that a stage of the 1910 Tour de France would cross the Col de Peyresourde, the Col d'Aspin, the Col du Tourmalet and the Col d'Aubisque. Interest was huge, Blanchet mended the roads, and Steines kept his mouth shut and fingers crossed.

To ensure the riders' safety and that no one would get left behind, Desgrange also wrote that he was introducing to the Tour de France the *'voiture balai'*, the broom wagon, a truck that would be the last vehicle on the road and would sweep up any stragglers. It occupies the same position today, a token one, as the last Tour vehicle on the road. And there's even a broom strapped to the back of it, but it's been a long time since a Tour rider's backside graced its seats. Modern Tour men who have to stop are whisked off to the finish in air-conditioned team vehicles or some other luxury transport to save them from the ignominy of the broom wagon.

All was set for the great day, but between May and July Desgrange began to worry again. He worried even more when he heard there had been some recent bear attacks in the region, and by the time the Tour started it's said that Desgrange was ill and confined to his bed.

Stage nine took the racers into the Pyrenees with some smaller climbs. Then came stage ten – the big one. Before it Steines briefed the riders. He told them not to take risks, and that the time limit that had been introduced, whereby a rider had to finish a stage within a percentage of the winner's time, would be suspended for the day.

The stage was 326 kilometres long between Luchon and Bayonne, and it had to start at 3.30 a.m. to ensure that there would only be a few tail-enders out on the mountains after dark. Battle raged between Octave Lapize and his team-mate, Gustave Garrigou, who won a 100-franc prize for climbing the Tourmalet without once getting off to walk. The two were well ahead at the top, which made what happened next look bizarre.

Alphonse Steines and a colleague, Victor Breyer, waited on top of the last climb, the Aubisque. They were expecting to see Lapize and Garrigou leading, instead an almost unknown rider, François Lafoucarde, wobbled into view. Breyer ran into the road and asked Lafoucarde what had happened – where were the others? He didn't reply but just plodded past, staring straight ahead. Quarter of an hour later the next rider was more vocal. It was Lapize. Exhausted, half stumbling, half pushing his bike, he looked at Steines and Breyer and spat out the word 'Assassins'.

He caught Lafoucarde, went straight past him, and won the stage. There were 150 kilometres still to ride from the top of the Aubisque, but from the way Lafoucarde dropped down the order, and the fact that he had been nowhere in contention on the Tourmalet, you can't help feeling that he must have had assistance in a motor vehicle to leapfrog into the lead. Lapize rightfully took all the glory and the stage – while still complaining about the brutality of the route – and went on to dominate the rest of the race to win the 1910 Tour.

Everyone raved about how the magnificent men on their pedalling machines had tamed the wild mountains. France wanted more, so in 1911 the Tour gave them more. This time it was the Alps, the real Alps and the mighty Col de Galibier on a classic stage that included the Col d'Aravis and the stepping-stone to the Galibier, the Col de Telegraphe.

It was also a classic battle, one between a strong man who could hammer out a rhythm on long rolling stages, the sort of racer the French call a *rouleur*, and a lightweight climber, or a *grimpeur* in French, a man who didn't so much pedal as dance uphill with wings on his feet. François Faber and Gustave Garrigou were the men. Faber had it his way in the early stages, but on the prelude stage to the Alps from Belfort to Chamonix, Garrigou pranced into the lead. Next day he was on another planet.

The Galibier, like the Tourmalet, is one of the great rendezvous of cycling, an iconic place, where the best do their best work. The classic side is the Telegraphe side, climbed from the Mauriennne valley. You go up the

Telegraphe, saving something for later on its measured bends and wooded slopes. From the top there is a five-kilometre descent into Valloire, a town now but a mountain outpost in 1911. Then it's the Galibier, a vast U-shaped valley scooped out by primordial ice with a tiny road wriggling up the middle of it.

A visit to the Galibier puts anyone in perspective with nature. Its scale dwarfs you. Then as you follow the road upwards there seems no way out of the valley – ahead is just a solid wall of rock, a dead end – but a sharp right turn heralds the last Calvary of the Galibier, a series of hairpins that for cars leads to a tunnel under the summit, while bikes still go where the first Tour racers went, right over the top of the natural pass.

This was a fitting place for Garrigou to stamp his authority on the race. Emile Georget won the stage, but Garrigou was the only rider who didn't have to walk on the Galibier. Strong men cried that day, and Garrigou took over the lead. His next challenge would be the Pyrenees, where he would have to cope with attacks from his nearest challenger, Paul Duboc.

Duboc was from Rouen, a city in Normandy on a big bend of the River Seine, and the people there have Viking blood in their veins. Duboc was their hero and they were outraged when he collapsed after leading the field over the Tourmalet. It appears that he'd accepted a drink from a spectator and that it was poisoned, because his collapse was quick and near total. He limped the rest of the way to the finish and was taken to hospital for emergency treatment. Duboc's fans immediately blamed Garrigou for his poisoning.

He had the most to gain; with his last challenger now far behind him Garrigou would win the Tour, so long as he could get through Rouen. Within hours of Duboc's collapse he received death threats from the city, and these grew in number as the race approached Normandy. Garrigou was terrified. He even talked about giving up on the eve of the Rouen stage. Then Desgrange confronted him. In his state of almost nervous collapse the Father of the Tour was sure that Garrigou wouldn't lie to him, so he asked him outright, had he poisoned Duboc? No, came the reply, and Desgrange was convinced.

Next day he had a make-up artist prepare Garrigou for the stage. He fitted a false moustache, a big hat, blue sunglasses, and he was allowed to change his racing colours and his bike. He was unrecognisable. Desgrange asked the riders to stay together until after Rouen. So the huge angry mob that was waiting couldn't pick out Garrigou in the middle of the fast-moving bunch as it sped through their city streets. Once safely through, Garrigou threw off his disguise and won the 1911 Tour.

The tenth Tour de France saw its first foreign winner. Cycling in Belgium was big by 1912. It had its own character based on aggression and speed as much as stamina, and those qualities were nurtured by a kind of bike race peculiar to Flanders called the *kermesse*.

Originally religious festivals, kermesses developed into an excuse for a fair and revelry. Every village and town had one, and they still do. There are fairground rides and kids' sports, the bars are open all day, and there's bike racing on circuits of around ten kilometres that use the main street for the start and then for the finish, after looping out into the countryside. Teenagers might do five laps, pros 16, or else they do a big circuit while the juniors race, then finish off with ten laps. And why ten kilometres? In the words of Jonny De Nul, the man who was King of the

Kermesses in the eighties and nineties, winning 20 or more of them a year: 'Ten kilometres is just enough time for a guy to watch the racers go by, drink a beer and order another before we go past again.'

Flanders is flat, or at least it has no mountains, so the key to winning races there is speed, because the only way to gap your opponents in a kermesse is to sprint hard out of corners or pour on the power in a crosswind section. They are tough races, and a pro in Flanders has to ride a lot of them, which means they make him tough too. These tough guys were well suited to the single-day Classics of the north, like Paris–Roubaix, and as the race grew their interest was sparked by the Tour de France.

But they brought more than speed and toughness to the race. Belgians were prepared to attack the moment the start flag was dropped and not stop until they were exhausted, or they had won. And the Flemish Belgians brought with them a huge grudge. Belgium's ruling class spoke French, and they looked down on the Flemish culture and language, which meant that Flemish cyclists hated anything French, including their bike racers. This class and language divide would surface throughout Tour history, but it was red hot in 1912.

A Belgian, Charles Crupelandt, won the first stage, and after a tough battle through the Pyrenees a Belgian took over the race lead. He was Odile Defraye and he raced for the French Alcyon team, sponsored by a bike manufacturer famous for the Kingfisher blue of its bikes and team kit. Then the race changed. Every Belgian began to work for Defraye, no matter what team he was in.

Teamwork is vitally important in bike racing, although it wasn't really allowed in the early Tours. Collusion, though, is very difficult to prove, especially between different teams. If one of Defraye's rivals attacked, the Belgians would work hard to catch him. Or if they found themselves in a move and Defraye wasn't, they would stop sharing the lead and driving the breakaway until their compatriot caught up. From being five strong, Alcyon now had 25 riders all committed to a Defraye victory. That duly came, but only after it got so bad that Octave Lapize and his whole La Française team withdrew from the race. It left Desgrange in a dilemma too. He didn't like trade teams, but nationalism was now affecting the fairness of his Tour.

The other problem was the points system. A rider could finish one hour in front of the next man on a stage but still gain only one point in the overall classification. Defraye was a consistent rider, not a great one. If the Tour had been decided on time in 1912, he would not have won. So Desgrange changed the rule. The 1913 Tour would be decided by the total time taken to cover the whole course, but the change ended up costing a very popular French rider the race – and it still produced a Belgian winner.

Eugène Christophe was the French rider. He had finished second in the 1912 Tour, but had actually ridden the whole route quicker than Defraye, so he started as the favourite in 1913. This was the first counter-clockwise Tour de France, which meant that for the first time the Pyrenees would come before the Alps.

As a good climber Christophe wasn't worried about that, and when Defraye took over the lead on stage three, Christophe shadowed him in second place. He was waiting for the Pyrenean stage, stage six, 362 kilometres from Bayonne to Luchon and climbing the Aubisque, Tourmalet, Aspin and Peyresourde in the opposite direction to 1910.

Christophe made an early move, taking seven riders with him, all of them good, while Defraye crashed and ended up so far behind by the Tourmalet that he decided to abandon the race. By then just Christophe and two Belgians, Philippe Thys and Marcel Buysse, the older brother of Lucien and Jules, were left at the front after a horrendous ascent of the Aubisque during which they'd been forced to get off their bikes and push through ankle-deep mud.

Buysse was quickly dropped on the Tourmalet, then later Christophe, leaving Thys to cross the summit alone. There wasn't much in it, so Christophe descended as fast as he dare. It must have been terrifying on those old bikes. Mountain descents are so steep that riders reach speeds of up to 80 kilometres per hour without trying. Slowing a 1913 bike down from that sort of speed with their flimsy brakes was no joke. Christophe's heart must have been in his mouth when ten kilometres down the mountain the forks on his bike broke.

He couldn't swap anything. The only way to continue was to repair the fork. Christophe had learned some black-smith's skills when he was younger, but the nearest forge was at the bottom of the climb in St Marie de Campan. So Christophe picked up his bike and began to jog down the mountain. Reports vary concerning the distance. *L'Auto* says that he ran for 14 kilometres to the village, but when Christophe took part in a 1960s reconstruction of the events in 1913, he said he did ten on foot.

Whatever, the run ended at the village blacksmith's, where Christophe stoked up the fire, took some metal tubing from the smith and used the heat and his skill with a hammer to join the two parts of his forks back together. It was difficult, though, as Christophe needed both hands for the repair, and the forge needed blasts of air to keep it hot enough to get the metal to the right temperature. He had to ask the boy who worked in the forge to operate the bellows for him, and that was noted by the gaggle of officials who had stopped to see that Christophe did the repair and completed the stage totally unaided. He knew he'd done wrong, he knew the officials had seen him and that they would penalise him, and that made Christophe angry. When one of them said he was going out to the village to get some food, since he was starving, Christophe spitefully growled, 'Stay there and eat coal. While you are watching me I am your prisoner and you are my jailer.'

For three hours Christophe worked in the forge, then set off to climb the Aspin and Peyresourde, eventually arriving in Luchon three hours and 50 minutes behind the stage winner, Thys. He'd been nearly 18 hours doing his unusual triathlon, 18 hours of riding, running and metal-work. Now there's a plaque commemorating Christophe's epic day in the village centre of Ste Marie de Campan.

Thys took over the lead, lost it next day to Buysse, but took it back again after Buysse crashed and had to run to a village to make repairs of his own on stage nine. Then Thys began to pull ahead with consistent rather than flashy riding in the Alps, to win his first Tour de France.

He won again the following year in a race that was contested under the gathering threat of the First World War. Archduke Franz Ferdinand was assassinated in Sarajevo on the day that the Tour started, and when the race ended on 26 July, Europe was eight days away from war. On 3 August the German army invaded Belgium and many of the men who had raced in the Tour were drafted into their nation's armies. Not all of them survived.

4. THE YELLOW JERSEY

The Great War left France paralysed. Nearly a quarter of her population had been drafted, and of them just over six million men and boys were killed or badly wounded. The Tour de France lost Henri Alavoine, Edouard Wattelier and Emile Engel among its notable regular racers, plus many who had taken parts as 'isolés', and Lucien Petit-Breton, François Faber and Octave Lapize among its winners. Lapize became one of France's first fighter pilots, but died when shot down during the Battle of Verdun.

The country was on its knees, and ordinary French people were almost starving, especially in the north where the fighting had been most fierce. The Somme, parts of the Pas-de-Calais and Le Nord were a waste land. Nothing grew, every tree had been blasted away and roads barely existed. It looked as though life would never be normal again in this living hell.

But life would be normal again, and just to help it along the Tour de France decided to go ahead in 1919. Not only that, it would run through the battlefields of the north, which, as it turned out, partly defined the race. It certainly wasn't a titanic athletic struggle. Most of the contestants hadn't ridden their bikes for four years, because they'd been busy trying to stay alive. And when the news broke that the Tour would be on, they had little time to prepare for it. Of the 67 starters only ten finished. The 1914 winner, Phillipe Thys, didn't even make it through the first stage, but the race was still remarkable for two things that are part of cycling today: the yellow jersey and the introduction of the phrase 'Hell of the North'.

Stage racing had become an accepted part of cycling. People understood it and liked the way a rider who had bad fortune one day could come back on another. That facet of stage racing reached the hearts and minds of working people in France, the majority of whom still earned their living from the land. Their life was dominated by overcoming setbacks; they expected them and had a gloomy suspicion of good luck. But the problem with stage races was that although fans could see the leader on the road when he passed through their village on any given day, they found it harder to identify who was leading the race overall.

It was suggested to Desgrange that it would help identify the leader if he wore the same distinctive jersey each day. He agreed and went off to buy enough for the leader to wear every day for the rest for the race. The official race history holds that yellow was chosen because *L'Auto* was printed on yellow paper, but the real reason is far more mundane. Desgrange needed 15 jerseys in different sizes, and they had to be the same colour, but the supplier only had that quantity in yellow, because yellow was his least popular colour.

And so the yellow jersey was born. Its first wearer was Eugène Christophe, the hero of the 'broken forks' episode on the Tourmalet – or so, once again, the official history has it. However, it's recently been discovered that in the

1950s, when he was quite old, Philippe Thys told a French cycling magazine that he'd been asked to wear a yellow jersey by Desgrange when he was leading a Tour before the war. Unfortunately, if it did happen any record of it has been lost, but Thys wasn't a man given to telling lies. Thys also added that he hadn't wanted to wear it, and reckoned that he only did so after Desgrange paid him. Christophe was none too keen in 1919 either, claiming that its distinctive colour made it easier for the rest to pick out where he was on the road, so he was easier to mark. But on stage 14 from Metz to Dunkirk the colour of his shirt was the last thing on Christophe's mind.

The stage went right across the north-east corner of France, from east to west, along what had just been the front line. The roads were awful, and the whole landscape was wrecked, prompting one journalist to describe the scene as the 'Hell of the North' when he saw the devastation around the industrial city of Valenciennes. It's an area famous for the cobblestone tracks that were used originally by farmers and miners to get around. The tracks are called 'pavés', and every year they form the crux of the single-day Classic, the Paris–Roubaix race. They are still rough, demand a special riding skill, and today are protected by law from upgrading, as listed buildings are in the UK.

The Paris–Roubaix jealously protects its Hell of the North today, but in 1919 Christophe would have happily seen all those pavés tarmacked over, because the rough, bomb-cratered road broke his forks again. This time he found a bicycle factory, not a blacksmith's, used their forge for the repair, and lost nearly two and a half hours because of it. He lost the Tour de France too. The winner was Firmin Lambot, the first Belgian from the French-speaking Walloon area to win the race.

Lambot was followed in 1920 by a compatriot, although a Flemish speaker this time, Philippe Thys. His victory made Thys the first triple winner of the Tour, and you can only wonder at how many he would have won had the war not stopped him in his prime. His third Tour win was a very intelligent, if unspectacular victory that showed traces of the modern way of racing the Tour de France. Thys only made big efforts when he had to, and was content to coast on less difficult days, even letting rivals get ahead, then chasing to reduce their lead to a less threatening level.

Thys may have raced the modern way, but the Tour was still tough and true to its roots. Desgrange once said that in his ideal Tour de France the route, race distance and conditions would combine to be so hard that only one man made it to Paris. To this end he tried to stop teams using any kind of tactics. He stopped riders in an escape group relaying each other at the front to share the pace, and prevented chasers doing the same. In his mind every racer should have made his own way to Paris in his own separate lane, which is simply impossible. And Desgrange still would not allow any outside help if a rider suffered a mechanical failure.

They had to carry enough spares to see them through each stage, and if a racer used those up he had to improvise, but still had to carry the broken piece of kit to the finish. Any help would be penalised. Another Belgian, Léon Scieur, felt the rough end of this rule when he had a bad day back in 1919 on a stage in Brittany. It was cold and wet, and he had to stop several times to warm his hands by the fires in roadside cafés. To add to his misery Scieur had several punctures. Eventually he used up all his spare tyres and now had to mend the tube each time it happened. Racers in the early Tours all used a type of tyre that is still very popular today called a tubular. The inner tube is sewn inside a canvas case, on to which the tyre tread is glued. To mend a puncture you have to unpick the stitching, remove the tube, glue on a patch then stitch it back inside the canvas case. After his fourth puncture a woman had invited him indoors to do the work, but he was still frozen and when his trembling fingers couldn't thread the needle he asked the woman to do it for him. That was against the rules, and the race official who'd followed Scieur inside the house told him that he would penalise him if she helped. Scieur took a deep breath, managed to gain control of his hands and completed the repair himself, all the while cursing the official. It helped him to keep warm.

The experience stuck with Scieur, a tough rider whom the press nicknamed 'the Locomotive'. He was on top form in 1921 and was leading the race with one day to go when the spokes began to break in his rear wheel. The rules that year stated that a rider could replace a broken item, but only if he could prove that it was broken beyond repair. When an eleventh spoke broke there was nothing more Scieur could do with the wheel, so he took a spare from inside the support truck that followed the race. But so fearful was he of the rules and the people who enforced them that he carried the broken wheel on his back for 300 kilometres. The teeth of the sprocket that carried the chain drives pressed so deeply and rubbed his skin so raw that Scieur carried a star-shaped scar on his back for the rest of his life.

Léon Scieur won the 1921 Tour, becoming not only the second Walloon rider to win but the second from the same small town that the 1919 winner, Firmin Lambot, came

from. This is such a rare coincidence that it's worth examining. Cycling in Belgium is a Flemish sport; fewer French-
speaking Walloon Belgians race, and very few have been
successful pros. Is there something about the town of
Florennes that makes Lambot and Scieur the exceptions?
Well there might me. Florennes is just on the French-
speaking side of the Taal Grenz, the area of Belgium that
runs along the southern edge of East and West Flanders
like a thin spit of land sticking out from the rest of
Wallonia, which is basically the south-east third of the
country. Florennes is Flanders in all but name.

Language conflicts aside, the Belgians were beginning
to dominate cycling. French hopes rested on the shoulders
of three brothers, the Pelissiers: Charles, Francis and the
mercurial Henri. The first two were good riders; Charles
was one of the first sprinters of road cycling; but Henri was
the star, a true talent but with a star's temperament too.
He was bright, witty and a good talker. Henri Desgrange
hated him, because he liked his racers to be a bit thick and
ill at ease with the press. That way he could control them
better, and write what he wanted about them. Henri was
happy talking to journalists and was always good for a
juicy quote, but he would insist that they wrote down
exactly what he said.

If Desgrange didn't like Pelissier very much, then
Pelissier didn't like the Tour de France at all. He said that
the long stages and huge overall distance made for boring
racing. Pelissier saw cycling as a sport of speed and tactical subtleties, which it is now, but Desgrange wanted it to
be a sport of toil, endurance and suffering. Pelissier liked
the single-day Classics as they were more his style, and he
constantly criticised the Tour, to which Desgrange once
responded by writing in *L'Auto* that Pelissier had a tiny

brain and was not made of the stuff that Tour winners were. Just what Henri needed to fire him up.

Firmin Lambot won again in 1922, the oldest ever winner at 37 and also the last Walloon Belgian to win. Eugène Christophe suffered another set of broken forks, a lot more mountains were introduced, and Desgrange still treated the race as his own personal dictatorship. When a Belgian rider, Hector Heuseghem, broke his bike so badly that he couldn't continue, a race official agreed that he could swap his bike for a new one. The rules said he could if the old one was too wrecked, but Desgrange still docked him an hour on the overall classification. Heuseghem had been leading the Tour until that point and might have won but for that 60-minute penalty.

Henri Pelissier sat out the 1921 and 1922 Tours, unable to accept racing as it was in Henri Desgrange's world. He was a potential Tour winner, though; second place back in 1914 proved that. He won a stage in 1919 and two in 1920, but Desgrange got on his nerves so much in those two Tours that Pelissier quit them both. Now Pelissier began to realise that he was the one who was losing out by letting Desgrange get to him and not having a serious go at winning the Tour. Meanwhile Desgrange goaded him in the press, saying he was scared and weak, so in 1923 Pelissier decided he would shut Desgrange up by winning the Tour de France.

He had a tough fight to do it with a young Italian who was new to the race, Ottavio Bottechia, but Pelissier seized victory with two good days in the Alps to become the first French winner of the Tour since Garrigou in 1911. And Desgrange? He was never one to let an opportunity slip, or fly in the face of public opinion. Pelissier was a popular winner, so Desgrange effused about his performance in

L'Auto, where he compared Pelissier's victory to the work of a great artist. Even Pelissier couldn't disagree with that, so a truce was called, until next year.

The long Tour stages in 1924 still started early in the morning, when it could be quite cold. Riders were allowed to wear as much clothing as they wanted, but they had to finish with every scrap they had on at the start. Henri Pelissier wore two jerseys for the first part of stage two, but as the day warmed up he removed one and threw it away. But he should have carried it with him to be checked in at the end, and because he didn't he was given a time penalty. Pelissier was furious. He found Desgrange and let go at him. Desgrange didn't like being shouted at by anyone, least of all a sweaty bike racer, so their feud was back on again.

At the start next day a race official walked up to Pelissier and without saying a word lifted the racer's jersey to see what he was wearing underneath. Pelissier protested – he wasn't to be treated like a schoolboy by some functionary. He complained to Desgrange, who just smiled. Later, when the Tour passed through Coutances on the same stage, the official stopped Pelissier again to count his jerseys. That was it. Pelissier got off his bike and with his brother, Francis, and another racer, Maurice Ville, stormed off into the nearest bar.

A journalist of a different kind was following the 1923 Tour. His name was Albert Londres and he wasn't a sports journalist at all. He wrote features, big features, and specialised in exposing injustice, corruption and state indifference. He'd just written a piece on the conditions in French penal colonies in Guyana that had rocked the country's conscience. He'd heard about the Tour, about the suffering and draconian rules, and smelled a story. Seeing that the previous year's winner hadn't come through the checkpoint after Coutances, Londres' instinct told him that the story was unfolding right now.

He drove back along the stage route, asking about Pelissier all the way, until he found him drinking hot chocolate along with Francis and Ville in the Coutances railway station bar. All Londres had to ask was what was wrong, because Pelissier was primed and ready to dish the dirt on the Tour. 'We can put up with the distance, with the suffering and hardship out on the road. That is what we do, but all these rules and vexations. My name is Pelissier, not Atlas,' Henri said for openers. Then he fished around in the pockets of his jersey. 'There. Look,' he said throwing some pills and potions on the table. 'Cocaine for our eyes, chloroform to rub on our gums, pills for strength. We run on dynamite.' There was more, a lot more. Londres wrote it all up in a piece called 'Les Forçats de la Route' (The Prisoners of the Road). The article caused a sensation, but instead of putting anyone off the Tour de France it just seemed to increase the public's fascination with the race.

The first link between doping and the Tour de France had been made, but nobody was put off, least of all the organisers. If anything the revelations made their race seem even more of a challenge. Pelissier talked about the injuries he lived with, running sores, all his toenails falling out, and the tablets he took to numb the pain and stay awake. And the public loved every gory detail of it.

Pelissier didn't finish another Tour, and later he said that he'd been playing with Londres, pandering to his need for an exclusive and taking advantage of the fact that he wasn't a cycling reporter to pull the wool over his eyes. But the subsequent history of the Tour de France suggests that Pelissier was probably trying to cover up what he'd said and sound respectable. Anyway, Londres had seen all those pills – what were they if they weren't drugs?

Maybe Pelissier also wanted to regain some popularity with his fellow riders, because his revelations did him no favours with them. There are things pro bike racers can talk about and things that they can't, and until quite recently the subject of drugs was taboo. To be regarded as a good pro and accepted as one of the boys, it paid to go with the *omertà*, the code of silence on doping that was deemed to be for the collective good.

Pelissier's fiery nature meant that he was the first to break that rule, but it also meant that he was difficult to live with. So difficult that in 1933 his first wife, Léonie, committed suicide. Then, two years later, a stormy relationship with his girlfriend, Camille Tharault, ended in a huge fight in which Pelissier slashed her face with a knife. In response Camille ran to fetch the same revolver that Léonie had used to kill herself and shot Pelissier dead with it. She meant it too, as five bullets were found in his body. By that time even the courts knew how difficult Pelissier was to live with, and Tharault was given a one-year suspended jail sentence on a plea of self-defence.

5. THE FIRST ITALIAN

Ottavio Bottecchia was second to Henri Pelissier in 1923, so when Pelissier blew his top and left the race, the way was clear in 1924 for Bottecchia to become the first Italian to win the Tour. He is also one of the few riders who have taken the yellow jersey on day one and kept it throughout the race.

Bottechia was another modern racer. Despite Desgrange's efforts to keep the Tour an individual contest, tactics were developing and beginning to play a bigger part, and Bottecchia was very astute. He made his moves on the stages that suited him and limited his losses on those that didn't.

He came from the hillier part of the Veneto region in Italy and served with the Austrian army during the First World War. He was a machine-gunner, but he was given a bike to carry his weapon around on so that he could deploy it quicker in the field. It was the first time Bottecchia had ever ridden a bike, but he found that he could ride it very quickly – he probably had to.

When he left the army Bottecchia thought that cycling might get him out of the poverty he'd been born into. It did, in a way. He won races almost from the start of his racing career, but the money went to support his extended family and he was always short of funds and equipment. When Bottecchia turned up for his first Tour de France, Desgrange could hardly believe that he was already a big winner. His racing clothes were rags, his shoes were falling apart and he was as skinny as a whippet. His ears stuck out too, so Desgrange christened him 'Papillon', the Butterfly. The only French Bottecchia knew when he first took part in the Tour was, 'No bananas, lots of coffee, thank you,' which is all he needed to get his daily rations for each stage.

He was a true innocent, but an innocent who quickly got tangled up in some of the turmoil that was going on in Italy at the time. After he finished second in the 1923 Tour, and Henri Pelissier had declared that Bottecchia would win in 1924, the Italian equivalent of *L'Auto*, the *Gazzetta dello Sport*, asked every reader to subscribe one lira each to Bottecchia so he could go to France in 1924 better prepared. Benito Mussolini, the leader of the country's fascists, was the first to subscribe.

Then a story appeared in the papers that Bottecchia had been seen reading anti-fascist material. They were political pamphlets that Bottecchia had only read to improve his literacy, but passions were raised in Italy at the time. Mussolini was marching towards power, and it wasn't popular to be seen as standing against him, which is how Bottecchia was seen, when the story got out. Bottecchia was so worried about reprisals from Mussolini supporters that he refused to wear the yellow jersey when a stage passed close to Italy in 1924.

The anti-fascist story damaged Bottecchia in Italy, but his engaging personality won him thousands of fans in France. He was also very popular with the other racers in the peloton, despite the fact that he made them look second rate by winning so easily. It is said that he sang snatches of opera as he raced along, and after every stage the few new French words he'd learned would be used on waiting journalists: 'Not tired, French and Belgians good friends, cycling is good job.' He loved cycling, loved making new friends and had simple needs. After the Tour finished, Bottecchia travelled back to Italy in a third-class rail carriage to save money, and he wore the yellow jersey under his street clothes all the way there.

But even Bottecchia's child-like joy in winning could not please grumpy Desgrange. He criticised the Italian for winning with ease and asked why, if he was so obviously superior to the other racers, he didn't show it with some more spectacular riding and win more stages and by bigger margins. Next year Bottecchia won the Tour again, and won four stages with it. Desgrange stayed quiet for once.

With two brilliant wins and still only 31, it looked as though Bottecchia would rule the Tour de France for years to come, but in 1926 he suffered a crisis of confidence. He abandoned on stage ten amid terrible thunder and lightning, when rain turned to ice on the Aubisque, Tourmalet, Aspin and Peyresourde climbs. His body hurt, his lungs ached and he was coughing so badly that blood dribbled from his lips. Bottecchia wept with pain and at the ignominy of having to give in. He was profoundly affected and fell into a deep gloom when he returned home to Italy. His depression wasn't helped by continued physical problems: his legs hurt and the congestion in his lungs would not go away. Bottecchia slowly became haunted by the fear that he had damaged himself by racing in those terrible conditions.

He continued riding and training, however, in the hope that one day he would recover, but he never did recover enough to race. Then, on 3 June 1927, Bottechia went out riding in the morning, as was his daily habit, but after a few hours he was found unconscious by the road, just a few kilometres from his home. The circumstances were mysterious. Bottecchia's bike lay some distance away from him and it wasn't damaged, but his skull was cracked and his collarbone broken. He died 12 days later in hospital.

There was an inquiry, which came to the verdict that Bottecchia had suffered from sunstroke, lost control of his bike and fallen. But that was unlikely. He was found in the morning and had set off from home at seven o'clock, saying he would be gone for three hours. It isn't very hot by then, even in Italy in June, and certainly not hot enough to trouble a man with dark, tanned skin who was used to riding for hours on end under a burning sun.

The conspiracy theorists stepped in. Some cited the anti-fascist leaflets and said that Bottecchia was murdered because of his opposition to Mussolini. However, Bottecchia simply wasn't political and never voiced an opinion, pro or anti anyone. Then an ex-pat Italian dying in New York was supposed to have confessed to killing Bottecchia in a Mafia hit. He even named the Godfather who told him to do it, but the police could find no trace of this Mafia man in their records.

The final twist to the riddle came years later, in 1948, and from another deathbed confession. An old farmer from Bottecchia's village told his priest that he had killed the great champion, and he made the priest swear that he would tell everyone about it once the farmer was dead. He said that he had discovered Bottecchia in one of his fields enjoying the sun and eating his grapes. Times were hard and the farmer flew into a rage; he'd had problems with locals raiding his fields before and this was the final straw. He picked up a large stone, crept up behind the intruder and hit him over the head. Then, when Bottecchia fell, the farmer saw who it was. He had mortally wounded the pride of the region, and in a bitter irony the farmer was one of his biggest fans.

But there are holes even in the farmer's story. It was true that he had been the man who ran into his village sounding the alarm, saying that he'd found Bottecchia lying in a ditch, but what about the grapes? Grapes aren't ripe in June, so why would Bottecchia have been eating them? His sad end remains a mystery today.

Bottecchia's death shook Italy, but it hardly got a mention from Desgrange when he previewed the 1926 Tour de France. Looking back from the distance of time, Desgrange sometimes seems very harsh, and you can get the feeling that although he loved cycling, he didn't really like cyclists very much, at least not the professionals. Maybe it was his experiences of their cheating in the first Tours, but he seemed to regard them as work-shy schemers who would always find a short cut if he didn't watch them. He suspected the team sponsors too. Cycling needed their money, Desgrange needed it too, but at worst he thought they were colluding to fix the result, and at best he considered they were becoming too powerful an influence on the Tour.

Desgrange didn't like flat stages either. He needed them to get from one set of mountains or hills to another, but he felt that under the influence of the teams the flat stages were becoming long, boring hauls where much of the field finished together, or at least spread over just a few minutes. Desgrange liked his riders to stagger over the line hours apart on every stage, as they did in the mountains. Anything else just was not racing.

The 1926 Tour had a lot of bunch finishes, stages that ended with many of the field fighting it out at the end in a mad dash for the line, stages where it was possible for the overall favourites to ghost in the bunch and save energy, especially if they were Belgians. Racing in organised, tight-knit groups was meat and drink to them. It was how their bike racing at home went. The particular Belgians who dominated the 1926 Tour were a band of brothers, the flying Buysses.

The Buysse brothers, Lucien and Jules, were born in Wontergem in East Flanders and were about as Flemish as you could get. They were short, stocky, tough and very fast racers who were as happy on the road as they were on the track. Lucien's first big cycling victory was in the Six Days of Ghent, which is one of a series of races that are held over six days on indoor tracks all over Europe. They're not a major focus of cycling nowadays, but in Buysse's time the six-days were as big as the Tour de France, and as well as in Europe there was a flourishing circuit of six-day races in America.

They were good training for the Tour. Riders raced around steeply banked wooden board tracks, which were sometimes as short as ten laps to the mile, for 144 hours non-stop. The first six-days were individual contests, where the rider who covered the most laps won, but because the exhaustion of the contestants deprived these races of spectacle, by the twenties they were contested as two-man teams in a constant relay race called a Madison. The name came from Madison Square Gardens in New York, where the first two-man six-day was contested.

The distances covered were huge. The six-day distance record was set by Krupkat and Huschke in the 1924 Berlin race with 4,544 kilometres ridden between the two of them. The Tour de France that year was 5,425 kilometres long, split into 15 stages and spread over three weeks. Six-day racers slept little, and after they had one or two of these marathons under their belts, the Tour de France didn't seem too difficult. At least they were out in the fresh air when riding the Tour, rather than the choking cigar smoke of an indoor velodrome.

Lucien Buysse's first go at the Tour de France was in 1914, when he was forced out by mechanical problems. Once he got his life back together after the war, Buysse was a stronger rider, finishing third in 1924 and second the following year, when he also won two stages. But his finish position wasn't his story of those two Tours, it was the role he played in them: that of a *super-domestique* to Ottavio Bottecchia.

In cycling *domestique* is the name given to a rider who races in the service of another, his team leader for example. The word was first used as an insult by Henri Desgrange, and was directed at Maurice Brocco. In the 1911 Tour, Brocco lost his chance overall when he had a bad day on the stage to Chamonix, but later he paced François Faber all the way to the finish of a stage. This was against the rules, but Desgrange couldn't really prove that was what happened because he didn't have enough witnesses. Brocco claimed that he was riding along at his own pace and he could do nothing about who followed him. Desgrange thought that Faber had paid Brocco, which was true, but he couldn't prove it. Not being able to disqualify Brocco, Desgrange poured scorn on him in *L'Auto* saying, 'He is unworthy, he is no more than a domestique,' which in the French of the time meant a servant, like a maid.

Brocco was a better bike rider than Desgrange portrayed him, and he had a fiery temper too. Before the next stage he walked up to Desgrange and said to him, 'Today I will make you eat that word, domestique indeed. We will settle accounts.' But being shouted at by bike racers wasn't something Desgrange liked, so he decided to follow Brocco on the stage to check that he was behaving, which is exactly what Brocco wanted Desgrange to do. He had a point to make.

After some early attacking the stage settled down and Brocco was in the second group climbing the Tourmalet, with Desgrange right behind him following in a car. So Brocco started. 'Am I allowed to ride with these men?' He asked Desgrange. 'No? Well then,' he added and attacked, quickly leaving them behind. On the next climb Brocco caught the leaders, still with Desgrange in tow. 'What about these, then? Do I have the right to stay with them?' he asked. 'No? OK,' and he dropped those riders too, racing away to win the stage alone by 34 minutes. His point was proved. Brocco was no domestique.

But as the years went by teamwork crept into the Tour de France, and Desgrange reluctantly allowed it. Teams recruited talented leaders, and they recruited other riders to help them by pacing them or working hard at the front of a group to catch a rival. Still, the time came in any Tour when the team leader had to step up and fight alone, especially in the mountains, where only the most talented stay at the front of the Tour. If a leader had a rider nearly as talented to help him on the climbs, that was a huge advantage, and so the term super-domestique was born, denoting a rider who could challenge for the Tour but instead was paid well to help someone else.

Lucien Buysse was the first super-domestique in a long line of similar riders. They are often young riders who are being groomed for stardom. Working closely with an established team leader is regarded as good experience for them. Greg Lemond for Bernard Hinault in the early eighties, and Miguel Indurain working for Pedro Delgado in the late eighties are two examples of such future champions that spring to mind. Lucien Buysse did his super-domestique apprenticeship in the 1924 and 1925 Tours, working hard for Ottavio Bottecchia.

Jules Buysse won stage one of the 1926 race, and another Belgian, Aimé Dossche, who would go on to open the most famous bike shop in his country, Dossche Sports, won stage two. Then on stage three something happened that shows how much life has changed since 1926. Lucien Buysse received news that his eldest daughter had died. He wanted to drop out of the race, but amazingly his own family encouraged him to carry on.

Lucien won the Tour by having two amazing days in the Pyrenees, one of them in the apocalyptic conditions that ended Ottavio Bottecchia's racing career. The second day went from Luchon to Perpignan, and the Buysse brothers scored a one-two, although seven minutes apart. Lucien rounded out the race by defending well in the Alps, and ran out the winner of the Tour by over 75 minutes from Nicolas Franz of Luxembourg.

It was a good win for Buysse, and an exciting race, but Desgrange still wasn't happy. He didn't think big field sprints were exciting, so in 1927 he declared that all the flat stages would be ridden as team time trials. This meant that no one could take it easy, especially the favourites. Each one would start the race with his team, and the teams started with a time gap between them, so the leaders did not know how their rivals were doing.

Up until 1927 there had never been a time trial in the Tour, either team or otherwise; now there would be 16 of them. It was an odd move, designed to make the Tour harder, and it did. Desgrange showed some pity for the riders by drastically cutting the length of each stage, but he also increased their number.

The race distance dropped to 5,321 kilometres in total, split over 24 stages, and the average stage length fell drastically to 222 kilometres from the previous year's 321. It was still a very different race from a modern Tour de France, though. The 2009 race was 3,459 kilometres long spread over 21 stages, making their average length 165 kilometres.

Cutting the stage distances, as they did in 1927, would eventually make the Tour a better race, but the team time trials didn't. They are another example of Desgrange's muddled thinking. He didn't like the teams' influence on the race. He didn't like big teams with plenty of money dominating his race, yet here he was handing the Tour to them on a plate. The powerful Alcyon squad kept Nicholas Frantz close to the overall lead until the Pyrenees, where he attacked on the by now traditional Aubisque, Tourmalet, Aspin, Peyresourde stage to virtually win the Tour in 16 and a half hours of racing.

Frantz was the second winner from Luxembourg after François Faber. The son of a wealthy farmer, he was the first Tour winner who didn't really need to race. Cycling wasn't his way out of poverty, as it was for many others; Frantz just loved it, having the talent to do it and an unbreakable body. And just to underline that point, Frantz won again in 1928, without the slightest bit of physical trouble.

He led from start to finish and only had one scary moment. It was on the 19th stage between Metz and Charleville, when Frantz crashed and wrecked his bike.

The rules now stated that a rider had to try and repair his bike before swapping it for another. The penalty for not doing so was one hour added to his time for the race.

Frantz was leading by 90 minutes, but he still didn't want an hour lopped off his lead, as he would lose time anyway because of the crash. Luckily his team manager came up with an idea. The rules specifically said that he couldn't swap his bike for an Alcyon team bike or any other brand being raced on in the Tour. They were all named, so there could be no excuses. But naming the brands was a loophole. It didn't prevent Frantz from continuing the stage on a lady spectator's bike – the only one to hand. The Alcyon manager bought it off her and Frantz finished the stage on that, only losing 28 minutes in the remaining 100 kilometres.

Frantz was easily the best of the pro racers in the 1928 Tour, but he was in a different world from those who took part as *touriste-routiers*. The category was created in 1923, basically for the riders who had entered as *isolés* before that. Henri Desgrange liked these racers. They were the battling amateurs he'd have liked every competitor to be. They bulked up the field, created interest and made his race look a bigger spectacle.

They really were the tough guys of the Tour. After each hard day in the saddle, and very often at night as well, the touriste-routier's struggle wasn't over when he got to a stage finish. They would be able to wash in the town baths, and theoretically their luggage would be waiting for them there. However, the van that was supposed to do the delivery often broke down or got stuck in the mud, especially in the mountains.

They then had to find a room. The organised racers booked by post before the race started, but many were illiterate and couldn't do that. They had to ride around town with their bags balanced on their handlebars, searching for a room, and when they found one they had to overhaul and clean their bikes.

Touriste-routiers ranged from rank amateurs, who couldn't last more than a day or two, to good competitors who but for a bit of luck could have won a place in a pro team. Some, like Benoît Fauré, who is known as the king of the touriste-routiers, even preferred racing as an individual because he didn't have to share any prize money he won with team-mates. It's a rule in cycling that all the prizes that team members win are put into a pot and shared out equally after the race. Faure, who raced in the Tour between 1929 and 1935 and won a stage in 1929, when he finished 15th overall, didn't want to do that.

At the other end of the scale there was Jules Deloffre. He was dead poor but a talented acrobat, so before he started looking for a room he would do tumbling tricks in the street and pass round his sweaty, threadbare racing cap to collect money to pay for it. Another touriste-routier, an Italian called Rossignoli, was so broke that he could only afford one pair of shorts, which he raced in without washing them for three weeks. His fellow racers eventually began to complain about the smell, but he just said that if they didn't like it they should let him ride off up the road and win, so he'd be able to afford some new ones.

The touriste-routiers came not just from France but from all over Europe. They had other jobs, in farming mostly, but fishermen, miners, factory workers all raced as well. One was a Paris policeman called Gelot, known in the press as the 'le Flic Volant', the Flying Copper. There was a teacher too, from Perpignan. His name was Bobo and his subject was geography. But one of the biggest groups in the touriste-routier class were bike shop owners. It stood to reason that if you had to choose between two or three bike shops in town, then the guy who had got himself though the Tour de France would know a thing or two that the others didn't.

A touriste-routier had nearly caused an upset in 1927. The stage in the Pyrenees that Frantz later dominated to establish his victory started in terrible weather at midnight. Conditions were vile, with rain lashing down, so an Italian touriste-routier called Giovanni Gordini decided to try something. He attacked from the start, and because of the poor visibility he literally disappeared up the road. Even Desgrange didn't see him go past his car, which was preceding the race.

Eventually Desgrange became puzzled at why spectators were shouting about a rider leading by 50 minutes, so he had his driver accelerate to see if this was true. It was, it was Gordini, and by the time Desgrange caught him he had an hour's lead and nearly had the yellow jersey. Desgrange got word back to the rest of the field, who stirred themselves. Gordini then had a series of punctures and Frantz caught and dropped him well before the finish to save the face of the professionals.

If Nicolas Frantz was the main story of the 1928 Tour de France, almost of equal interest were the first competitors from outside Europe. They comprised the Rovat-Dunlop team and were a New Zealander, Harry Watson, and three Australians, Perry Osborne, Ernest Bainbridge and Hubert Opperman, later to become Sir Hubert Opperman but forever known affectionately in Australia as Oppy.

Opperman's cycling started with his first job, which was delivering telegrams by bike. He finished third in his first race, and by the age of 23 was the best in his country and a triple national champion. It was clear that he needed a bigger stage to play on, so the Melbourne *Morning Herald*, along with the *Sporting Globe*, and the *Sun* in New Zealand, started a fund to raise enough money to send Opperman and three of the best riders from their two countries to Europe to race, with the ultimate aim of taking part in the Tour de France.

Watson, Bainbridge and Osborne treated the trip as an experience, but Opperman really wanted to show how good he was. He did well in the warm-up races, including taking third place in the Paris–Brussels event behind Nicolas Frantz. However, come Tour time, with four riders instead of the ten that other teams had, the Australians were at a disadvantage during the flat team time trials. Every day Opperman had to go ahead of his team-mates so he didn't lose too much time, but he impressed a lot of people. The mighty Alcyon team took him under their wing and their manager gave Opperman a lot of advice. He eventually finished 18th in the Tour and won the admiration of everybody, readers of *L'Auto* even voting him Europe's most popular sportsman in 1928.

When he didn't need a team, Opperman excelled. He won the Bol d'Or 24-hour track race in 1928, even after his bike was sabotaged by a rival and he had to stop for repairs. He got back on terms by riding for 17 hours straight before nature called and forced him to stop for a break. Opperman's career peaked in 1931 when he won the longest race of all, Paris–Brest–Paris, before dropping out of the Tour de France with dysentery. After that Opperman turned his attention to breaking cycling records, until the Second World War ended his racing career.

But cycling was only half of Hubert Opperman's life and fame. After the war he joined Australia's Liberal Party and in 1949 he was elected MP for the Geelong district. He was called to government in 1960, and between 1963 and 1966 he was Australia's minister of immigration. He was given an OBE in 1953 and knighted in 1968 after service as Malta's High Commissioner.

To round off the second decade of the Tour's existence a Belgian, Maurice De Waele, won the 1929 Tour de France. Sense had prevailed in the offices of *L'Auto* and the team time trials were reduced to three. However, Desgrange was still in charge, and to show it he brought back the rule specifying that a rider had to finish with the bike he started on, or prove that it was broken beyond repair.

This partly proved to be the undoing of Victor Fontan, a strong rider from the Pyrenees who had been shot during the First World War and didn't get back to racing again until 1924, when he was in his mid thirties. By 1929, though, Fontan was one of the best racers in the world, and before the Luchon to Perpignan stage was leading overall. He should have had a great day on his home turf, but he crashed on an early descent and smashed up his bike. It was still dark and he had to knock on doors to try and find someone who would lend him a bike. Then, when he found one, he strapped the wreckage of his old bike on to his back and rode for 150 kilometres over Tourmalet and Aspin climbs before realising that his situation was hopeless and he retired.

De Waele didn't have it all his own way either. He fell ill during stage 14, a big one in the Alps, and had to be pushed and shoved by his team almost all the way to Paris to win the Tour. That was the last straw for Desgrange. The trade teams had gone too far. 'My Tour has been won by a corpse,' he blasted from the pages of *L'Auto*. It didn't matter that De Waele was ill, that he couldn't eat solids, or that the rest of the field agreed he was the strongest and the moral winner until he fell ill. Desgrange decided that teams sponsored by businesses were history in his Tour de France. The 1930 race would be for national teams and individual touriste-routiers only.

6. THE RISE OF NATIONALISM

Some say that sport is a metaphor for life, and that was certainly the case in the Tour de France during the 1930s. To kick off a decade that would see Europe and then the world at war, Desgrange introduced national teams to the Tour. Belgium, Italy, Spain, Germany and of course France lined up for the first edition of the thirties, each fielding their eight best riders. The rest of the race was made up of 85 touriste-routiers, either amateur individuals or full-time pros who raced for trade teams for the rest of the year.

No rider was allowed to show a trace of advertising on his clothing, which had to be the approved national uniforms for each team, and plain tops and shorts for the rest. And the whole field raced on identical bikes, all painted yellow and supplied by *L'Auto*. The race was to herald the era of a pure, fair Tour de France, free from the machinations of sponsored teams, or at least that was the theory.

Barring the trade teams from the Tour, however, meant that Desgrange not only had to buy 150 bicycles, *L'Auto* also had to foot the hotel and food bills for all the national teams. To fund this Desgrange introduced the publicity caravan. The Tour would have advertising – it couldn't work without it – but it would roll along ahead of the race.

The caravan has grown over the years, and now it really is something to see. Companies pay for a place in a file of vehicles that precedes the Tour wherever it goes. Up and down mountains, across flat plains, in rain or shine, wherever the riders go, the publicity caravan goes before them. In the early days vehicles were just plastered with their sponsors' names, but soon willing volunteers would hang out of windows throwing freebies to the crowds, and the vehicles became more and more absurd.

Now the caravan consists of giant flies on wheels, huge cheeses on the back of lorries, mobile giant waste bins and gas canisters, washing-up liquid bottles, chocolate bars and bottles of drink, all motorised and all staffed by vacationing students who chuck plastic novelties, free sweets, hats and all sorts of cheap and cheerful stuff to the crowd. And they love it; woe betide you if you get in the way of a Breton granny or a kid from the Limousin when they are trying to score some free sweets.

France and Italy had by far the most formidable teams in 1930, but after dominating the first part of the race the Italians fell apart on a huge 222-kilometre team time trial between Bordeaux and Hendaye. Their star rider, Learco 'the Human Locomotive' Guerra compounded a terrible day by crashing and losing over an hour.

France took the lead after that. Charles Pelissier proved to be the first of a long line of great sprinters in the Tour de France by winning eight stages, four of them in a row. And the overall winner was André Leducq. The French were the stars thanks to two great individual performances backed up by a huge team effort.

Leducq took the yellow jersey in the Pyrenees by means of some consistent rather than spectacular racing. Then, while he was riding really well on the biggest stage in the

Alps, he crashed on the descent of the Col du Galibier, which in 1930 was climbed by its more unusual south side. He was knocked out cold and took 15 minutes to come to his senses, by which time most of the French team were off their bikes and crowded around him.

They got him going again, but on the short ascent of the Col de Telegraph a pedal broke on Leducq's bike and he came crashing down again. Marcel Bidot, a team-mate who would eventually manage the French team, was alongside him when it happened. He stopped, dragged Leducq to the side of the road, propped him up against a stone and examined his injuries. When he touched his knee, which was ripped to bits and in a real mess, Leducq screamed, saying that it was broken, but Bidot just picked up his foot, pushed it upwards to bend his knee and told him that it wasn't. Then, leaving Leducq writhing in agony, Bidot took a spanner to a spectator's bike, removed one of the pedals and bolted it to Leducq's.

Leducq was still in no condition to continue. He was crying with pain, but if he was looking for sympathy he didn't get any from Bidot. 'Stop blubbering,' he told him. 'The yellow jersey never gives up. Look, the whole team is waiting for you. We will take you to the finish.' And that's what they did, pacing Leducq to the stage finish in Evian and saving the Tour for him. Antonin Magne was third overall, Bidot fifth and Magne's brother Pierre sixth. It was a superb result for France, and the new team formula was deemed a great success.

It was the beginning of a golden era for the French in their biggest bike race. They provided the next four winners in Antonin Magne, who won in 1931 and 1934, Leducq again in 1932 and George Speicher in 1933. Of them all Speicher's win was the least eventful, as it was due more to the crushing strength of the French team than anything special from Speicher.

Instead the main story of the 1933 Tour was that it was the first year of the King of the Mountains contest. This is the one where points are awarded to the first few over all the Tour's climbs and, nowadays, the leader wears a polka-dot jersey. That wasn't introduced until 1975, though, when its sponsor was the Poulain chocolate company, whose wrappers were white with red spots. The 1933 King of the Mountains was a Spaniard, Vincent Trueba, who weighed less than 50 kilograms and was so tiny that the journalists called him the 'Spanish Flea'.

While the Tour was on, Adolf Hitler became chancellor of Germany without the average cycling fan noticing too much. The following year he declared himself Führer and head of state, and by then people had seen newsreels of the Nazi rallies and the iconography of Hitler's political party, and were starting to get worried.

Antonin Magne's win in 1931 was also a brilliant French team effort, but it left him so shattered by nervous exhaustion that he didn't start in 1932 or '33. However, Magne was back to full strength in 1934, and ready to head another strong French team. Magne took the yellow jersey early on, but when the race reached the Alps a first-timer in the French team, René Vietto, proved that he was stronger.

Vietto's story is typical of a lot of working-class young men who succeed in cycling, especially in the early days of the Tour. He was from Cannes, and his first job was as a lift boy in one of the big hotels there. It wasn't a bad way of life, but the work didn't pay well, and when Vietto found out in local bike races that he had a flair for cycling, he grabbed the chance of a new life with both hands.

Every morning at four o'clock he went out on the hilly roads that are the backdrop of the Côte d'Azur, riding over 100 kilometres before work. He progressed quickly, got a pro contract and left his job, improved some more and was finally selected for the 1934 French Tour team.

Vietto was totally in awe of Magne. He liked his leader's dedication, he liked his nickname 'the Monk', and he admired the way he conducted himself, but perhaps he admired him too much. After two Alpine stage victories, one at Grenoble and one at Digne, Vietto proved he was riding better than Magne. He led the King of the Mountains competition, and the newspapers not only took it as read that he'd win that contest, but also predicted that Vietto would take over the yellow jersey from Magne in the Pyrenees.

Everyone believed it, maybe even Magne, but not Vietto. He refused to attack his leader, and when Magne crashed descending the Col de Puymorens, Vietto was right next to him to offer him his wheel. Equipment exchanges between team-mates had been allowed since Desgrange kicked out the trade teams, so Magne grabbed the spare and set off in pursuit of the leaders, leaving Vietto stranded.

Next day Vietto did the same thing again. He was forcing the pace on a climb for Magne, trying to draw some sting out of their rivals' legs, when he became aware that his leader was no longer near him. Magne had punctured, so when Vietto found out, he stopped in the road, did a U-turn and rode back down the mountain to give Magne his wheel. Service vehicles were allowed on the thirties Tours, but mountain roads were still bad, there was little radio communication, and the French car was much further down the climb looking after another rider. Vietto lost nearly half an hour waiting that day, but he saved Magne's Tour.

Magne was a worrier and had a very cautious nature, so much so that he irritated his French team-mates when they shared a room with him. All he could talk about was what could go wrong on the next stage, or what had gone wrong on the one they'd just done. And when he wasn't talking about that he'd be moaning about the price of stuff.

Magne carried his caution and miserliness into his second career in cycling as a team manager, or *directeur sportif* as they are called in France. In his day a directeur sportif ran a team, and this remained the case until quite recently, although with the addition of assistants. However, teams are now so big that they have a senior figure, usually someone who has earned his spurs as a directeur, in overall charge of logistics, and several directeurs sportifs answerable to him who take control on the road.

Magne directed some great riders during his career, including the man who first scored a hat-trick of Tour victories, Louison Bobet. He also directed Raymond Poulidor, who although he never won the race is just about the most popular French cyclist ever. Magne did his job with the same dignity he displayed as a racer, and that brought him the Legion of Honour in 1962, but he worried about everything that went with the job, including his budget.

Britain's Barry Hoban raced for Magne's team in the sixties and remembers: 'Every other pro team had jerseys with zips in them. They were all made from fine wool, so were hot, but a short zip did at least let some air in at the front. Magne wouldn't buy them, though, because the zips cost one franc more. And he would never supply us with silk tyres, which were faster than cotton ones for time trials. We had to buy our own, and 28-spoke lightweight wheels to put them on if we wanted to do a fast time trial, or if there was a sprint finish on a smooth track, where faster tyres are an advantage.'

Mind you, Magne maybe had cause to worry and be cautious, because he was very unlucky too. For example, if Vietto hadn't saved the 1934 Tour, Magne would certainly have lost it through no fault of his own. The French team supplied his tyres, so Magne wasn't using the cheap ones he'd have probably preferred. In 1935, when he was still strong enough to win the Tour again, Magne was hit by one of the race vehicles and crashed out of the race, ending up finishing the stage on the back of a farmer's truck.

That stage also saw the first fatality of the Tour de France. Magne crashed on the descent of the Col de Telegraph. From there the riders climbed the Galibier, and it was on the following descent that Francisco Cepeda met his death. He was a member of the Spanish 'individuals' team. National individuals were new concept in the Tour, a category designed to cater for riders who weren't quite good enough for their national team, but were a cut above the touriste-routiers. Cepeda was descending quickly in wet conditions on the top part of the Galibier's south side, which joins the Lautaret pass after a few kilometres. The top part is very twisty and Cepeda seems to have gone into a bend too quickly, and simply run out of road. He crashed and cracked his head on a rock, fracturing his skull. He died in hospital three days later.

Cepeda's was the first of just three deaths to date in the Tour de France which, given the risks involved, is a quite amazing statistic. Hurtling down mountains on two skinny tyres, often with a rock face on one side and a drop of many thousands of feet on the other, is a recipe for disaster. So are huge field sprints with 100 or more highly motivated professional athletes desperate to either win or ensure that their team's sprinter crosses the line first. Then there is the sheer human exertion of racing for three weeks over huge distances through anything from snow to boiling sunshine. That there haven't been more deaths is a tribute to the racers' skill, their fitness and, it has to be said, the organisers of the Tour de France.

A Belgian, Romain Maes, took the initiative early in 1935, winning the yellow jersey on the first stage and keeping it until the end. He led a Belgian whitewash, with Félicien Vervaecke taking third overall and the King of the Mountains trophy, while Sylvère Maes, who was no relation to Romain, was fourth and Jules Lowie fifth. Vervaecke later opened a bike shop in the Woluwe-St-Pierre suburb of Brussels where a young Eddy Merckx lived, and became Merckx's first coach, setting him on the way to becoming the first Belgian to win the Tour since the thirties.

The resurgence of Belgium was the sporting story of the Tour de France in the run-up to the Second World War. The organisation story, though, was the transfer of power from Henri Desgrange to someone who had been groomed for the job, the son of *L'Auto*'s company accountant, Jacques Goddet.

Goddet was highly educated and spoke several languages, including the English that he learned when studying for a short period at university in England. He walked straight into the editor's job at *L'Auto* when he finished his studies in 1931, and began covering the Tour de France. Goddet would also cover many Olympic Games and football World Cups in his long career.

By 1936 the Tour organisation was a full-time job for several members of *L'Auto*'s staff, and Desgrange, although he had reached his early seventies by then, was still in charge of it. He started out as race director on the 1936 race too, but suffering from the after-effects of kidney surgery he had to stand down after a couple of stages to be replaced by Goddet, who would lead the Tour, and French sports journalism, well into the eighties.

The political story for the 1936 Tour was that Italy refused to send a team. The French, along with the British, had been scathing about Italy's empire-building, which was a bit two-faced really considering the two countries' own imperialist record. There was an attempt to start by a group of Italians who claimed French residency, including one of the best sprinters of the time, Raffaele Di Paco, but pressure was put on them and they withdrew at the last minute.

The race began in terrible weather, with floods and torrential rain affecting the first seven stages. Sylvère Maes worked his way into second place, and then on stage eight, a big one in the Alps, he more or less drifted into the yellow jersey.

Antonin Magne was the best of the French at that stage, and he went on the attack next day but could not shake Maes. He tried again the following day, and the next, but Maes stuck to him like glue. Eventually, on the Pyrenean climb of the Tourmalet, Magne paid for his efforts and began to slow, whereas the inexorable Maes just stuck to the same pace and rode away to win the stage and the Tour.

When he returned home to Gistel in West Flanders, Maes used his winnings to build an art deco style café, sited on the town's main crossroads, which he called 'The Tourmalet' to celebrate where he won the Tour. It's still there, but today it's an Irish Bar, which the current owners have renamed 'The O'Tourmalet'.

They say a new broom sweeps clean, and that is exactly what Jacques Goddet did on the first Tour de France where he was fully in charge. Derailleur gears had been used for years by cyclists all over the world, but not in the Tour. Desgrange had relented slightly a few years earlier and allowed the touriste-routiers to use them, but not the pros. Desgrange said that easy gear changes made bike racers soft and, like warm baths and silk sheets, Derailleur gears eroded a man's character. Pro racers in the Tour still changed gear the way they had since 1903. They had a choice of two gears, one for uphill and one for down. To change they had to dismount, undo their rear wheel and turn it around to engage the different-sized single sprocket screwed on to the other side.

Derailleurs ended that and they changed the tactics of bike racing. It became more closely contested, and distancing a rival depended as much on tactical sense and strength as on knowing when to change gear. The peloton became the moving base of operations for every race, from which attacks and efforts were made to cause splits.

The Italians returned to the 1937 Tour, and they returned with Gino Bartali, a Tuscan racer who is still regarded as one of the toughest and best from Italy. Bartali started badly but triumphed over the Galibier on stage seven to lead the race. Next day, however, a team-mate made a mistake while taking a corner, crashed and knocked Bartali off the road and into a river. He hit a submerged rock with his chest and was winded, causing several of his team-mates to jump in after him. They hauled him to the bank, where covered in mud and blood he remounted. They pushed him almost all the way to the finish to save the yellow jersey, but Bartali was in trouble.

Next day was another tough one, with the south Alpine double of the Vars and Izoard to contend with. Bartali couldn't keep up with the leaders and lost over 22 minutes. In bygone Tours that wouldn't necessarily have been disastrous, but as the overall standard of the Tour's participants grew higher time gaps had closed, and Derailleur gears had closed them even further. Sylvère Maes took over the lead, with Bartali out of it. But then, gradually, a Frenchman called Roger Lapébie, who was as much a scallywag as he looked, crept into the picture.

Now, I'm not saying Lapébie cheated to win the 1937 Tour, but according to reports no one has been pushed so far around France by spectators than this wily former track rider from Bordeaux. The Belgians, who can be a bit wily themselves, protested constantly at the blind eye the race judges, who were all French, seemed to be turning to Lapébie. The Belgians claimed that Lapébie not only encouraged spectators to push him up the climbs, but also would hang on to motor vehicles that were part of the race on flat stages. Finally, rumour has it, the Belgians decided that if making official complaints was getting them nowhere, then they'd have to take matters into their own hands, and they allegedly mounted an operation the newspapers called 'Get Rid of Lapébie'.

While Lapébie was riding to the start of stage 15 in Luchon, his handlebars snapped in two. On examination it was found that they had been sawn nearly through from underneath. With the uppermost part still intact, Lapébie couldn't see this, but the handlebars came apart as soon as he applied pressure to them. It was lucky really that it happened before the stage, and not when he was up to racing speed.

New handlebars were fitted, but thirties racers carried their water bottles in holders on their handlebars, and there was no time to fit one. As the day wore on, Lapébie began to suffer from dehydration, because he couldn't carry any water and there were strict rules that said he could only be given some in the official aid stations along the route. Eventually he was reduced to stopping at mountain streams for water, which was allowed.

Somehow, though, Lapébie kept going, but he had lost seven minutes to Sylvère Maes by the top of the Col du Tourmalet. What followed was one of the most heroic descents in Tour history as Lapébie shot down the Tourmalet and caught Maes 15 kilometres after the climb.

Maes and Lapébie started the final climb, the Col d'Aubisque, together, and as the better climber the Belgian was expected to drop Lapébie. Or at least he would have done had Lapébie not got hundreds of pushes from the crowd. When the judge warned him, Lapébie said he couldn't help it and that he was asking people not to push, but Maes contradicted him, telling the judge that Lapébie was asking for pushes.

To cap it all, Lapébie won the stage in Pau, where the Belgian team mounted another official protest. The race organisers investigated, found Lapébie guilty but handed him a measly 90-second penalty, at which the Belgians were outraged. A bad-tempered Tour was about to get really messy.

Maes still had the yellow jersey from Lapébie by just over three minutes; there were no climbs left, and it looked as if the Belgian would win in Paris. The next stage was to Bordeaux, but about half-way through it Maes punctured and Lapébie attacked. Not terribly sporting, but within the rules. Once he'd fitted a new tyre, Maes chased with the help of Gustaaf Deloor. Deloor wasn't pushing him or anything, just sharing the pace, but although Deloor was a Belgian he was in the Belgian 'individuals' team, and not part of the national Belgian team. Maes was in the national team, and the rules did state that he couldn't have help from anyone who was in another.

Then, when the two Belgians were gaining on Lapébie, a signalman let the Frenchman through a railway crossing and closed the barrier in front of the Belgians. There was no train, so Maes got off his bike and crawled under the barrier to continue his pursuit. He finished the stage one minute 40 seconds behind him and in a really bad mood, asking if he had to fight not just French bike racers to win the Tour, but the whole of France.

And Maes said that before the judges handed him a 25-second penalty for working with Deloor, bringing Lapébie to within 25 seconds of the lead. It was too much for Maes, who said he wasn't going to pedal to Paris while being slowly robbed of victory, and he and the whole Belgian team withdrew from the Tour, leaving Lapébie the winner.

It had been a scrappy race, but at least it left Lapébie happy. He became a great character of French cycling, and even when he stopped racing he could never stay away from the Tour. He loved telling tales about how he won, and in his later years the old rascal would brag about all the pushes and tows he got in 1937. His view was that the help he got from spectators and the officials' leniency were both simply due to his popularity, and no one ever contradicted him, except maybe one or two Belgians. The Tour de France is still like that, though. It looks after its own, and even the most washed-up ex-pro who has made a hash out of life after racing can still get a job for three weeks doing PR, or maybe driving one of the hundreds of official cars on the race. It's like a big old boys' club.

Higher and faster have always been key words in the Tour's history, especially higher. In its early days the staff of *L'Auto* constantly visited the mountains to talk to locals about which climbs were the toughest. They also kept in touch with road-building departments, who were always working to create new vehicle routes or improving old ones through the Alps and Pyrenees. For 1938 they found the highest pass the Tour had climbed so far, the Col d'Iseran. At 2,770 metres its road surface was rough and a terrifying prospect for anyone riding a bike.

Gino Bartali was the hot favourite to win, and he didn't disappoint. The Belgians put up some resistance, but the French team was full of older riders who were past their prime.

Bartali rode conservatively in the Pyrenees, which came first that year, and went on the attack in the Alps. The stage where he chose to make his move ran between Digne and Briançon and climbed the Vars and Izoard, which by now were a familiar part of the Tour. Bartali followed the leaders on the Vars, and then as they started the Izoard he decided to push a little harder on the pedals, just to see what happened.

Immediately he was on his own, and when he looked round to see where the others were on the long straight up to the village of Brunissard, he could see no one. Later he recalled: 'I didn't see anyone behind until the first of the hairpins near the top, then I got a view down the valley and below me I saw two dots that looked like little ants crawling along the road.' The dots were Mario Vincini and Mathias Clemens, who finished behind Bartali in

Briançon five and six minutes back respectively. The best of the rest were 11 minutes behind. Bartali made those gaps in the time it took to climb and descend one mountain. He was cycling in another dimension that day, and the big effort he made virtually won him the Tour.

Europe was heading for war by 1939. Italy, Spain and Germany could not send teams, which left lots of space for the French. Unfortunately the home country was in one of its periodic cycling troughs. This one coincided with a national crisis of confidence as France felt threatened and was in two minds about German aggression. There were some strong riders, such as René Vietto, who had made a return to top-level cycling after having made some bad investments, but there was very little depth.

Vietto took up the challenge by taking the yellow jersey early in the race, but then he developed a problem with his knee and had to have pain-killing injections every evening. He kept fighting, though, and held on to the yellow jersey until stage 17, when the Izoard proved a mountain too far. Vietto's knee all but gave way and Sylvère Maes took 17 minutes out of him to take over the lead, which he kept to Paris.

In many ways the 1939 Tour was a race that had to be got out of the way. By September the Second World War had started and France was an occupied country. Many of the Tour's racers were drafted into the army and, just as it had in 1914, it looked as though life would never be normal again.

7. THE TOUR AT WAR

L'Auto published a tentative plan for a 1940 Tour de France in August 1939, but it was shelved once the Germans invaded. At first the whole country was thrown into confusion, but some order was restored when the Germans decided to divide France. They would occupy and administer the north, which bordered the English Channel, because that is where any invasion from England would come from. Meanwhile they would let the Free French under Marshal Philippe Pétain, a First World War hero, run the south from a base in Vichy.

Early in the occupation *L'Auto*'s Paris office was raided by the Germans, its records were seized and a lot of Tour de France history was lost. Goddet kept writing, however, and the paper kept being published. He appears to have collaborated with the Germans as well, at least at first. He supported Pétain, who wanted a kind of peaceful coexistence with Germany. The worst thing Goddet did, though, was hand over the keys of the Vélodrome d'Hiver, the indoor cycle track in Paris, to the Germans, who interned thousands of Jews there before shipping them off to concentration camps.

Goddet hardly mentions that in his autobiography, *L'Equipe Belle* (The Beautiful Team), but in his defence

Goddet didn't roll over and do everything the Germans wanted. In 1942 their propaganda machine thought that they could win the hearts and minds of French people by returning life to as normal as possible, so they asked Goddet to organise the Tour de France for them. At no small risk to himself, Goddet refused.

However, an ex-colleague at *L'Auto*, Jean Leulliot, who managed the French national team in the 1937 Tour and was now the sports editor of another newspaper, *La France Socialiste*, was more open to the German request. In the autumn of 1942 Leulliot put together a race that ran through the occupied and free zones of France, which he called the Circuit de France. Goddet would not let him use the 'Tour' title.

It had eight stages, travelling from Paris to Le Mans, then to Poitiers, Limoges, Clermont-Ferrand, St Etienne, Lyon, Dijon and back to Paris for a 4 October finish. Sixty-nine professional cyclists lined up to take part, but they weren't all willing volunteers. This race was going to work, the Nazis had decided, and more than one rider received visits from the Gestapo to help them make up their minds. One of them, Emile Idée, told the journalist Jean Bobet years later: 'I was very afraid. The Gestapo made it clear that my family would be in danger if I didn't race.'

The Circuit de France was won by François Neuville, but it was a false, forced affair that created more bad feeling than it did good. The Germans wouldn't sanction another Circuit in 1943, and Leulliot and Goddet feuded for the rest of their lives over that one edition, even though Goddet did an about-face and organised the Grand Prix du Tour de France in 1943 and 1944. Maybe he too had a persuasive visitor. However, he stressed in *L'Auto* that the

Grand Prix was a series of nine separate races and not a real Tour de France.

Goddet's assertion about the Grand Prix being no Tour was brave, considering that *L'Auto* had fallen under German control. To be fair to him, as many people were at the time, Goddet went as far as he dared against the Germans, but he was also trying to stay alive during the occupation. He paid for having helped the Germans too. When the Allies liberated Paris, *L'Auto* was closed because it was deemed to have submitted to German control.

A lot of scores were settled in France just after the war, and Goddet had a torrid time. Out-and-out collaborators received rough justice before law and order could be established by the Allies, but others who were merely suspected of helping the enemy faced many obstacles in their careers and daily lives. Goddet started another sports newspaper, *L'Equipe*, in an office across the street from his old one, but the knives were out for him and for a while he had to write for it anonymously.

He also found that he didn't have automatic control of the Tour de France either, despite the fact that Goddet had retained the rights to the Tour de France name. When a dummy run for a full Tour was mooted for 1946, Goddet and *L'Equipe* had to share the organisation with a rival paper, *Le Parisien Libéré*. The winner of that race, the Course du Tour de France, or Monaco–Paris as it is sometimes known, was a young racer called Apo Lazarides.

Lazarides had an interesting war. He was born in the north of France, in the Pas-de-Calais, and had Greek blood. When he was a child his family moved to the south, where he began cycling under the expert guidance of René Vietto. Lazarides quickly developed into a formidable climber, and owing to his short stature was known throughout his life as the 'Greek Kid'.

He was devoted to Vietto, though, and when his mentor suffered sepsis in his toe during the first post-war Tour in 1947 and had to have it amputated, Lazarides had his toe removed too, claiming that they would now both be a little lighter and able to climb that bit better. It's one of those Tour stories that sounds like a tall one, but apparently Vietto's toe is preserved in formaldehyde in a bar somewhere in Marseilles. Unfortunately, though, nobody I've asked knows which bar.

Living in the initially free south meant that Lazarides could race throughout the first part of the war, and he was a regular sight on the hilly roads behind the Côte d'Azur. After a while, despite their promises not to do so, the Germans had to occupy the south because the Allies invaded North Africa in November 1942. Now Germany feared an invasion from the Mediterranean as well as from the north.

But the south, with its mountains and remoteness, proved difficult for the Germans to police, and the southern wing of the French resistance, or Maquis, were very effective in the area. Lazarides kept riding, and after initially stopping and searching him whenever they saw him, the Germans got to know who he was and accepted that his long bike rides into the hills were part of his training. That is when the Maquis recruited him. Once the Germans were used to Lazarides, and their patrols and checkpoints ignored him, his training rides took on a deadly purpose. Now, instead of having his pockets stuffed with food to sustain him on long rides in the hills, Lazarides filled his pockets with ammunition for the Maquis, who fed him when he made his deliveries.

Many other cyclists were involved in similar work in their own regions and countries, and much of it remains unsung, but the most celebrated resistance fighter was Gino Bartali in Italy. Not that anyone knew the full extent of his involvement until after his death. His sons had heard things and would ask their father, but Bartali, a devoutly religious man, would just say, 'One does these things and that is that.'

After their father died, Bartali's sons had to sort out his affairs and go through the papers he'd kept secret from them. What they found pointed them in the direction of more research, and the result of that was revealed to me by a more recent Italian champion, Maurizio Fondriest, the 1988 world road race champion, who knows the Bartali family well. Fondriest says:

'The Germans wanted Italy's Fascist government to round up all the Jews in the country, but many Jews were taken into hiding by monks in monasteries,' Fondriest told me. 'The Italian resistance wanted to try and get the Jews out of Italy and to a safe place, but they needed forged documents to do it. One group of monks set up a printing press in Lucca, but they needed photographs of the Jews who were hiding in other places. Bartali volunteered to transport the photographs and documents.

'He would leave his home in Florence wearing a racing jersey with his name printed all over it, and set off on what looked like a training ride. He was so famous that at first he was never even stopped at the road blocks, so he cycled around the monasteries picking up the photographs and delivering the forged passes that were ready.

'Eventually, though, the Fascists grew suspicious, but they still did not dare arrest Bartali because there would have been a public outcry. Then the Germans became suspicious. They couldn't understand why so few Jews were being handed over, and they put pressure on the Italian Fascists to find out what was happening. They knew Bartali was involved, so they had to arrest him. He was threatened and beaten, but he told them nothing, and once they let him go he carried on as he had done, only more so. He became involved with the Assisi underground and even led Jews out of Italy himself.

'He made a trailer with a hidden compartment in it. A Jew would hide in the compartment, and if Bartali was stopped he said that he was pulling the trailer on his bike as part of his training. Even if the guards looked inside it they couldn't see the hiding place. Bartali was a hero but he never spoke about what he did afterwards.'

There are other stories too of cyclists as heroes during the war. André Leducq was part of the French resistance, along with his good friend André Bertin, a bike importer from the north of France. Bertin was decorated after the war but later sent his medal back in disgust because of all the people who were claiming to be resistance but weren't.

Goddet came out of it OK. He wasn't trusted totally at first, but he had organisational flare and was soon once again at the helm both of the Tour and of *L'Equipe*. However, Goddet was better with a pen than he was with an adding machine and its finances were always rocky. In 1965 he was forced to accept an offer from Emilien Amaury, who had been a bona fide resistance hero, for *L'Equipe* – and the Tour – to become part of his huge publishing empire. After Amaury's death his son Philippe took over, and the sporting side of their interests has since morphed into ASO, one of the biggest events organisers in the world, who run not only the Tour de France but many other top European cycling events, and events in other sports such as the Paris Marathon and the Paris–Dakar Rally.

The war stopped the Tour de France, just as it had between 1914 and 1918, but it didn't damage it. It was too much a part of the fabric of French life to die, and the government wanted the race back as soon as possible to give the people something to unite behind and look forward to, rather than dwell on the injustices of war.

8. IL CAMPIONISSIMO

Fausto Coppi was the first superstar of cycling. There had been great riders before, great athletes capable of astonishing performances, great characters and personalities too, but Coppi transcended his own athleticism and his sport. He was the first cyclist who constantly featured in the gossip columns, whose life away from cycling sparked as much interest as his brilliant sporting achievements did.

And he was brilliant. Some say, and there's merit in their argument, that Coppi is still the greatest bike racer ever. He didn't win as much as Eddy Merckx, or as many Tours de France as Lance Armstrong, but Coppi's greatness lay in the margin of his victories. When he was on form he simply rode away from the rest and won by many minutes, and he could win almost every kind of race, which is another mark of cycling greatness.

Coppi didn't have an auspicious start in life. He was born in 1919 in the town of Castellania, which is in the Alessandria region of northern Italy, just inland from the Mediterranean coast. Nearly ten per cent of the town's population is called Coppi today, and the house in which he was born is the Coppi museum, decorated in the way it was when he grew up in it.

Life was hard in Castellania, and when Coppi's schooling ended at the age of 12 there was no job for him. Luckily he had a couple of well-connected uncles: Giuseppe, who was a tugboat captain in Genoa, and Fausto, who was a captain in the merchant navy. Giuseppe got young Fausto a job as a butcher's boy in a nearby town, Novi Ligure, and when Fausto senior heard tell that his sickly-looking nephew flew like the wind on his delivery bike and wanted one day to become a bike racer, he bought him a racing bike.

Coppi was a cycling genius. Tall, gangling and quite clumsy on two feet, on two wheels he had all the poise, balance and grace in the world. Where others pushed their pedals around, Coppi stroked them with his feet. He began racing in 1935, and four years later he was a semi-professional fighting it out with the greats of Italian cycling, including Gino Bartali.

Coppi and Bartali's relationship began with guarded respect, and respect was always part of it, but it became one of the hottest rivalries in cycling, a rivalry that didn't end until the Tour de France of 1949 and the Col d'Izoard. It was one of the key talking points in cycling throughout the forties, and in many ways mirrored the rivalry of two French riders, Jacques Anquetil and Raymond Poulidor, in years to come. Coppi represented modern cycling and modern Italy, whereas Bartali was the standard-bearer for the old ways.

Coppi couldn't take part in the first two post-war Tours de France. He had raced during much of the war, building a huge list of victories including the Giro d'Italia, several national titles and several single-day Classics, and he set a new world hour record. Technically he was in the Italian army during this period, but when things got tough for

Italy as the war dragged on, Coppi was called into active service. He was no soldier, though, and when he went to fight in Tunisia he was quickly captured by the Allies. He ended up in a prisoner of war camp for two years, which left him below par when the Tour de France resumed.

The first post-war Tour took place in 1947. The previous year's Course du Tour de France hadn't been easy. Cyclists and their entourage consume food and fuel, and both were in short supply in a country that was on its knees. An appeal for help was made in the pages of *L'Equipe*, not for money but for food and petrol, and bike fans sent enough for the race to go ahead. The result was of less interest than the fact that the race had taken place at all, and no one took much notice of the winners, let alone the short, awkward-looking man with a lot of attitude who had finished third: Jean Robic.

But Robic won the 1947 Tour de France, and he did it in the most dramatic way possible by taking victory on the final stage. René Vietto had been the favourite. He had sacrificed his chances in the Course du Tour de France for his protégé Lazarides, hoping that Lazarides would return the favour once the Tour proper began again. Surprisingly, though, Lazarides didn't make the French national selection, which meant that the mercurial Vietto started off feeling persecuted.

Nevertheless he took the race lead by winning the second stage of 130 kilometres from Lille to Brussels. Vietto held the yellow jersey for five days, lost it and then regained it in the Alps by winning in Digne-les-Bains. He still had the jersey six days later as the race left the Pyrenees, where his most dangerous rival was an Italian, Pierre Brambilla.

Nothing changed until three days before the finish in Paris, when there was a massive 134-kilometre time trial between Vannes and St Brieuc in Brittany. Vietto feared this stage. He was a climber, and although Brittany is lumpy it doesn't have any mountains. He would need every bit of help he could get, so Vietto bought a special yellow jersey made of silk, which would slip through the air more easily than the standard race issue wool one. But these were still the days of draconian rules, and a Tour official refused to let Vietto wear it.

What happened next was pure comedy. Vietto totally lost it. He was 33 by then, and he looked it. A slight but tough-looking man with a sergeant-major's wiry haircut, he tore off the jersey, threw it at the official's feet and on live radio denounced the Tour, its organisers and anyone who had anything to do with it as liars and cheats who were conspiring to defeat him. He stormed over to his team car, packed his belongings in his suitcase, took it into his hotel and refused to start. Some officials followed him, picked up his case and threw it back outside. You do not leave the Tour when you are leading it, they told him. But Vietto was having none of it and he marched outside, picked up the suitcase and took it back in, whereupon the officials threw it outside again. Eventually Vietto started the time trial and, grumbling to himself all along the route, proceeded to lose 15 minutes and his final chance in a race he'd been trying to win since 1935.

Pierre Brambilla took over the race lead after the long time trial, with Robic, who was from Brittany, in second place. And that looked like that. Robic was second at nearly three minutes right up until the final stage and the final hill of the race, but then the Miracle of Bonsecours happened.

Bonsecours is a climb out of the Seine valley in Rouen. If Robic was beaten then nobody had told him. He attacked all day and did so again on Bonsecours. Brambilla and his Italian team-mates had answered everything Robic threw at them, but just when they couldn't afford to they made a mistake. Brambilla was boxed in by other riders when Robic played his final card. Once Brambilla untangled himself he nearly caught Robic, but was attacked himself by a Frenchman, Edouard Fachleitner.

Fachleitner shot past Brambilla, caught Robic and went by him, but the little Breton sprinted desperately after Fachleitner and just caught on to his rear wheel, and they were gone. Brambilla's effort didn't bridge the gap. He held it for a moment then blew wide apart, losing 12 minutes to the pair who rode hard together to move into first and second in the Tour. Brambilla never recovered from the beating either; it was weeks before he could even look at a bike. In fact there's a rumour that he buried the one he'd raced on during the Tour in his garden.

Robic was called 'Leatherhead' by the fans, because he'd had so many crashes in his career and broken so many bones that he always wore a leather crash hat to protect an old injury. He loved cycling, and he loved the recognition that winning the Tour gave him so much that he raced as a professional until he was well into his forties. And after that he became an amateur again. He even raced on the last day of his life. In 1980 he had taken part in one of the races for old pros that are popular in France. Driving home late at night he lost control of his car and was killed in the crash. There's a memorial to Robic now on Bonsecours Hill, commemorating his 'miracle'.

The 1948 Tour was won by Gino Bartali, who not only became one of the oldest winners at 34, but also set the record for the widest spaced pair of victories – ten years apart. He was leader of the Italian team because Fausto

Coppi had refused to race in the Tour, still upset at what he thought was a conspiracy against him during that year's Giro.

These were still turbulent times in Italy. During the Tour de France their communist party leader, Palmiro Togliatti, was wounded in an assassination attempt and civil unrest broke out. The Italian team was on the verge of withdrawing from the Tour when their prime minister phoned Gino Bartali. He told the cyclist that the country needed a distraction, that a stage win or if possible overall victory would save Italy from revolution.

Bartali had been called to arms before, and had answered the call to do the right thing for his country when he helped the Assisi Line during the war, and now he did it again. At the start of the 13th stage he was nearly 20 minutes behind in eighth place overall. There weren't many days left to make up time, and Bartali had just two big Alpine stages to work with. The first was from Cannes to Briançon, but the last climb on that stage was the mighty Col d'Izoard, where the Italian had dominated ten years before. On a cold, wet day Bartali attacked the front group early on the Izoard. The climb is a huge theatre that welcomes virtuoso performances, and Bartali made the most of it. He soared away up the long straight valley that leads up to the village of Bruinissard, then danced between the rock pinnacles of the Casse Déserte and around the hairpins at the top to descend into Briançon and win the stage by six minutes.

Louison Bobet, a young Breton riding his second Tour de France and destined to have a big future with the race and on the Col d'Izoard, still had the yellow jersey, but Bartali moved up to second place. Next day he repeated the performance on a huge stage with the Lautaret,

Galibier and Telegraphe climbs. He bided his time during the first half of this 263-kilometre mountain marathon that took him nine and a half hours to complete. Then he attacked and rode solo over the Col de la Croix de Fer, and the Porte, Cucheron and Granier cols to win by six minutes again. The Tour was Bartali's and some peace was restored in Italy, but Bartali's victory did nothing to appease the war that had been going on inside Italian cycling.

Coppi and Bartali had got off on the wrong foot almost from the day they met. Bartali was a great and brave man – his activities during the war proved that – but he was first and foremost a competitor and subject to all the insecurities that brings. Coppi was the same, and if you throw in some mild paranoia he was probably worse. Bartali was unhappy at being usurped by the younger man, and Coppi blamed a Bartali conspiracy every time he lost. The whole thing came to a ridiculous head when, despite both racing for the Italian national team in the 1948 World Championships, the pair marked each other so closely that they ignored what was happening at the front of the race and got totally left behind. A three-month suspension by the Italian cycling federation brought them somewhat to their senses, but it still didn't bring a truce.

Their fans didn't help either, often hurling abuse at each other during races. They were two distinct social and age groups, so they didn't like each other anyway. Coppi fans tended to be young city folk, free thinkers or the well heeled, while Bartalists were older, from the country, religious and less well off. This division also brought about another factor that would widen the division between the two great Italians.

One of Coppi's most ardent supporters was a doctor called Locatelli. He loved sport, loved cycling and thought that Coppi in particular was both admirable and fascinating. His wife Giulia didn't share his enthusiasm at all, until she met Coppi. And then she fell in love with him.

What timing that was. Coppi won the 1949 Giro d'Italia and the Italian national coach brokered a kind of peace between Coppi and Bartali, so they both started the Tour de France as equal leaders of the national team. They would finally bury the hatchet during the race, but with that little war behind him Coppi's relationship with Giulia would grow to cause a storm no one could have imagined.

Despite the peace deal, distrust simmered in the background of the Italian team for the first half of the 1949 Tour de France, but as the race wore on Coppi gradually proved that he was the stronger. Bartali finally accepted the fact on stage 16, ironically on almost the same route as he had begun his push for the yellow jersey the year before.

Their team-mate Fiorenzi Magni had the yellow jersey, but it wasn't in the Italian script for him to keep it, so Coppi and Bartali attacked on the Izoard, which was again the last climb of a long day. They quickly got a gap and had set about putting distance into the rest when Coppi clumsily rode over a hole in the road, punctured his rear tyre and crashed. Bartali was ahead of Coppi overall, so could have forged on ahead, but instead he waited. Once his wheel was replaced Coppi continued, quite surprised by the actions of a man who he thought hated him. The pair continued to gain time, but then Coppi's pace proved too much for Bartali, who was feeling his 35 years. He had to accept the inevitable and ask Coppi to slow down, which he did. With Bartali's acceptance and with Coppi's point proved, their rivalry disappeared and Coppi, knowing that the day was Bartali's birthday, let him take the stage.

Bartali still had the yellow jersey, but now it was only on loan. Coppi and Bartali attacked again next day, but Bartali had bad luck, crashing twice. Coppi waited the first time, but after Bartali's second fall their team manager, Alfredo Binda, knowing that with Coppi's form the time was right to gain a lot of time on the rest, ordered Coppi to continue alone. He won the stage by five minutes from Bartali and had ten on the rest. Fausto Coppi had won his first Tour de France. It was also the first time anyone had done the Giro-Tour double and won both Grand Tours in the same year.

Coppi won many more races that year, and waiting at the end of each of them was a fan he began to recognise. Giulia Locatelli had become infatuated with Coppi. Stalker wasn't a word that was used in the late forties, unless you were hunting, but Giulia stalked Coppi until he noticed her. Coppi was married, but that didn't put her off. Giulia's infatuation grew until, in 1950, she used the opportunity of Coppi being in hospital with a fractured pelvis after a crash to get close to him.

Her visits sealed their fate. Coppi fell for her and maybe was a little flattered. Giulia was attractive, from a good family and she had married well. Could she be interested in a butcher's boy from Castellania? It was obvious that she was, and when she wrote a letter to Coppi in hospital each day, he sent one back each day. The affair that would cause scandal in Italy and see them both excommunicated from the Catholic Church had begun.

Coppi could not race in the 1950 Tour de France, as he was still recovering from his injuries. Ferdi Kubler of Switzerland won after the Italian team was attacked by a French mob and withdrew from the race while Fiorenzi Magni was winning it.

The attack happened on a stage in the Pyrenees, which lived up to the wild image that journalists had been fond of promoting since the early Tours. It kicked off when Bartali crashed into a photographer at the top of the Aspin climb. Some fans rushed to help the Italian up, which upset some other fans and a fight broke out. The angry spectators even kicked and punched Bartali. When Jacques Goddet arrived on the scene he was horrified and laid into the crowd with a big stick. The police helped extract the riders, and Goddet, and the race resumed, but the Italians were furious. Relations between the two countries were still not good after the war, and Italian cycling victories set against the poor performance of French riders did little to alleviate a strongly held French belief that Italy, who were on the losing side and had been the aggressors, had done better than France out of the war.

Argument and debate went back and forth all night between the Italians and the French organisers, with Bartali adamant that both the Italian A and B teams should withdraw. Poor Fiorenzi Magni was leading and expressed a desire to continue, but Bartali would not be appeased, so they all left the race. A stage that was due to finish over the Italian border in San Remo was quickly re-routed too, after angry Italians promised that no Frenchman would leave the town without a good kicking.

The Italian withdrawal was a terrible shame for Magni, who said little during the debate as he didn't want to influence anyone, and to his great credit didn't create a fuss when the decision was made, even though it probably cost him the Tour de France. Magni was a great rider and a great personality. He still is, and at the age of 82 is still very involved in Italian cycling. He was a strong, bruising sort of racer, the first Italian to win a northern Classic when he scored the first of a hat-trick of victories in the Tour of Flanders. Magni also won the Giro d'Italia and was such a hard man that once, when he broke his collarbone in a stage race and could not pull with his right arm when going uphill, he simply tied some tape around the right side of his handlebars, stuck the other end between his teeth and pulled on that.

With the Italians gone, the way was clear for Ferdinand Kubler to win the Tour, which was also notable for the first appearance of a North African team, and for the story of Abd-el-Kadir Zaaf. Zaaf was Algerian who was used to racing in heat. The hottest stage of the 1950 race was between Perpignan and Nimes and no one wanted to race except Zaaf and his team-mate Marcel Molines. They built up enough lead for Zaaf to be the virtual yellow jersey, but with 15 kilometres to go he began to zigzag all over the road. Eventually Zaaf collapsed and was laid down under a tree, where he passed out. When he came round a few minutes later he groggily realised he was riding the Tour de France, jumped on his bike but began pedalling in the wrong direction. The crowd stepped in and stopped him, but Zaaf was so confused that he was taken to hospital.

The Tour made him famous overnight, and afterwards he made a lot of money from appearances in criteriums, which are round-the-houses exhibition races where Tour racers are paid to appear, and continued racing for a few more years. Later, he lost all his money after a dispute with the Algerian authorities and his life went downhill fast. Zaaf was shot in the leg during an argument, sent to prison and ended up a penniless, almost blind tramp in Paris in 1981, where he was recognised one day years later by a Tour de France journalist. The readers of the journalist's cycling magazine responded to an appeal and donated money to get Zaaf back on his feet and pay for an eye operation. He died four years later.

Kubler's Tour victory proved to be the first of a Swiss double as his compatriot Hugo Koblet won the following year. What a contrast in style those two were, though. Kubler was as strong as a horse, larger than life, and a man who had the annoying habit of telling his competitors where he planned to attack, then doing just that and winning the race. He was such a one-off that the journalists called him the 'Pedalling Madman'. Koblet was Kubler's opposite. Understated and elegant, he was smooth, polished-looking and so proud of his appearance that he kept a comb and a sponge soaked in eau de Cologne in his back pocket with which to spruce himself up just before a race finish. He was nicknamed the 'Pédaleur de Charme'. It means charming pedaller but it sounds better in French.

Kubler didn't ride the 1951 Tour de France, which made Coppi the favourite, but he had been hit by personal tragedy. His brother Serse, who was also a pro rider, good enough to have taken joint first in the Paris–Roubaix Classic, had a terrible crash during the 1951 Tour of Piedmont and died from his injuries. Coppi started the Tour but his morale was too low for racing. This left Koblet almost unopposed and he won the race by 22 minutes from Raphael Geminiani.

Coppi managed to drag himself through the Tour, but his morale was not improved by his wife Bruna constantly nagging at him to give up cycling. She feared the worst after Serse's death, especially since Fausto had many crashes during his career and had already been badly injured several times. He took her worries as completely misjudging the situation and not understanding what cycling meant to him, and what it had meant to his brother. Giulia did understand, of course, and she and Fausto were writing to each other on an almost daily basis. They had seen each other too, although everything was platonic at this stage.

Koblet dominated the 1951 Tour, but he was never the same rider after it. He liked to travel and visit new places, so after doing enough post-Tour criteriums to put some money in the bank he took up an invitation to race in Mexico and South America. Unfortunately, he caught a virus in one of the countries he visited and it affected him for years. He began to have money difficulties because of bad investments and had to race more often in small events that paid for him to start them. Koblet began a downward spiral that ended in a fatal car crash, with only him involved, on a highway near Zurich in 1964. Suicide has never been ruled out.

The Tour visited two new places in 1951 that would feature large in its mythology in years to come: the Massif Central and Mont Ventoux. The Massif Central stage to Clermont-Ferrand in the heart of countryside that was once a fiery ring of volcanoes was won by a local rider, Raphael Geminiani. He would make a big impression in the Tour de France in years to come and in many ways. In fact he's still making one in his eighties, opinionated and every bit as fiery as the region he comes from.

Mont Ventoux also has a volcanic past, although it is much less visible. The mountain is just that, a mountain. It stands 1,912 metres above Provence, a lump of shattered limestone that was pushed upwards by volcanic action deep in the earth's crust millions of years ago. It's unlike most other Tour de France climbs in that the road over it is not a mountain pass, because it serves no other purpose than crossing the summit. The peak dominates the region to such an extent that its bare white top was used as a beacon by sailors in the Mediterranean, but the heart of Mont Ventoux is its weather.

Like a beautiful diva, Mont Ventoux has its moods. In perfect conditions it can be a beguiling place of bright sunshine and gentle breezes, bathed with the scent of Provençal herbs wafting up from the plain below. On other days it will be a furnace where the heat of the sun burns on its way down, then bounces off the glaring white surface and burns again. Then there is the mistral wind. If this blows over Mont Ventoux it drags freezing cold air from the snowy peaks of the Alps then blasts it across the top of the mountain. On any July day, the temperature on the top can range between 0 and 35 degrees Celsius, and wind speeds of 290 kilometres per hour have been recorded there. Lucien Lazarides led the Tour over on the 1951 stage from Carcassonne to Avignon, and everyone got down safely. It wouldn't always be so.

The Tour really spread its wings during the fifties when it came to finding new climbs to race up, and new for 1952 were two of the most iconic in cycling, L'Alpe d'Huez and the Puy de Dôme. Coppi was back to full strength and the 1952 Tour de France was one of his crowning glories.

The first week was enlivened by an incident which looking back seems funny but really indicates something of the feudal structure of pro cycling that existed in the fifties. The most loyal of Coppi's domestiques, or *gregari* as they are known in Italy, was a brick wall of a man called Andrea Carrea. He was a model of the type: tough, stocky, able to ride hard for hours on end and then at his leader's whim go on 'la chasse à la canette', or the hunt for extra drinks that domestiques got by ram-raiding wayside bars.

Carrea won very few races in a long career that was spent entirely in the service of Coppi. One of his jobs was to ride near the front of a race, evaluating what was happening, and on the ninth stage Carrea was getting increasingly agitated about the constant attacking going on and the fact that the Italian team wasn't sending anyone with them. Carrea kept drifting back through the peloton to report to Coppi, who was having a bad day and seemed distracted. Eventually Coppi got fed up with Carrea and said, 'Look, you go with the next move if you are that worried.' So Carrea did.

But then the breakaway stayed away and Carrea took over the lead of the Tour de France. He had done nothing to help the move, but as the yellow jersey was being pulled over his head Carrea was in tears at the thought of being accused of betrayal by his team or, even worse, by Coppi. Instead of celebrating, Carrea waited on the line for Coppi to finish, and when he did Carrea was the first to get to him to tell him he was sorry. It was a strange moment, but it served to break the tension that had been growing in the Italian team over Coppi's lethargy. Since the Tour started Coppi simply hadn't been at the races, but the inci dent seemed to snap him out from wherever he was and into the here and now. Finally switched on to the Tour, next day Coppi went on the rampage.

This was the first-ever stage to L'Alpe d'Huez, a place that has become famous through the Tour de France. L'Alpe d'Huez is a ski station that nestles on the shoulders of the Grandes-Rousses, and the climb is the 13-kilome- tre stretch of zigzag road that links the station with the town of Bourg d'Oisans deep in the Romanche valley below. Today, when the Tour visits the climb, upwards of 300,000 fans line the route like the tiered audience in some gigantic theatre. And they have witnessed some of the most exciting moments of the Tour de France, because L'Alpe d'Huez is a road to nowhere so it is always the last climb of what is usually a tough day.

The Alpe in 1952 was nothing like the place it is today. In fact it took an artist, a local man called Jean Barbaglia, to see its potential. He saw the theatre, he saw tier upon tier of people who one day would flock here to cheer for their heroes. They now come from all over the world. The hardy ones in camper vans arrive on the Alpe three days before a stage, just to get a good place. From then the crowds swell until they have the 24-hour party that is race day.

They spill out on to the road, forming an impenetrable looking barrier that the riders just aim at; it parts continuously just in front of them. The noise is deafening: shouting, screaming, air horns, cowbells, the clackety-clack of television helicopters hovering above. The racers bury themselves in this tunnel of sound, using it to fuel their desire and push back the pain. To be on the Alpe on race day is to feel the earth tremble and collective enthusiasm almost take on a living form.

It was nothing like that in 1952. Barbaglia persuaded the owner of one of the few hotels at L'Alpe d'Huez, which then was just a ski lift, a few runs and some timber lodges, to help him lobby the Tour organisers. They were intrigued; they'd never had a mountain-top finish before, and they agreed to give it a go, especially since the hotel owner, Georges Rabon, was prepared to stump up some cash. Being a Tour stage town is an honour, but it is one that's paid for.

The stage didn't attract huge crowds, as the Grandes Rousses were still quite remote, but those that were there on the day saw Fausto Coppi at his very best. Little Jean

Robic, the Tour winner in 1947, attacked before L'Alpe d'Huez and began to climb it alone in the lead. But after a few hundred metres of ascent Coppi began to spin his long legs a little quicker and set off in pursuit of him.

Coppi's climbing was something else. I've only seen a bit of grainy black and white film, but his climbing style looked effortless. He didn't attack, he just accelerated. He didn't get out of the saddle, but instead just poured a little more power into the pedals. And he hardly moved his body, it was all his legs and lower back. 'Pedalling with your kidneys' is what the old pros used to call it, meaning that is where they felt the power starting from, in their kidneys or lower back. We know it today as core power.

Coppi quickly caught Robic, rode with him for a while, then dropped him to win the stage and take the jersey. The margins weren't big, but Coppi had only turned the wick up for 13 kilometres. Next day he would give it full gas for longer and the margin would grow.

It was another first. For the first time a stage finished at a ski station just over the French border with Italy at Sestrières. This time Coppi went from the start. He topped all of the day's climbs in the lead and romped home well ahead of anybody else. On the morning of this stage Coppi was ahead of second place, his team-mate Carrea, by just five seconds. Six and a half hours later he led the Tour by 20 minutes.

He kept drawing ahead, even on flat stages, and he won a stage in the Pyrenees. Victory in the Tour slowly became inevitable, but Coppi also had his eye on a prize a little further into the race: another first summit finish on the Puy de Dôme.

This climb is spectacular. You can see it for miles, sticking up like a huge thumb above the volcano-shaped hills of the

Massif Central. The city of Clermont-Ferrand sits at its base, and the usual approach is to thread through the western suburbs, climbing all the time to a plateau. There the riders draw breath before what is the crux of the climb: four and a half kilometres of 11 per cent average gradient, with a 13 per cent maximum, corkscrewing around a rock pillar that millions of years ago was the inside of a huge volcano. The journalists loved it in 1952 – racing up the inside of a volcano at the end of a huge 245-kilometre stage that took the best riders over nine hours lent itself to the flowery writing that was still their style of cycling reporting.

As a proposition for the riders, though, the Puy de Dôme was extraordinary. Fifties racers didn't have the low gears that Tour riders use today. Their bikes were still quite heavy and made from steel too. The gradient soon exceeded their lowest ratio, and even the best were reduced to weaving across the road to lessen the slope, or lunging from side to side on their bikes so that every muscle of their body helped them climb upwards. Except Coppi. He started the steep part a little behind the leaders, but as the steepness strung them out he picked off his rivals one by one. Even the Puy de Dôme didn't break his style as he stroked his pedals around and simply rode right past everyone, winning the stage from a lanky blond Dutchman called Jan Nolten. Coppi caught Nolten just 400 metres from the line, but from then put nearly two minutes into him. Two minutes in one quarter of a mile. If you want to measure how good Coppi was, that statistic isn't a bad place to start. Gino Bartali was third and the names of the first three are recorded on a granite plaque by the line right on top of the Puy.

The 1952 Tour was over, Coppi had tied it up in Sestrières really. He took it easy in the final time trial, losing three minutes, but he could afford them. He finished the Tour next day 28 minutes ahead of the Belgian Stan Ockers, whose progress in this race was followed by a seven-year-old boy in Brussels called Eddy Merckx, who became aware for the first time in 1952 of a race he would win five times. Italy won the team prize and Coppi was the King of the Mountains.

Coppi went on to more legendary victories, but he never won the Tour de France again. His relationship with Giulia grew, and he left his wife, and Giulia her husband, so they could live together. They were the Posh and Becks of their day, filling as many column inches about their lives – where they were seen and what they were doing – as Coppi did through his racing.

Not everyone was happy about the relationship. Part of Italy was very upset by the thought of any couple living in sin, never mind a national sports star who was supposed to be a role model for their children. And when Fausto and Giulia had a son, Faustino, the Catholic Church excommunicated them.

Coppi's fellow racers never changed the regard in which they held him, but as time passed they could see that Giulia was high maintenance. The media interest and the Church's decision affected Coppi, and as he grew older he went on racing when he should have rested more. Eventually some of his friends grew so concerned that they advised Coppi to stop racing, but he wouldn't. The rumour was that he couldn't because he needed the money.

At the end of 1959 Coppi and Giulia went to North Africa with a number of other top racers and their wives for a series of exhibition races. They enjoyed a bit of sun, got plenty of exercise and came home happy. Then, just before Christmas, Coppi told Giulia that 1960 would be his last year of racing. She wasn't disappointed. It was time, past time really; he was 40 years old.

But then Coppi fell ill. He was diagnosed with flu, but he didn't respond to flu treatment. A series of doctors were consulted, each more senior, but each stuck to the original diagnosis. Even when Raphael Geminiani, who had also been on the North African trip, got in touch to say that he had malaria and was being successfully treated for it, they refused to alter their opinion. But as Coppi's condition worsened, even the doctors began to wonder. The position was now serious: if untreated, malaria can kill enough red blood cells in eight days to cause death, and with the delays through misdiagnosis that amount of time had already gone. Sure enough, at 8.45 a.m. on 2 January 1960, Fausto Coppi passed away in his sleep.

9. THE FIRST HAT-TRICK

Coppi changed cycling, he upped the ante. Top racers made good money before him, enough to maybe open a bar in their town when they retired. Some even did it in style. Locals from the West Flanders town Gistel, whose grand-parents were around at the time, still talk of Sylvère Maes, who after winning the 1937 Tour built a landmark café on the main crossroads. Its patrons knew the owner was home when they saw his huge American station wagon parked outside.

But Coppi was bigger than cycling; the mystique and interest that surrounded him transcended his sport. Interest in him and support for him bordered on mania, and it drew in strands of society other than the traditional working-class fans of cycling. This made cycling a bigger market. The Tour de France was still contested by national teams, but the trade teams that the pros raced for during the rest of the year were beginning to attract interest from businesses outside the sport who wanted to be sponsors.

The result of this interest was that the rich got richer – the top riders earned more. They made friends with politicians, entertainers and even film stars. They became sophisticated and not hamstrung by class. But for every

Coppi, for every Hugo Koblet driving around with his model wife in a Studebaker motor car, there were 100 other pro racers, some of them pretty talented but not mega-stars. Coppi's popularity did little for them. Most made enough to see them through the summer, but many had to work at other jobs during the winter.

Jean Bobet was a Tour de France rider in the fifties, an intelligent man with a university degree who loved cycling. He was also the younger brother of Louison Bobet, who by 1953 was already a world champion and Classics winner and was set to become the next big thing in the Tour de France.

Jean wasn't as talented as his brother on two wheels, but with a pen he is in a class of his own. After his racing career was over, Jean became one of the most respected journalists in cycling, and he is still writing today as an award-winning author. Having been a pro gave him unique access to riders, his racing experience gives him excellent insight, but he brings something else to writing about cycling, because Jean Bobet writes like a poet. To give you a taste of his unique style, this is how he describes being caught and passed by Fausto Coppi in a time trial stage of the Tour of Italy: 'One day, in a cloud of golden dust, I saw the sun riding a bicycle between Grosseto and Follonica.'

Nobody speaks or writes better about his racing era than Jean Bobet, and here's how he saw the division of earnings at the time:

There was what I call the G4 of riders: Coppi, Koblet, Kubler and Louison Bobet. The Belgian Rik Van Steenbergen won enough to make it a G5, but somehow he wasn't seen by the elite as being one of them. He was too much of a mercenary perhaps, although in truth his earning power ranked him at the top. It wasn't just a question of money, though. Maybe the four didn't trust that Van Steenbergen would go with the accords that they agreed on, and they were probably right.

The G4 earned good money, more than ever before, but for the rest of cycling it was largely the same. Retainers from sponsors were quite small for an ordinary rider, and his income depended on winning races or gaining some other notoriety, then getting into the criteriums and track meetings, or even the winter six-days, which all paid good appearance money.

Below the good riders who could win races, there was another layer. Honest men, good guys who loved cycling, loved the life, but who were just trying to keep their heads above water. Many of them had no contract at all and no guaranteed income. They were engaged by the teams on a race by race basis, what we called racing '*à la musette*'. A musette is the food bag handed up during a race so a rider could replenish the supplies in his pocket. We'd say they were racing for a food bag. Some of these riders rode the Tour de France, many of them did. They never made any money and would have to work during the winter, as lorry drivers say, or even postmen. They were good guys though.

Going into 1953 Louison Bobet was under the press cosh. No one is better at telling sports people what they should and shouldn't be able to do than journalists. Bobet, they said, should have won the Tour de France by now, and began to suggest that maybe he wasn't the right kind of rider to do it.

There was added pressure because this was the 50th anniversary of the Tour and France wanted a French winner. Coppi wasn't riding, because he wanted to prepare for the World Championships in Lugano, which would be run on a course that really suited him, so he had other plans for July. He was going to train for the worlds in a controlled manner, the way all pro racers do now, and based himself in the Italian Alps while the Tour was on. Also, Giulia Locatelli would be with him. Their affair was in full swing, but the press were still largely unaware of it.

Coppi wanted to see his friend Bobet triumph in the Tour. They were part of the G4, it was Bobet's time, and it was the 50th anniversary of a race the French invented and gave to the world. A Frenchman had to win, because it was good for cycling. Good for the G4 and their control too. And Coppi knew exactly *where* Bobet would win it.

The Col d'Izoard has huge significance in French cycling, and much of that stems from what Bobet did on the climb. It is a beautiful place, made iconic for France and for the whole cycling world by Bobet, and by Coppi before him. They both had some of their finest racing moments on this road that soars upwards from a deep gorge, though lush meadows and into a barren shattered landscape at the top called the Casse Déserte, the broken desert. Here the boulders and scree are punctuated by towering rock pinnacles, one of which is adorned with the silhouettes of Bobet and Coppi and is their shared memorial. This is and always will be their mountain.

The crucial Alpine stage of the 1953 Tour went from Gap to Briançon and ended with the Col de Vars and the Izoard, twin climbs whose names have been made inseparable by the Tour. When the Spanish climber Jesus Lorono attacked on the Vars, Bobet pounced like a hungry cat. He hurtled down the other side, distancing the Spaniard, then set off up the Izoard alone and in the lead.

His riding now was majestic, almost otherworldly, and Coppi was waiting to see it in the Casse Déserte. He had ridden there that morning with some close friends as part of his training. Giulia was there too, a Coppi trustee having driven her up the climb to meet him so they could watch Bobet together. The two G4 riders were close, and Bobet knew Giulia and about her affair with Coppi.

When Bobet saw Coppi he shouted, 'Thanks, thanks for coming!' The Tour boss, Jacques Goddet, saw Coppi too and stopped his car to shake his hand, while the Italian nodded up the road towards Bobet's fast disappearing form and said, 'That was beautiful.' Nobody but Bobet noticed the woman in a white coat standing next to Coppi, and nobody noticed the warmth in their smiles when Coppi and Giulia looked at each other. They would notice soon enough.

Bobet won the Col d'Izoard stage by more than five minutes and later won a long time trial to tie up his first Tour de France victory. It was a glorious triumph for France, and for Bobet it was about time. Being the best French rider of any generation brings a lot of pressure. Bobet had to win the Tour de France, it was expected. This pressure, or more a sense of duty, lasted until 1986 when French cycling lost its confidence. They haven't won the Tour de France since and don't look like doing so any day soon. Marion Clignet was a French world champion with eight titles to her credit. Today she coaches a French Tour de France team, and she puts the lack of French success down to confidence. 'We were fine when the sport was limited to Europe, but when it went world-wide French riders lost confidence in themselves. The just don't have the "can do" attitude any more to compare with the Americans and Australians, and the British, for example.'

The 1953 Tour also saw the introduction of the points competition, although the green jersey for the points leader did not appear for some years. The competition was created to give another kind of rider a chance to go for something overall. Points are awarded down the finishing order on each stage, and because there are more flat stages in any Tour than mountainous ones, the prize usually goes to a sprinter, one of the type who excel on flat and rolling stages. The first winner was Fritz Schaer of Switzerland.

The fifties were a time of innovation in the Tour, and 1954 saw the first foreign start, in Amsterdam. From there the race went down through Belgium, and local riders were looking for glory. They got some, but Bobet wasn't letting anyone get very far from him and on the fourth stage he took over the lead.

It was too early. Bobet was the favourite, but this was a tricky Tour. Coppi was riding, as were Kubler and Koblet, and the Swiss had some other troublesome talent in their team. Then there was the Spaniard, Federico Bahamontes, the best climber the Tour had seen until that point, and still one of the greatest ever. Luckily Bahamontes only wanted the climber's prize and was first to the top of several famous mountain passes, once sitting down to eat an ice cream on the summit while he waited for the others to catch up. It was a great publicity stunt which added to Bahamontes' popularity, but there was a practical reason for waiting too. In his early Tours the Spaniard wasn't confident about descending, and he preferred to follow others down the mountains so he could copy their lines through the corners.

It was a tough Tour, 4,800 kilometres that included the Pyrenees, the Massif Central and the Alps, with some huge flat stages thrown in. It was a Tour for biding your time, and Bobet did just that, slowly letting the race come to him. He played things defensively, losing his early lead then taking it back by stealth in the Massif Central. Then on stage 18, again on the Col d'Izoard, Bobet wrapped up his second Tour de France, ahead of compatriot Jean Malléjac. He climbed the Izoard alone, just as he had done the previous year, but this time he was wearing the yellow jersey. It's this image that still haunts French cycling. Only one Frenchman has equalled it, Bernard Thevenet in 1975, but winning on the Izoard in yellow is still the Holy Grail of French cycling.

Bobet was at his peak in the mid fifties. He won the World Championships in 1954, then showed more of his all-round ability by winning the Tour of Flanders the following year. He was the world number one by a mile and odds-on favourite to win the Tour de France again in 1955.

It was a shorter Tour, 400 kilometres less than the previous year, because Jacques Goddet felt some of the long, flat stages were beginning to drag. The public wanted an incident-filled race with dramatic stages and cared less about how far the racers had ridden. In 1955 they got a stage that was more than dramatic – it was apocalyptic.

Mont Ventoux was in a very angry mood on stage 18. Jean Bobet, who was selected to help his brother in the French national team, remembers the sense of trepidation: 'The peloton was quiet. Normally, riding in the sun on an undemanding route, which the approach to the Ventoux is, there will be constant chattering in the peloton. They are a bunch of young men doing what they enjoy and getting paid for it. They are exuberant, joking all the time, but not this day. We knew what the Ventoux would be like.'

When a race runs over flat terrain to the foot of a big climb, the start of the climb can cause mayhem and bring an element of lottery to the game. Riders try to squeeze through gaps that aren't there, gears slip, riders fall. And worse still, chancers with no climbing ability at all might attack, only to come to a standstill a few hundred metres up the road when they run out of talent. If a favourite gets knocked off or stuck behind this free-for-all, he can lose the Tour. But the French team knew this and they had a plan.

'Louison told us to start riding hard 20 kilometres before Ventoux,' says Jean Bobet. 'Not just ordinary hard but very hard so we'd pull the peloton out into a long and orderly line, even cause splits if we could and sap some of the other climbers' energy. Pure climbers don't like riding in a big gear on long false flats, like there are before Ventoux, it fries them. Then Louison said he needed us to continue going hard for one or two kilometres on the Ventoux, by which time only the favourites would be left at the front and they could sort out things for themselves from there.'

The plan worked well. As they hit the climb Ferdi Kubler had a slight lead, but the French team had Raphael Geminiani with him. The other French national riders with enough strength were giving it flat stick at the front of the peloton, about one minute behind, with Jean Bobet in there, riding himself inside out for his brother. He knew it was worth the exceptional effort he was making, despite what he recalls his brother had been saying.

It's funny looking back. All the way from Carpentras to the foot of the climb in Bedoin I was riding and riding. I was giving my all for Louison, but he kept coming up alongside me and whispering that he wasn't feeling so good. He gave us the plan so he can win the Tour, then he doubts that he can do it. You would think that would be demoralising to me, but it wasn't. His complaining and doubt were music to my ears. Louison was like that – if he sounded confident he was bluffing, if he complained about how he felt he was flying. I knew we didn't have to worry when we hit the climb and I heard his voice just behind me shout, 'Right, just two more kilometres at maximum, boys.' He had taken control, the nerves and doubts were gone, he was psyched and ready.

Yes, and ready for one of the most dramatic stages of any Tour de France. Up front Ferdi Kubler kept attacking, and kept telling Geminiani when he was going to do it. The Ventoux was like a furnace, and out of respect for the older champion, Geminiani told Kubler to cool it, to ride with him. 'The Ventoux isn't like any other climb,' Geminiani counselled, to which Kubler replied, 'And Ferdi isn't like any other rider,' and attacked again. Exasperated, Geminiani shook his head, shouted 'Ferdi is an idiot,' and let him go with 15 kilometres left to climb. A few kilometres later the Swiss champion was riding at a snail's pace and weaving all over the road. 'Ferdi is dead. Ferdi has killed himself,' he gasped as Geminiani pedalled by. Casualty number one was down.

Further back the field was really spread out, and another drama was about to kick off. Jean Malléjac, a top man in the French team, who had done the same as Kubler, slowed dramatically and was wobbling all over the place. But now Malléjac collapsed and lay stricken and delirious by the roadside. The Tour doctor, Dr Dumas, was quickly on the scene, but Malléjac was in a bad way.

Heatstroke, they said as he was carted off to hospital, but plenty in the peloton knew otherwise. It was amphetamine.

Louison Bobet fought his way through this mayhem and then he attacked, a difficult thing to do on a climb where everyone was riding hard, especially on the Ventoux. Matching the pace of others is difficult, but attacking can cause a rider to suffocate on this climb. No one knows why. It's not the altitude; at just over 2,000 metres the Ventoux isn't high enough for that. It's not every day that it happens either; on some days the Ventoux is like any other tough climb and obeys the same natural laws. But on others it doesn't, and this was one of them.

The attack cost Bobet, but he made it stick. How much it cost him, his brother Jean discovered later. The stage ended in Avignon. Bobet won, desperately holding on to the one-minute advantage he clawed from the Ventoux, but he suffered to do it. The French team were delighted. Their manager, Marcel Bidot, welcomed each member as they staggered into the team hotel, which was close to the finish line. No matter how far down they had finished on the stage, each had done his job.

They made their way to their rooms, exhausted but happy with their triumph. It felt good, the team were on a high, but the man who was responsible for it was nowhere to be seen. Eventually Jean tracked Louison down to his room, and there he saw how much it costs to win the Tour de France.

The room was in darkness, the shutters closed and curtains pulled so no direct light could enter. It wasn't pitch black, though. This was Provence in the summer and there was a suffused light with which, when my eyes got used to it, I could see a shapeless body laid on the bed.

It was Louison, and he was still fully clothed. I congratulated him but he beckoned me over and whispered, 'I'm done.' I said, 'We're all done, all of your rivals are done.' But he wouldn't have it. 'They will attack me tomorrow,' he groaned. I ignored him then I noticed he hadn't even removed his shoes, so I did that for him. Every time I touched him he groaned with pain, but I could not see him lie there with his shoes still on.

It was a pitiful sight. The difference between winning and the rest was brought home to Jean in that hotel room that day. How deep you have to go to for victory – only a winner and those close to him experience that. And the insecurity of a great champion was laid bare too. Exhausted, hurt and whimpering, Louison wasn't celebrating, he wasn't satisfied about what he'd done, but instead he was still obsessing about the opposition.

Like most great champions, Louison was insecure, but it's that insecurity that helps make them what they are. They should worry about their rivals, it's their job, it's what gets them up in the morning and sends them out training. Jean wasn't worried about the attacks coming. He was the rational half of the Bobet family, he knew everybody was cooked, but he was worried about how deep Louison had gone. 'I think he surpassed his own strength on several occasions in his career, and one of them was on the Ventoux,' he says today.

As Bobet left his brother's room he met his trainer and physio Raymond Le Bert going in. 'Don't worry about your brother, young Jean, I will get him all right,' he said. And Jean knew he would. Le Bert was a man ahead of his time in the fifties. He was self taught, as all the trainers and masseurs were in cycling, but Le Bert was so good, so well-informed that without seeking them he had received honorary medical qualifications.

Cycling was full of strange beliefs in those days, and full of strange characters who looked after cyclists. They were called *soigneurs*, from the French word *soigner*, meaning to care for. They still are, but a soigneur today is a far cry from the men – and it was only men, a woman didn't do this job until 1986 – of the fifties and before. They ranged from the good, honest and well trained like Le Bert, to out-and-out charlatans and witch doctors, with drugs pedlars somewhere in between. One of the many good things that came from the revelation in 1998 of doping deep inside the Tour de France was the policing of soigneurs and their role.

Le Bert was probably the best of his generation, and he was often scathing about others doing the same job, particularly about the drugs pushers. It cost him work too. Later in his career Le Bert was hired by a young racer who was already a world pursuit champion and the hour record holder, Roger Rivière. It was 1960, by which time Jean Bobet was a journalist and Louison was almost at the end of his racing career. Rivière and Jacques Anquetil were the next generation of top French racers, and it was obvious that the drugs race had gone up a step. Early in their relationship Rivière asked Le Bert to give him his best pick-me-up, but when Le Bert supplied him with what he'd always given the Bobets, a preparation based on strong coffee and sugar, Rivière told him that it wouldn't even get him from the hotel to the start line, and sacked him.

Louison Bobet lived his life by his trainer's rule, and it was a life that made a monk's look like that of a teenage clubber in Ibiza. Bobet trained hard but he dieted even harder. Some say he wasn't as naturally talented as a Coppi or a Hugo Koblet, who when he was at his short peak just made racing look easy. Louison Bobet was a self-made champion. No stone was too small to turn if it made him a better racer. He dieted rigorously and lived his life by a strict code. Raphael Geminiani sums up Bobet when he says, 'Even in the off-season, if Louison wanted to drink a beer he would beat himself up for days for wanting it, then beat himself up for days after for drinking it.'

Despite his monk-like existence Bobet was no automaton obsessed with cycling. He was a charming and very intelligent man with numerous projects on the go outside the world he worked in. He loved gadgets, and he had the money to indulge that love. He loved business and used his winnings to set up sea-water treatment spas that are a major business today. He also loved flying, becoming a qualified amateur then a professional pilot.

He flew with great confidence, although – in those far-off days when the skies were emptier – not always with great attention to the rules. He used his plane to go to races and to business meetings, but at first he was only cleared to fly in conditions of total visibility.

That didn't stop him, though. Once, with his brother as navigator and a cloud level of only 150 metres, they flew using a railway line as their route marker. When the rails stopped just short of the airfield they were aiming for, Bobet performed hedge-hopping circuits to find his landing strip. Another time they didn't find the airfield at all, put down in a field nearby, and cycled to the race. Today Bobet's son is a senior pilot with Air France.

But going back to 1955 and that hotel room in Avignon, Le Bert got Bobet back on his feet and Jean was right:

everyone was fried by the Ventoux. No attacks were mounted, and his brother enjoyed a triumphal march into Paris as the first man to win the Tour de France three times in a row. It was a first time for others too, most notably for British cycling.

After a Briton, James Moore, won the first-ever bike race, cycle racing became quite popular in the British Isles. Big track meetings attracted huge crowds and races were held on the open road, just like the ones in France and the rest of Europe. But as the racers were mounted on unstable and virtually brakeless penny-farthing bikes, these races were pretty scary affairs. Soon a racer scared someone's horse, and the rider, a lady from a well-to-do family, was thrown off and hurt quite badly. The authorities banned bike racing on the open roads, or at least racing in a bunch was banned. Cyclists found they could still compete if they started at minute intervals from secret locations referred to by a numbered code, so as not to attract attention. Each racer's effort was timed and supposed to be done entirely under his own steam: he wasn't allowed to shelter in the slipstream of any rider he caught or who caught him. And so the time trial was born, but cycling in Britain had to go undercover to do it.

'Private and confidential' became the watchword of British cycling, and just so that the riders wouldn't spook any horses, or their lady riders, by exposing any flesh, racers competed in identical top-to-toe black outfits. As world cycling developed, British racers could hold their own on the track, but once a world road race championship got going the British competitors, living on a diet of individual time trials, were at a great disadvantage when racing in big groups. Bunched racing was eventually allowed on closed circuits, like airfields and motor race tracks, but it still wasn't the open road. Road racing as such didn't come back to Britain until the late forties, and even then not without a fight.

But as soon as it did get under way road racing attracted men who had already come under the spell of the Tour de France. French cycling magazines like *Miroir du Cyclisme* and *But et Club* were available in Britain after the war, and for a few, for reasons they probably don't even understand themselves, the sepia-toned pictures of Coppi, Bartali, Koblet and Kubler had them yearning to race like the Europeans.

One such young man was a trainee builder from Yorkshire called Brian Robinson. He is 78 now and still rides his bike 100 kilometres twice a week. He is still passionate about the sport, and is thoroughly enjoying the success of today's British road racers. He is their founding father after all.

His older brother introduced Robinson to racing. He subscribed to the magazines and had even raced in Europe, but Brian was somehow called to go further and try to make this alien sport his career. He was very talented, very hard-working and very intelligent. By 1955 he made such a name in the few British races there were that he was an automatic selection for an ambitious project. Great Britain would put a team in the 1955 Tour de France for the first time ever.

Ten men started, but only two survived. Robinson was one of them and finished a very creditable 29th overall out of 69 finishers. The last man, the *lanterne rouge* as the French called him after the red lamp that was hung on the back of French railway trains in days gone by, was the other British finisher. His name was Tony Hoar, but last place was no dishonour, because with 130 starters, in effect he beat 61 other riders to get to Paris.

It was a good start for Britain, good enough to inspire a British bike company called Hercules to sponsor a team of British cyclists to race on the continent for a year. In a story that was to become depressingly familiar in the coming years the team were hopelessly underfunded and the money ran out before June, but looking back today Robinson also feels that there were shortcomings in the riders.

'It was a good set-up, we started out on good wages, and even though the team folded half-way through the year it should have been the start for a lot of British riders on the continent, but to my mind they weren't dedicated enough. We were living in France, so my philosophy was to live like a Frenchman, but right from the pre-season training camp we had on the French Riviera in February the others were thinking of home. They were always grumbling about the food, saying things like "I wish we could get some Yorkshire Pudding." That was no good. You had to put all thoughts of home out of your mind and get on with it,' he says.

Robinson did get on with it. He stayed on when the others came home after the team's demise, riding '*à la musette*' as Jean Bobet described, hiring his services for teams in stage races. 'I preferred them because you stayed in hotels on stage races and the team paid for that, so I raced in as many stage races as possible and stayed with acquaintances between them. For a year I didn't have a home, but I saved money. Maybe I was lucky I could live like that. I could live anywhere, it didn't bother me. I was trying to be a French racer, and the only way to do that was to live and race in France. I succeeded because I had to win money to pay my way,' Robinson explains.

His persistence paid off with a start in the 1956 Tour de France as the only Briton in the race. He was part of a team called Luxembourg-Mixte, which was basically the best riders from Luxembourg plus some other nationalities to make up the numbers. It was a cut-throat gang, as Robinson remembers: 'The leader was obviously Charly Gaul, he was by far the best, but because of that he didn't want to share any money he won with the whole team. It wasn't like a proper team, you see. Gaul's argument was that only a couple of us were good enough to help him, so why share with anyone else? He had a point, but it didn't lend itself to team spirit, or to a happy atmosphere at the dinner table.'

The 1956 Tour was also a first for Ireland, with Seamus Elliott riding the Tour. He was another man who felt drawn like Robinson to racing in Europe, and who had made a big impression in French amateur races the previous year. Elliott raced for the Ile-de-France team. He didn't finish the Tour, but Robinson improved to 14th place overall by the end. Both would be back for more, and both would make their own piece of history, with Robinson as the first British stage winner in 1958 and Elliott the first Irish yellow jersey in 1963.

The French team looked good on paper in 1956, but the defending champion Bobet was out after surgery for a saddle injury that had affected him during the previous year's Tour and for a while afterwards. His brother Jean explains:

The criteriums were the problem. Louison was paid good appearance money, the best in cycling in 1955, and he had to cash in. He raced 39 times in the two months after the Tour, then nearly every day in October. And the races weren't grouped in one area then another. I went with him to most of them and we would do one in the west of

France, then one in the north, then next day the Midi.
From there we went to Milan maybe, or Spain. Then back
to France and up to Belgium. Driving and racing all of the
time. It was memorable, but taxing; very taxing for
Louison, who had already given everything to win the
1955 Tour. After that period Le Bert examined Louison
and pronounced, 'He is no longer an athlete but a shell.'
He was exhausted. He had an operation on his crotch,
which because of his poor physical condition took a long
time to heal.

Leaderless, the French national team underestimated a
breakaway on stage seven that gained a lot of time. In it
were 31 riders, with several strong ones from French
regional teams and only one, Gilbert Bauvin, from the
national squad. At the end of the day a regional rider,
Roger Walkowiak, had the yellow jersey, and the country
boys from the regions felt they had put one across the city
slickers of the national team.

André Darrigade restored some pride for the top French
riders when he got the jersey back a few days later, but he
was a sprinter and although he put up a good fight he
eventually crumbled in the Pyrenees. The French team
seemed not to know what to do next, or who to get
behind, and meanwhile Walkowiak slowly levered himself
back into the picture, eventually running out the victor.

After Bobet's glorious three-year run the 1956 Tour had
been a damp squib, and the crowd at the Parc des Princes
finish showed what they thought by booing and whistling
at the French 'A' team when they did their lap of honour.
It was a shame for poor Walkowiak, because he never got
the respect he deserved. He had won the Tour de France
after all, and that has never, ever been easy. And to add

further insult to him, if anyone looks like winning the Tour by stealth and the mistakes of others, writers call that winning 'à la Walkowiak.'

Louison Bobet rode the Tour again in 1958 and finished seventh. Then in 1959 his Tour career ended on the Col d'Iseran when he just stopped racing and left for home. Looking back at the helpless wreck his brother found in that darkened hotel room in Avignon back in 1955, you can't help thinking that is really when Bobet's career ended, on the day he gave too much on the Ventoux.

It wasn't a sad exit, however. The Bobet brothers were too talented for that. Both went on to very successful careers in other fields, Louison in business and Jean in journalism. They fell out over their careers too for a while, but their love of cycling brought them back together again. They would ride every Sunday morning in Brittany, and at other times they visited special places with their bikes, such as the Col d'Izoard, warmly and good-naturedly reliving their triumphs.

That ended when Louison succumbed to cancer at the age of 57. To mark his passing Jean did what he did best and wrote about his relationship with his brother in a poignant and very beautiful book he called *Tomorrow We Ride*.

10. MAÎTRE JACQUES

Jacques Anquetil was a law unto himself. Whether it was winning his first Tour de France as almost a raw novice, his attitude to cycling, or his unusual domestic arrangements, if the rule book didn't suit him, Maître Jacques just ripped it up.

Maître Jacques was the nickname his fellow racers gave Anquetil. *Maître* means master in French and is a title of substance, one that they give to lawyers, who as a body are held in high esteem in France. What is more, Anquetil was Maître Jacques from early on in his career. His peers recognised his authority as soon as they saw it, and never questioned it afterwards.

But the easy authority that commanded respect within the peloton left many fans cold. They saw in Anquetil what they saw later in Eddy Merckx and in Lance Armstrong, only with bells on. To some Anquetil was imperious, cold, aloof, and just too dammed clever for his own good. But he was also an enigma. His accomplished manner was a veneer; underneath he was superstitious, he hated meeting new people, had a fear of crowds and a really morbid premonition that he would die young. He hardly spoke about these things, but they were real, and there were people, particularly his first wife, that Anquetil leaned on very heavily to get by.

Anquetil's outward qualities as a person and as an athlete endeared him to modernists, to city types and sophisticates. His friends were politicians, actors and pop singers. But France in the fifties and sixties was still a very rural place. Farm labourers and factory workers were the big fans of cycling. They lined the roads to watch the Tour go by, they read about it in the papers and followed cycling all year, and a lot of them didn't really like Anquetil.

They preferred Raymond Poulidor, the 'Eternal Second', the man depicted in history as a latter-day St George who tried to slay Jacques the dragon, but always got eaten. He was younger than Anquetil, and their Tour de France careers only overlapped for four years, but somehow their rivalry left a big and disproportionate impression on the race. Poulidor was a shy, naive country boy. A nice guy, the sort you'd like your daughter to come home with. People liked him, but although he was physically strong his tactics gave his team-mates grey hairs, and if Poulidor hadn't had bad luck he wouldn't have had any luck at all.

At its height Anquetil and Poulidor's rivalry split France, just as Coppi and Bartali's had divided Italy. It was seen as a battle between the old and the new, the country versus the city, a historic France against a modern France. Even their beginnings, although agricultural, represented two different worlds.

Jacques Anquetil was born in Normandy, a blond ancestor of Viking invaders, the son of a hard worker who turned a couple of fields into a farm that he owned and eventually employed several people. Poulidor was the swarthy son of Limousin peasants, who were part of a feudal system where some of their produce paid the rent on their fields, and who in their whole life never broke the chain of subservience.

There was little money but a lot of love in the Poulidor household, and although Raymond remembers his father as a kindly soul, there were still tough lessons to be learned. 'My brother and I were wrestling once and accidentally broke a pane of glass in our bedroom, but my father refused to replace it until the end of winter. A Limousin winter is no joke and we would sometimes wake up with snow on our beds, but my father wanted to teach us that things cost money,' he once told me.

His father certainly taught Poulidor the value of money, because even when he was a successful racer with big earnings, Poulidor's tightness was legendary, as his teammate, Britain's Barry Hoban, remembers: 'Poulidor could peel an orange in his pocket and eat it without anyone knowing, and in the nearly 20 years I raced and trained with him I never once saw him pay for a coffee.'

Ernest Anquetil was a much more severe father. For even the mildest transgression he made Jacques go into the garden and kneel on a log with both his hands behind his head. Try it – it's the sort of stuff special forces soldiers are subjected to during interrogation training. But although he ran a tight ship, Ernest had a weakness. When he was young he had wanted to be a bike racer, but his parents wouldn't let him. Consequently he did everything he could to help Jacques when he took an interest in the sport.

He encouraged Jacques to race, helping him to buy a suitable bike. Later, when Jacques finished his apprenticeship and found his employer unwilling to let him train with the local cycling club on Thursday afternoons, Ernest gave him a job on the farm and all the time off he needed.

But he did a deal with him. Jacques had to win by his third race or it was back to work full-time.

He did win, then rocketed through the amateur ranks, quickly becoming a pro and almost as quickly winning his first big race against paid riders, the 1953 GP des Nations. He was still only 19, but Francis Pelissier, one of the famous Pelissier brothers and now a respected directeur sportif of the La Perle team, saw something in Anquetil. The skinny blond-haired youth was still a boy in his physical appearance, but his ice-blue eyes burned with pride, and he had a cycling gift. Well, two actually, but they go together: Anquetil was an amazing time triallist and could out-suffer the toughest penitent.

The time trial in cycling demands special qualities. Alone against the clock, which is an unforgiving competitor, a cyclist must spread his or her effort equally along any given stretch of road, hilly or flat, long or short, it doesn't matter, just to the point where exhaustion is reached by the finish and not a moment before or after.

It requires a certain type of body, and crucially a certain type of mind. Your muscles must support a high constant effort, and you need a brain like an airline black box to monitor the feedback from them continuously. Jacques Anquetil had those things. The directeur sportif behind his greatest exploits, the former Tour rider Raphael Geminiani, once described Anquetil as 'the combination of a still, a jet engine and a computer'.

The young athlete raced for a cycling club, AC Sotteville, which was based in the city of Rouen, not far from Anquetil's home village of Quincampoix. One person who helped Anquetil there was a doctor, Dr Boeda, who was interested in the training of sports people. The doctor was recommended by André Boucher and Sadi

Duponchel, both key members of the cycling club. Boucher remained Anquetil's trainer for the rest of his career and Duponchel a friend, but one whom Anquetil trusted throughout his life. Jacques Anquetil didn't make friends easily, but when he did they were friends for good.

Dr Boeda's wife was his former nurse, Janine, who was five years older than Anquetil. At first she didn't like the young cyclist because, like many top sports people, Anquetil was a bit of a hypochondriac. When the only tool you have for your job is your body, you can get a bit cranky about it. But Janine had seen really sick people and couldn't understand why her husband lavished so much time on this skinny kid who had nothing wrong with him, except that some days he couldn't ride his bike as fast as he wanted to. However, over the early years of Anquetil's racing career she began to know and understand the man inside the young racer.

Then, in the spring of 1957, they met by accident while Anquetil was training and Madame Boeda was on holiday on the French Riviera, and for the first time Janine saw the Anquetil only a few ever did. Gone was the preoccupied sportsman; the man she discovered was relaxed, charming and honest. Confident, accomplished, but at the same time vulnerable. He made a big impression on her, and she had already made one on him.

By then Anquetil was 23, and he'd won every major time trial in an era of cycling when one-off races against the clock, such as the Grand Prix des Nations and the Grand Prix de Lugano, were very popular. Anquetil was also the world hour record holder, but he hadn't yet won a single-day Classic or even ridden a Grand Tour.

France was on a roll in its big bike race. Admittedly Louison Bobet's triple was followed by the blip of Roger

Walkowiak, who was thought to have stolen the race while the star-studded national squad bickered and couldn't unite around a single leader, but French cyclists and their fans still went into their national race expecting to win. So, being the boss of the French national team was a pressure job, just like being a national team football manager.

In the 1950s the French boss was the thirties racer, Marcel Bidot, and because of 1956 his job the following year was just that bit tougher. Who was going to be in the team was one problem, but who would lead it was even tougher. Louison Bobet was now past his best but he still wanted a big say in the French team, and he wanted to be its leader, but Bidot wanted to give that role to Jacques Anquetil and build a team around him. Luckily, while Bobet was vainly battling the whole of Italy in an attempt to become the first Frenchman to win the Giro d'Italia, he told the press there that he wouldn't ride the Tour de France.

Bidot felt insulted but relieved at the same time. Protocol, manners even, said that Bobet should have spoken to him before announcing his decision, because Bidot had promised the country a French winner of the Tour from a national team with Anquetil and Bobet in it. Bobet had made Bidot look as if he didn't know what was going on in his own team, but his withdrawal was a blessing in disguise. Bidot was sure Anquetil could win whereas, despite his experience, Bobet wasn't the racer he'd been in 1955. Still, Anquetil was the only first-timer in a very experienced and talented squad, and Bidot didn't name him as the leader at the start.

The 1957 Tour was a hot and sleepy race for the first week or so, but Anquetil liked that; he soaked up heat like a lizard and was far more vulnerable in the cold and wet. He took the yellow jersey on the stage five to Charleroi, but the heat didn't help Anquetil's tendency to inattention. In later years his wing man was Jean Stablinski, a tough, street-fighting type of bike rider with a tender heart and a brilliant racing brain, who had witnessed his Polish father being shot dead by the Nazis when he was only ten years old. A few years before his death in 2007 Stablinski told me, 'On long stages with no obvious points to cover like big mountains, Jacques would just go to sleep at the rear of the peloton. I don't know how many times I had to go back and haul him to the front because the peloton might split or we needed to cover a break, or get Jacques with a move in case another team forced things.'

The field was decimated by the heat. Cyclists didn't drink enough in those days, which can and did have disastrous consequences. In the 1957 Tour two big favourites, Charly Gaul and Federico Bahamontes, were forced out by dehydration. They were two of the best climbers the sport has ever seen, and were expected to trouble Anquetil where he'd never been tested before, in the high mountains. With them out of the way the new French star cruised over the giant Col du Galibier, by far the biggest climb he'd ever ridden, to keep tight hold of his lead.

Anquetil won a short time trial in Barcelona, looked vulnerable in the Pyrenees but battled through, won the final time trial and tied up his first Tour de France victory. It was very professional. Anquetil didn't put a foot wrong once in three weeks. It was a cold execution, and one headline writer realised what was to come when he wrote, 'Anquetil wins his first Tour.'

But confirmation of Anquetil's talent proved elusive. The next two years showed that a really brilliant climber could cause him problems. The 1958 Tour was won by Charly Gaul, a former butcher from Luxembourg who once threatened to take his knife and turn a rival into sausages, but who pedalled uphill with such grace that the press dubbed him the 'Angel of the Mountains'. He won by dominating the first-ever time trial up Mont Ventoux, and having one superb day in the Chartreuse amid terrible weather to come back from being right out of contention.

The Ventoux is one of the Tour's most iconic climbs. It's always scaled by its south side, but even this has many faces, and they are all due to its capricious weather. Essentially the climb is 22 kilometres of almost constant nine per cent gradient through a forest of stunted cedars to an expansive bald summit of shattered limestone, but the Ventoux has moods. Even in summer it can be freezing cold when scoured by the fierce mistral wind. But if the air is still, or worse, if a warm wind blows from the south, climbing the Ventoux is like being roasted slowly on a spit.

Gaul dominated the Ventoux in 1958, setting a record that stood for many years. He lost the yellow jersey next day but won it back in the Chartreuse when pouring rain and freezing cold gave Anquetil a nightmare that troubled him for years to come. In it Anquetil would be riding along and then see a cyclist up ahead. He would make a huge effort to catch the rider. Then when he drew level he'd see that it was Charly Gaul, made out of a million raindrops. These would disappear, then reform ahead of him. Anquetil would chase again and the dream would repeat itself until he woke up.

His defeat in 1958 hurt Anquetil, and no one knew this better than Janine, whom he had now married. By the time he won his first Tour, Jacques and Janine were deeply in love. They knew it, and eventually Dr Boeda realised it. Things came to a head in the spring of 1958. Anquetil was training in Cannes and Janine was at home in Rouen, but they could no longer live apart. He jumped on a plane, borrowed a friend's car in Rouen, and knocked on her door in the middle of the night. Janine knew why, she put a fur coat on over her pyjamas and the couple set off for Paris, where she bought new clothes on the Rue de St Honoré and began a new life with Jacques.

What Jacques wanted, Jacques got, or so it seems. But although she was totally in love with him and still is, despite what he did to her in later years, Janine, although blonde, sophisticated and very attractive, was no trophy wife. Cycling in Anquetil's era, and for a long time after it, was a man's world where women, even wives, were at best regarded as the support team at home and at worst as pure distraction. But Janine Anquetil literally stood by her husband's side throughout his racing career, the only woman in a male world, and nobody even noticed. 'She could walk into a changing room with everybody naked and no one thought the slightest thing about it,' Jean Stablinski told me. 'And what a driver, and a negotiator; when we raced in the post-Tour criteriums Janine drove us everywhere, arranged the hotels, the meals and sorted out the money. It was like Jacques had married his manager,' Stablinski added.

Jacques and Janine were inseparable. She would stand in for him at public functions. If you couldn't get Jacques you got Janine, and no one complained. She helped him make decisions, gave the interviews that he didn't want to give. If a journalist came away with a notebook full of quotes from Janine he knew his editor would be happy. I

say 'his' advisedly: there aren't many women in today's
Tour de France press corps, but there were none in the
sixties. Janine was simply accepted as one of the boys.

She had incredible presence. She doesn't give interviews
today, mainly for the reason I'll go into next, but Helen
Hoban, the former wife of Tom Simpson, the first British
yellow jersey and arguably the most talented British bike
racer ever, knew her well. 'Janine was attractive, very
feminine, but she had such a personality that she was part
of cycling. When I first married Tom I used to read all the
cycling magazines just to try and learn who was who, and
Janine's picture was plastered all over them. She was
simply the other half of Jacques Anquetil, or so it seemed,'
she remembers.

So if that was the public face of Janine Anquetil, why
did she let Jacques rule her in private to the extent that
after he stopped racing, when at last he had the space in
his head to think about his life, she let Jacques have a child
with her own daughter?

It seems incredible but that's what happened. Janine
had two children with Dr Boeda. Jacques became their
stepfather, helped bring them up, but owing to a medical
problem subsequent to the birth of her second child,
Janine could have no more children. While he was racing
Anquetil had no time to think about this, but when he
retired he decided he wanted a child. Incapable of keeping
anything that was on his mind a secret from her, he
discussed the problem with Janine, and even told her that
he was considering hiring a prostitute to bear him a child.

Janine would not hear of that, so she volunteered her
daughter, Sophie, instead. And that is what happened. In
a twisted kind of Gallic expediency Jacques and Sophie
had a child, Christopher, and Jacques and Janine brought

him up as their son. But then sex with Sophie continued, with the full knowledge of Janine. And later, not content with two in his harem, Anquetil turned his attentions to the wife of his stepson, eventually living with her for the final years of his life. By then, though, it had all got too much for Janine and Sophie, and they had left.

But all that was in the future. Anquetil and the French suffered another defeat by a climber, Federico Bahamontes, in 1959. Bahamontes was called the 'Eagle of Toledo' for the easy way he seemed to soar over the mountains. By 1959 he was a seasoned pro, and looking for more than the mountains prize from the Tour. He no longer waited for others to catch up at the top and lead him down the descents, but used his uphill power to get away and stay away from the rest. His more rounded ability won him the Tour, but inter-team French rivalry helped him too.

A young rider, Henri Anglade, had snatched the national championships from under the noses of the French stars one week before the Tour. Anglade had shown promise and was already selected for the Tour, but in the Centre-Midi and not the national team. National pride was placed in the legs of Anquetil, the talented young Roger Rivière and the ageing Bobet.

But Anglade marched into the Tour and took control. The French team were caught off guard and let him, but when they found they were out of contention they conspired to help Bahamontes win. It wasn't pride that made them do it, it was money.

One of the most powerful men in pro bike racing at the time was Daniel Dousset. He was a former racer of limited ability who had a good brain, so he set himself up as a rider's agent. Dousset arranged the contracts with teams, and negotiated with the criterium organisers who paid the

racers to ride exhibition races all over Europe on small-
town circuits that the public paid to watch. The criteriums
were big business, and top riders commanded fat fees to
race as many as 30 or 40 of these races in the two months
that followed the Tour de France.

Business was so good that by 1959 Dousset had a rival,
Roger Piel, and Anglade was one of Piel's men, whereas
all the French national team belonged to Dousset. It was
Dousset who dictated that Anglade couldn't win.
Bahamontes was one of his men too, so he told the French
national team to make sure the Spaniard won. That way
he and not Piel would get ten per cent of the Tour winner's
fees, and the national team members would all earn too,
because Dousset would ensure that. No matter who you
were it didn't do to go up against Dousset.

At the finish in the Parc de Princes, Dousset was the
only happy Frenchman there. The bike fans smelled a rat,
and although they gave Bahamontes a sporting cheer
during his lap of honour, they booed and whistled the
French team. Anquetil was shocked, he didn't expect this,
and although he wore a thin, almost shy smile when he
did his lap of honour with the team, he was hurt. He didn't
realise people cared so much about cycling and, just to
remind himself that they did, he named the luxury speed-
boat he bought out of his 1961 Tour winnings 'Sifles 1959'
– Whistles of 1959.

One man in the Parc de Princes that day was oblivious
to the bad feeling directed at the French team. Brian
Robinson finished with another top 20 overall placing. He
had won a stage in 1958, and he won one again in 1959,
but this time by a huge margin. In doing so Robinson
sealed his place in cycling as the first Briton to be an established part of the European pro circuit.

Robinson made his pioneering way with a mixture of athletic ability and tactical savvy, and by immersing himself totally in the *métier* of being a European pro racer. His tactical savvy and knowledge of European racing was clear when he won on the long, lumpy road to Chalon-sur-Saône in 1959, as he recalls:

> It was the day before the last big time trial, so there was three days before Paris. I'd seen how much a Tour stage meant in terms of criterium contracts the previous year. I also knew that the top men would be saving themselves for the next day. So I decided to ride my time trial a day early. I asked the team mechanic to put my 28-spoke wheels with silk tyres on my bike, which were the only special equipment we had for time trials in those days, because I planned to attack.
>
> I was in an International team, which was the usual mixed bag of riders and we had nothing to ride together for, but my trade team-mate, Gérard Saint, was quite high up in the King of the Mountains competition, so he asked me to lead him out for some hill points. I did, Saint got the points and I flew down the other side. Another Frenchman, Jean Dotto, was following me and I could hear him shouting 'Wait, wait,' but I wasn't waiting for anyone. I risked crashing with those light tyres on a twisty gravelly road, but I needed to get a gap quickly. Once I got one I set to, pacing myself like I was riding a long time trial.

Robinson set to so effectively that he won the stage by over 20 minutes, and became a well-respected Tour de France rider.

Anquetil's next rendezvous with the Tour was in 1961. In 1960 he tried to win the Giro d'Italia but finished a

gallant second after every Italian in the race rode against
him, and the partisan Italian fans pushed their men up the
mountains in front of him. After his first Giro experience
Anquetil said, 'If the fans could have got away with
putting the Italian riders in their cars and driving them to
the top they would have done it.' The battle left him
exhausted and he didn't ride the Tour in which young
Rivière broke his back and ended his racing career. The
race was won by Gastone Nencini of Italy.

By 1961 Anquetil was 27, the uncontested leader of the
French Tour de France team and a totally changed man.
His racing that year took on a new confidence, and his
whole demeanour suggested he had fully grown into his
Maître Jacques sobriquet. He had won every big time trial
in the world, most several times; he had won the Tour de
France and twice finished second in the Giro d'Italia, but
the Anquetil era, the age of his domination, only really
began in 1961.

The Tour started in Rouen and, maybe a bit carried
away with being on home turf, Anquetil announced that
not only was he going to win the Tour but he would take
the yellow jersey on day one and keep it until Paris three
weeks later.

And he did it. By winning the first stage, then using the
time trials to put a headlock on the race, he wrestled it into
submission. Having the strong French national team behind
him helped, but Anquetil was quite sublime. On the stage
to Chalon-sur-Saône, a break took a dangerous lead that
the peloton weren't making much headway in reducing, so
Anquetil rode on the front for 30 kilometres without relief
to reduce the gap to a more comfortable margin.

He won easily, repeating a feat that only Ottavio
Bottechia, Nicolas Frantz and Romain Maes had ever done

before, and they didn't dare predict it. France was stunned into admiration, but not warmth. If anything Anquetil's cold execution of their beloved race only distanced him from the majority of fans, the working classes. They were used to struggles and setbacks in their own lives, so they didn't understand how someone could do something so difficult with such ease.

Of course it wasn't easy. In 1962 the Tour organisers succumbed to pressure and changed from national teams to trade-sponsored ones again. Anquetil began his long association with Raphael Geminiani as his directeur sportif. Geminiani was one of the few people, along with Janine and maybe Jean Stablinski, who knew which buttons to press with Anquetil. He studied him, worked him out and measured his spirit and abilities. Asked to sum Anquetil up in a sentence Geminiani says, 'His courage defied the imagination, but nobody noticed because his style was so perfect.'

In terms of facing pain and physical discomfort, of having unbeatable pride when it mattered out on the road, Anquetil was amazing. Neither could he stand pussy-footing around when it came to questions about his profession. Drug use hadn't been spoken about in cycling much, but it was rife. The Pelissier revelations of the 1920s first revealed it, then Fausto Coppi, when he was asked in a 1940s interview if he ever used drugs said, 'When they are necessary.' 'And when is that?' asked the interviewer. 'Almost always,' Coppi said.

Anquetil made full use of what riders then euphemistically called medical aid, and he was outspoken when dope testing was brought into cycling during the second half of the sixties. He claimed that testing was a breach of his civil liberties. He said that no one tested his friend the French singing star Jonny Halliday after he gave a performance. Anquetil reckoned that professional sportsmen were entertainers, just like TV celebrities and pop stars, and should be left to take anything they needed to help them perform. After all, they knew what they were doing, he asserted.

But did they? Anquetil triumphed again in the 1962 Tour de France, but during that race a little bit of history was made. On the stage to St Gaudens, after a battle in the Pyrenees, a young Englishman called Tom Simpson became the first English speaker to wear the yellow jersey. He only kept it a day, but stayed in contention throughout the race, moving up to third overall before a crash on the last mountain descent of the race dropped him down to sixth at the end.

Simpson was an engaging, talkative live wire who inspired people to like him. His talent, speed and attacking spirit made him one of the best single-day bike racers in the sixties. He won where no Briton had won before, becoming world champion in 1965. He won three of the five monuments of the sport, where only Mark Cavendish has won one since, and as I write we are still waiting for another British world road race champion. With little or no interest in cycling in his own country, Simpson's achievements and personality were such that he became the BBC Sports Personality of the Year in 1965. It was already a remarkable story, but Simpson wanted more. He wasn't physically suited to three-week stage races, and never had a strong enough or dedicated enough team to help him, but Simpson wanted to win the Tour de France. He once said that he wanted to go down as one of the greats, and the greats all won the Tour. His drive to achieve that would collide with doping and prove fatal.

Simpson didn't ride the 1963 Tour, concentrating on the Classics and World Championships instead. Anquetil won his third Tour in a row, becoming the first man in history to win four, but he had to lean on his courage more than ever to do so. Federico Bahamontes was the obvious problem, the mercurial Eagle soaring in 1963, but less obvious was Anquetil's health and a problem he had inside his own team.

Earlier in the year Anquetil won the Tour of Spain, but he had been ill and a strong German former world track champion, Rudi Altig, a member of Anquetil's own team, ended up his closest rival. Altig fought hard in Spain, giving his more senior team-mate a tough time. Anquetil didn't really want to ride the Tour after that, even though his team's sponsors needed him to, although on Raphael Geminiani's advice they fell short of demanding it. 'You could not order Jacques Anquetil to do anything he didn't want to do, but you could still get him to agree if you knew what to say, and I knew what to say,' Geminiani remembers, before adding, 'I also got them to throw in a lot of extra money to get Anquetil to the Tour.'

Once they were on the road, the diplomat in Geminiani quelled any potential revolt from Altig. Anquetil won the first rather short time trial and a stage in the Pyrenees but went into the last mountain stage, from Val d'Isère to Chamonix in the Alps, three seconds behind the race leader, Bahamontes. The stage suited the Spaniard, and he knew it, so he attacked all through it. With a 54-kilometre time trial to come, Anquetil could afford to lose a little more time, but not much, and he looked to be wilting under the pressure from Bahamontes.

But Anquetil still held on. The Spaniard had one climb left to distance him, the tough Col de la Forclaz, 13 kilometres at an average eight per cent, with steeper bits and a rough surface thrown in, that took the race back into France after a short excursion to Switzerland. Two men, two different styles and two different objectives: one had to break the other, and the other had to stop him. Twelve times Bahamontes attacked on the Forclaz, and 12 times Anquetil hauled himself back up to him. By the top Anquetil was still there, the only one left with Bahamontes after he'd torn the race to shreds. Anquetil was white as a sheet and looked like a corpse. Bahamontes looked as if he'd discovered a puzzle to which there was no answer.

And there was no answer to Anquetil, who then dropped the Spaniard on the descent to win the stage. A few days later Anquetil won the remaining time trial and the Tour by nearly four minutes from Bahamontes. He hadn't been at his absolute best but he still won, and that is the mark of a real champion.

Anquetil's best years in the Tour de France were probably 1961 and 1962 – which incidentally was the year a co-organiser, Félix Lévitan, was thrust on Goddet by the Amaury organisation to look after the commercial side of the race – but his most famous victory was his last, in 1964. It was the year that Raymond Poulidor came closest to beating him, so close in fact that Anquetil seemed to bear him a grudge for the rest of his career.

As in 1963, Anquetil again came to the Tour tired, this time because he'd just won a tough Giro d'Italia. He was worried about Poulidor and worried about a visit he'd made to an astrologer who had told him he would die on the 14th stage of the race. Anquetil took that sort of stuff seriously and again Geminiani had to weigh in with logic, and just a bit of wit. 'Another thing with Jacques was to

Maurice Garin arrives in Paris to win the
1903 Tour

Crowds cheer the riders on the Toulouse-
to-Bordeaux stage, 1903

Henri Desgrange, the editor of *L'Auto* and
credited by history as the 'Father of
the Tour'

Geo Lefèvre, *L'Auto*'s cycling reporter and
the man who really invented the Tour
de France

Au Reveil Matin, the café in Montgeron where the first Tour started in 1903

Louis Trousselier, the 1905 Tour winner poses with his bike

René Pottier led over the first mountain climbed by the Tour in 1905

Lucien Petit-Breton gets help in 1907 – he's docked time but still wins the Tour

François Faber, the heavyweight winner in 1909

Racing on the hot dusty roads of Les Landes from Bayonne to Bordeaux in 1908

TOUR DE FRANCE
Passage du peloton de tête à Cannes

TOUR DE FRANCE 1910
Cruchon et Ernest-Paul à l'arrivée de Bordeaux

Top: One of the first colour pictures – Tour riders in Cannes, 1910

Left: Ernest Paul, the stage winner (right) and Charles Cruchon, second, arrive in Bordeaux, 1910

Right: Octave Lapize reaches the summit of the Tourmalet in 1910

Artist's impression of Eugène Christophe repairing his forks in 1913

Top: Firmin Lambot climbs the Galibier in 1913

Left: Gustave Garrigou pushes his bike between snow banks on the Galibier, 1911

Right: Eugène Christophe on his way to winning the Chamonix-to-Grenoble stage of the 1912 Tour

Paris at 3am, the start of the 1914 Tour

Loneliness of the long-distance cyclist: an unknown rider pedals through the Alps in 1935

Roger Lapébie captured on the cover of *Le Miroir des Sports*, waiting for the 1937 Tour to start

Sylvère Maes leads on stage 15, Luchon to Pau in 1937

Top: Gino Bartali leads alone through the Casse Déserte, Col d'Izoard 1938

left: Roger Lapébie wins in 1937 after leader Maes retires in protest at the help the Frenchman gets from fans

Right: Sylvère Maes enjoys telling a radio reporter about taking his revenge on Lapébie by winning in 1939

Henri Desgrange (to Bartali's right) poses with the 1938 Tour winner

René Vietto rides by the wreckage of an aircraft in 1947; the plane was hired by *L'Equipe* to take aerial shots of the Tour, but crashed into the mountain side

Jean Robic crests Bonsecours on his way to victory in 1947

The broom wagon, vintage 1948, sweeps up some customers on stage 11 from Marseille to San Remo

Louison Bobet congratulates race winner Bartali on the final stage in 1948

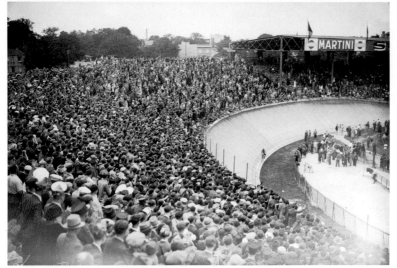

1949, the first televised Tour de France stage finish, and a nice shot of the Parc des Princes velodrome

Their feud is over – Bartali accepts Coppi is better as they ride together over the Izoard

Racing the train in the 1950 Tour de France

Abd-el-Kadir Zaaf collapsed before waking and trying to pedal off in the wrong direction, 1950

Fausto Coppi is encouraged along the road by his team manager, Alfredo Binda in 1952

The local priest helps out with a crash in his village; Tour director Jacques Goddet is on the far left.

Louison Bobet digs deep on the Ventoux to win his third Tour in a row, 1955

Hugo Koblet, the 'Pédaleur de Charme',
winning the 1951 Tour

Hugo Koblet (right) and Raphael
Geminiani climb the Ventoux in 1951

Jesus Lorono (left) and Louison Bobet
begin their chase of Jean Robic on the
Peyresourde in 1953

Roger Walkowiak, whose under the radar
Tour win in 1956 gave cycling the phrase
'à la Walkowiak'

Top: Fausto Coppi, the first winner on l'Alpe d'Huez, 1952

Left: The final round of Anquetil versus Poulidor being fought out on the Galibier in 1966

Right: Jacques Anquetil winning the first of his five Tours in 1957

Louison Bobet (second left) poses with his brother Jean (far right) and two French team-mates

Charly Gaul during his 1958 Tour-
winning escape through the Chartreuse

Gaul versus Mont Ventoux, setting his
1958 time-trial record that would stand
for many years

The Angel and the Eagle: Gaul (front left)
leads Federico Bahamontes (front, yellow
jersey) in 1959; Roger Rivière is on
Gaul's left

President De Gaulle shakes hands with
1960 Tour winner Gastone Nencini when
the race passes through De Gaulle's home
town, Colombey les Deux Eglises

Britain's first Tour stage winner, Brian Robinson, racing in the 1960 event

Anquetil re-establishes his authority by leading from start to finish in 1961

The first British yellow jersey, Tom Simpson leads the Tour in 1962

Jacques Anquetil climbs in total control of the 1962 Tour de France

French team-mates Jacques Anquetil (left) and Rivière (centre) try to put Bahamontes under pressure in the Alps, 1959, with little effect

Aloof, cool and totally in charge: Maître Jacques in 1963

Two rivals but only ever one winner: Raymond Poulidor and Jacques Anquetil take time out for the cameras in 1964

Self-imposed suffering: Anquetil digs deep on the Envalira in 1964, encouraged by team-mate Louis Rostollan

Felice Gimondi beats Raymond Poulidor (left) in 1965

'Chasse à la Canette': riders raiding a parked drinks lorry in 1965

Tom Simpson in his world champion's rainbow jersey, and German rival Rudi Altig, in yellow, entertain the crowd at a stage start in 1966

1967 Tour de France winner Roger Pingeon explains how he did it

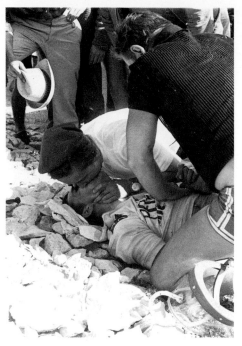

Efforts to revive Tom Simpson after collapsing on Mont Ventoux in 1967 are to no avail and he becomes the second fatality of the Tour de France

Barry Hoban rides to victory at Sallanches-Cordon in 1968 to become the first British winner of a mountain stage in the Tour

Who is the fairest? Raymond Poulidor examines his injuries in 1968

Already leading by many minutes, Eddy Merckx storms the Pyrenees in 1969 to win by many minutes more

Dutchman Joop Zoetemelk finishes second in the 1970 Tour, his first; it will take him ten more years to win

Zoetemelk and a Swedish rider, Gosta Petterson, want Merckx's 1970 yellow jersey; they won't get it

Zoetemelk climbs the Izoard in 1972, together with Frenchman Raymond Delisle

Maybe the greatest Tour climber, Lucien Van Impe in 1972

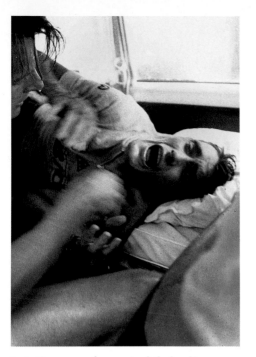

Luis Ocana crashes out while leading in 1971

The Holy Grail of French cycling, to lead the Tour alone on the Col d'Izoard in the yellow jersey – Bernard Thévenet does it in 1975, and ends the reign of Eddy Merckx

The mighty TI Raleigh team in 1978, Jan Raas (left) and Gerben Karstens lead in the team time trial

Bernard Hinault, champion of France, wins his debut Tour in 1978

Luis Ocana, simply the best in 1973

Joop Zoetemelk winning at last in 1980, and winning on a British-made Raleigh bike

The brilliant, mercurial Freddy Maertens winning a stage in 1981

Peter Winnen of Holland, on his way to winning on L'Alpe d'Huez in 1981

The last '*Patron*', Bernard Hinault during the Martigues time trial in 1982

Australia's Phil Anderson in 1982, wearing the white jersey awarded to the best young rider

Laurent Fignon time trialling to victory in 1983

Lucien Van Impe on a rest day in 1983 showing off his King of the Mountains jersey; the green one on his knee is the Tour of Italy's mountains jersey

Robert Millar time trialling in 1984

Sean Kelly time trials in 1985 on his way to winning his third of four green jerseys for Ireland

Bernard Hinault, battered bruised and black eyed but determined to win, after his 1985 crash

Lemond lends Hinault a hand in 1986

Tour winner Fignon (left) and Robert Millar, King of the Mountains in 1984; Millar is still the only British racer to have won outright a jersey of the Tour.

Greg Lemond (left) and Bernard Hinault on L'Alpe d'Huez in 1986

Bernard Tapie congratulates stage winner Jean-Francois Bernard on top of the Ventoux in 1987

Bernard gave everything to win the time trial to the top of Mont Ventoux in 1987

Kvetoslav Palov of the British ANC team passes the Tom Simpson memorial on Mont Ventoux in 1987

Stephen Roche is checked over by medics after his dramatic 'save' at La Plagne in 1987

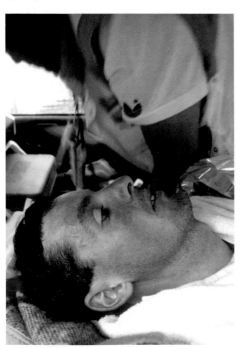

Sean Yates wins the time trial at Wasquehal in 1988, the first British winner of a Tour time trial

Pedro Delgado wins the 1988 Tour

Laurent Fignon losing the 1989 Tour by eight seconds in Paris

Greg Lemond, the valiant winner in 1989 of arguably the most exciting Tour de France ever

Gilbert Duclos-Lasalle tries some cool headgear on a red hot day in 1991

Maurizio Fondriest riding the prologue time trial in 1992

Miguel Indurain dominates in 1992, as well as in '91, '93, '94 and '95

All American, Lance Armstrong on his Tour debut in 1993

Armstrong as world champion during the 1993 Tour

Chris Boardman warms up for prologue victory, and the yellow jersey, on his Tour debut in 1994

Another fleet-footed climbing genius, the brilliant but ultimately tragic Marco Pantani in 1994

The Tour gives, but it takes too – an exhausted Laurent Jalabert showers after a stage in 2001

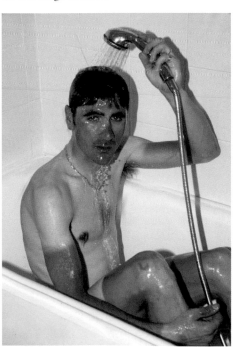

Lance Armstrong at the 1999 Tour start – he's been through the ravages of cancer, now he's ready to win the race

Air shot of L'Alpe d'Huez in 2000

Marco Pantani and Lance Armstrong break away on the Draguignan-to-Briançon stage in 2000

Johan Bruyneel and Lance Armstrong after winning in 2002

Unveiling the Casartelli memorial on the Portet d'Aspet during the 2002 Tour

Armstrong in 2003 after his toughest Tour, when he was pushed hard by Jan Ullrich (left); Alexandre Vinokourov is the third man on the podium

Racing through the Alps in 2003

Jan Ullrich takes the fight to Armstrong in 2003

Lance Armstrong riding the L'Alpe d'Huez time trial, 2004

Same place, another Alpe shot: Armstrong on his way to breaking the five victories ceiling in 2004

The final yellow jersey, or is it? Armstrong bids au revoir to the Tour de France with his children in 2005

Floyd Landis on the fateful stage to Morzine in 2006

Michael Rasmussen answers questions about his 'whereabouts' in 2007

Before hitting the streets of Paris for a final burn up the riders relax on the final Tour stage; Fabian Wegmann has a Bart Simpson moment in 2007

Bradley Wiggins, Mont Ventoux, 2009 – riding to fourth place, the British racer passes where Tom Simpson died 42 years before; later Wiggins reveals that he had a small photograph of Simpson taped to his bike as inspiration

Floyd Landis (centre) on L'Alpe d'Huez 2006

Armstrong returns, digging deep behind Wiggins in 2009

The 2009 podium: first Alberto Contador, second Andy Schleck (left), third Lance Armstrong (right)

make him laugh. You had to make something he was worried about appear ridiculous. I told him that he didn't need to beat Poulidor as Raymond always beat himself. He would crash or put himself out of contention in some other way. I'd already noticed that trend with Poulidor, and he would do it with other adversaries later. The image of Poulidor, the strong but clumsy country boy, made Jacques laugh and gave him confidence,' Geminiani told me.

Barry Hoban was a new pro in 1964 and riding his first Tour de France in Poulidor's team. He can testify to his leader's cack-handedness and loose grasp of tactics:

> Towards the end of the stage that started with a climb of the Col d'Envalira, the one where Anquetil was in trouble early on, Poulidor was with the leaders on the flat run-in to Toulouse when a spoke broke in his back wheel. The wheel buckled but it wasn't bad – all Poulidor had to do was loosen his brake quick release to stop the wheel rubbing on the brakes and carry on. But no, Raymond had to stop and change the wheel. Of course Anquetil was at the front with all the other leaders by then, and they were going like the clappers. It was a mountain stage so we, his team, were all behind and couldn't help Poulidor catch up, so he didn't catch up. He lost more time that day than he lost the Tour by. I'm not saying he would have won, because Anquetil would have still found a way to beat him, but it shows that Poulidor, lovely guy that he was, just couldn't think around a problem.

The Envalira stage that Hoban talks about was one of the most famous in Jacques Anquetil's career, and it's a story that is regularly told when people are trying to explain how unique Anquetil was. There was a rest day in Andorra in 1964, which is where the Envalira, a huge climb that goes up to over 2,400 metres, begins. Tour riders on a rest day always ride their bikes. If they don't their bodies, having accumulated a lot of metabolic stress, go into healing overdrive. Next day it would be like trying to start a ceased motor, so 70 or 80 kilometres of easy riding are squeezed between press duties, visits from family, and in Hoban's day washing their socks. He says:

> 'It was one of the things you did. You got a week's supply of new kit at the start of the Tour, but by each rest day it needed washing. Sometimes the hotel would do it for you but not very often. My wife always packed a box of washing powder with my Tour kit and we got on with it ourselves if the hotel had no facilities. The bath was the washing machine. For a spin dryer you wrapped each jersey or pair of shorts in a towel and with your room-mate holding one end and you the other, you both twisted the towel in opposite directions to squeeze water out of the jersey. Then they were hung out to dry on a window ledge.'

Of course Jacques Anquetil didn't do his own washing, he had people for that, but on this rest day neither did he do any cycling. 'Let the others train on their holidays, we're going to a party,' he told Geminiani when he politely enquired why Anquetil wasn't in his riding kit. Geminiani thought he'd better go too, so he followed Jacques and Janine off to a barbecue that a local radio station had put on for guests. Once there Anquetil, a man who when asked by a magazine to provide his number one dietary tip said, 'Never drink cheap champagne,' got down with the best of them and quickly knocked back a few glasses of bubbly, then a few more. It was strange behaviour, even for Anquetil, and he must have known that it would have consequences – Anquetil wasn't a fool. But next day was stage 14, so maybe he was thinking about what the astrologer had said, and was determined to spend his last 24 hours exactly how he wanted to.

At next day's stage start Anquetil was a wreck. Stiff, hung over and morose, he couldn't even ride himself in as the stage was uphill from the start, and Barry Hoban remembers, 'Bahamontes attacked before we had even tightened our toe straps.' It was carnage, the Tour was strung out up the climb, and last man on the road was the second-placed rider overall, Jacques Anquetil. His domestique, Louis Rostollan, a fellow Norman who was a good climber, tried to rally him, but Anquetil was on the point of retiring from the Tour. Then Raphael Geminiani arrived in the St Raphael team car.

'Jacques whimpered something to me about feeling like he was going to die,' he remembers. 'So I said, "Well get to the front and die there – a man like Jacques Anquetil doesn't die in front of the broom wagon." What I said was absurd, but it made him laugh. I had thrown the switch again and the real Jacques came back. He pulled himself together and got down to it.'

By the top of the climb Rostollan was having difficulty keeping up with Anquetil, and on the descent it was impossible. Like all great Tour winners, Jacques Anquetil had racing driver reflexes and a downhill skier's eye for the right line. He flew down the Envalira and chased for 120 kilometres, passing the various groups that the race had been split into by Bahamontes. Eventually Anquetil reached the front, where Poulidor handed him a gift by stopping to change his buckled wheel.

The Tour was saved, but Anquetil still had to win it. Poulidor dragged himself back into contention next day by winning a stage. Then Bahamontes did what he did best, going on an all-day climbing spree over five mountains to haul himself up to second overall and knock Anquetil and Poulidor down one notch each.

Anquetil won next day's time trial to take the yellow jersey by 56 seconds from Poulidor and establish himself three and a half minutes ahead of Bahamontes. The next two days were for the sprinters, so there was no chance of time gains or losses there. The time trial into Paris on the last day was Anquetil's for the taking, but before that he had to survive one last obstacle, the Puy de Dôme.

The stage was a long one, 237 kilometres of hot, sticky, undulating roads, punctuated by spiteful climbs. And at the top of each one the riders would catch a glimpse of the giant Puy getting nearer and nearer. As the favourites approached the end, Bahamontes must have known that even he could not gain the five minutes he'd need on Anquetil to have enough of a cushion for the time trial. The 1964 Tour had boiled down to a battle between Anquetil and Poulidor, a calculating time triallist versus a spirited climber, town versus country, and all the other baggage each carried as their feud intensified in the coming years.

The first man on to the steep section of the Puy would be able to dictate, so Poulidor had Barry Hoban make the pace from the penultimate climb, the Col de la Ventouse, and Anquetil asked Rudi Altig to do the same for him. 'Rudi and I were both track pursuiters as amateurs, so we could really make it go,' says Hoban. 'I hammered it so hard that I hit the Puy in first place, but I was cooked by then. I swung over, shifted down to bottom gear and survived as best I could. I did my job, though. There was a big split behind us, so only the favourites hit the climb together.'

There were five of them: Anquetil, Poulidor, Bahamontes, a talented rider from Italy called Vittorio Adorni and the new Spanish climbing sensation, Julio Jimenez. Jimenez attacked first with four kilometres to go, and Bahamontes went after him. Anquetil and Poulidor instinctively upped the pace, distancing Adorni, but neither did anything decisive. Anquetil didn't have to. He had a 56-second lead and he knew he would add to it in the time trial. Poulidor, though, had to attack.

In his spare time Anquetil loved playing poker, and that is just what he did with Poulidor next. He moved up alongside Poulidor, but as he felt his rival begin to dig to see how strong Anquetil was, Anquetil surprisingly moved ahead of him. This was Anquetil's bluff. Poulidor couldn't see his face if he was in front of him; he couldn't see how strong he was or if Anquetil was suffering; and Anquetil was suffering. His face was ashen and his eyes looked lifeless, staring blindly ahead, willing the summit to come.

The bluff worked. Poulidor admits today that had he known Anquetil was in the state he was, he would have attacked earlier. 'But when he went half a wheel ahead of me about two kilometres from the summit I really thought he was stronger,' Poulidor says.

Anquetil kept up his bluff for 700 metres, then dropped back slightly. Seeing his cue, Poulidor got out of the saddle as if to attack, but Anquetil managed to find something more to match him and he stayed alongside for another 300 metres.

That was it, though. Poulidor had cranked up the pace to such a pitch that even Anquetil could no longer hold on, but by then there was only 900 metres of the climb left. Following in the team car Raphael Geminiani wasn't worried. 'Inside the final kilometre I knew Anquetil was safe. He was slowing down because Adorni caught and passed him, and it was possible that Poulidor could have taken the jersey, but that didn't worry me because it was too late for him to take enough time to stay ahead of Jacques in the time trial. Having said that, though, Jacques told me later that evening he would have gone home had Poulidor taken the jersey. That's how strongly he felt about losing anything to Raymond,' he says.

Anquetil lost 42 seconds in the last 900 metres of the Puy, ending the day with just a 14-second lead over Poulidor. He added to that by winning the time trial into Paris and his fifth Tour de France by 55 seconds from Poulidor, the narrowest margin ever at that time. As he accepted the applause and circled the Parc des Princes velodrome, Anquetil seemed to take his time, and to look long and hard at the people cheering and applauding politely. He also looked tired and confused, and years later said he was quite upset by the contrast in the crowd, by the warmth they showed Poulidor compared with the muted respect when Anquetil did his lap of honour. 'He never understood that,' says Geminiani, 'He never understood how you could lose and be liked better for it.'

He certainly bore Poulidor a grudge, and although Anquetil never won the Tour again he relentlessly tried to do down his old rival. In 1966 he was instrumental in Poulidor losing the race. They didn't like each other at all, but when Anquetil retired, and especially later in life, they became friends. Jean Bobet watched the change in Anquetil with interest. 'Racing was war for Jacques but he mellowed as he grew older, and especially when he lived with Dominique,' he says.

Dominique had been Anquetil's daughter-in-law and had moved into his château at Neuville Chant d'Oisel shortly after Janine and Sophie left. I met Dominique at Anquetil's home a few years ago, a huge place that she was keeping going by renting it out for weddings. There was little furniture in the rooms and Anquetil's trophies had to be removed because they had started to go missing after some guests had been.

Dominique told me about an Anquetil the public never saw: 'He was very gentle, a nature lover who would sometimes stay up all night walking in the forests on this estate. He knew all the sounds and tracks made by animals and birds and worked tirelessly to build up the stock on our dairy farm. He would never harm anything, and when he went on hunting trips with his cycling friends, he never loaded his gun. He also knew a lot about the stars and studied them with a telescope.'

Dominique said that she sometimes thought Anquetil knew his life would be shorter than most, and that is why he tried to fill each day with experiences. When he was diagnosed with cancer in 1987, at first no one knew except Dominique. 'He said that if he died it was of no great consequence because he had seen and experienced such things that he'd already lived five times more than many other people had,' she told me.

When there was no hope Anquetil put his affairs in order and was visited by friends. Raymond Poulidor, who by then had been beaten so often in the Tour and by such a wide variety of riders that he was called the 'Eternal Second', was one of the first to his bedside. When Anquetil saw him he said, 'Sorry, my friend, it looks like you are going to be second again.' He also admitted to Poulidor that he had really had him in trouble on the Puy de Dôme in 1964, although he said that his suffering that day wasn't as painful as cancer.

Then when he became so ill that he didn't want people to remember him in such a weakened state, Anquetil stopped anyone visiting, except for Dominique. He died at seven o'clock in the morning on 18 November 1987. His funeral was a huge one at Rouen Cathedral, but he is buried in the churchyard of his native village, Quincampoix.

11. THE RETURN OF NATIONAL TEAMS

By 1965 Jacques Anquetil's official line was that he didn't need to win the Tour de France any more. He had already won it five times, two more than anyone else in history, and the criterium organisers and team sponsors could only just afford him now. What would winning another Tour bring him? Not any extra money, that's for certain. Glory? He was admired for his five victories, but ordinary French people preferred Poulidor.

Deep down that upset Anquetil, and he just couldn't understand it. On Planet Anquetil winning was every-thing; he admired winners and simply could not see why anyone else wouldn't. He had taken Poulidor apart in 1964, yet the crowd at the Parc de Princes finish applauded him politely but went wild when Poulidor did his lap of honour. Anquetil was better than Poulidor, he could outride and out-think him – why didn't people warm to that?

And then, in the back of Anquetil's mind was the thought that he was getting older, and the Tours he'd won had exacted a toll on his body. What if Poulidor actually beat him in the Tour? The situation was abhorrent to Anquetil, and to make sure that it didn't happen he

decided not to risk riding the Tour in 1965. He had nothing to gain and everything to lose. Why put himself
through it if nobody even cared?

But there was a problem with that. The St Raphael
drinks company, who had sponsored Anquetil's team for
three years, pulled out of cycling at the end of 1964.
Raphael Geminiani searched for a replacement and
managed to negotiate a huge deal with the French wing of
the Ford Motor Company. Ford wanted expansion in
Europe, and to help them do it they wanted Jacques
Anquetil to ride the Tour de France. That was part of the
deal, but Geminiani signed it knowing that he probably
couldn't deliver.

He knew how to win Anquetil over, but Geminiani also
knew when he was hell bent on not doing something, and
Anquetil was hell bent on not riding the Tour de France in
1965. Geminiani had to think of something to replace the
world's biggest bike race, so he came up with something
impossible. If Anquetil could do something that everyone
thought was impossible, and do it just before the Tour,
then nobody – not even Ford – would care whether he
was in the race or not. He would be bigger news than the
Tour winner anyway.

Bordeaux–Paris has gone from the racing calendar now,
but in 1965 it was still a very big race. It was a marathon
that harked back to the early days of bike racing as it was
587 kilometres all in one go, raced between the far south-
west of France and the capital. The first part was ridden
solo, but for the rest each rider raced behind a Derny
pacing bike. Dernys are strange-looking mopeds that
cyclists use in training and racing. Paced races were very
popular when cycling started, but are less so now. The
pacers, usually ex-racers who have put on a pound or two

since their prime, sit upright to give the following rider maximum shelter, which increases their racing speed. An engine provides the power to a Derny, but the pacers also pedal because that helps them increase or decrease the Derny's speed with more precision than by using the throttle on its own.

Bordeaux–Paris was an extreme test of stamina and concentration in its own right, but Geminiani planned to make it even harder. In 1965 it was preceded by the Dauphiné Libéré stage race, which then as now was an important warm-up event for the Tour de France. It has several tough stages in the Alps, and usually a hard time trial. It's like a mini Tour really. Geminiani wanted Anquetil to ride in both races, and he wanted him to win them both too.

The thing is though, Dauphiné Libéré finished on a Saturday afternoon and Bordeaux–Paris started at two o'clock the following morning, so that meant seven days of tough racing through the Alps and Massif Central, then a dash right across France for the start of a race that makes the toughest Tour de France stage look like a walk in the park – and no sleep in between.

But Anquetil did it. He won a hard and very wet Dauphiné Libéré, beating Raymond Poulidor into second place, just to make his point. Then, with the help of a rally driver in a Ford Mustang, President De Gaulle's private jet and two team-mates, Jean Stablinski and Britain's Vin Denson, who almost had to push Anquetil through the night portion of the race, Anquetil won Bordeaux–Paris.

It was all part of the publicity stunt. Anquetil was driven through the Alps to Lyon airport in Ford's flagship sixties sports car. The drive was originally meant to be all the way to Bordeaux, but when the President's office found out they were alarmed at the flagrant flouting of speed limits required to do it, and De Gaulle genuinely wanted to help, so they lent Anquetil his jet.

The President was a real Anquetil fan, and when reviewing the list of recipients of the Légion d'Honneur in 1964, the year when Anquetil became the first man to win five Tours, De Gaulle asked why Anquetil wasn't on it. The high-ranking civil servant who had drawn up the list said it had been decided that the government could not be seen to be rewarding a man whose name had been linked with taking drugs. De Gaulle was outraged and asked, 'How many times has this man caused the French flag to be raised and the national anthem to be played? How many times has he caused French people to be proud and the world to respect France? Put him on the list immediately.' And so Anquetil was given France's highest civilian honour.

But back to the great double. Anquetil was dead beat by the time he reached Bordeaux but very much alive and kicking by Paris, and there is probably a pharmacological reason for that. Also, the rumour goes that his closest true rival in the race, Tom Simpson, made his challenge look a lot tougher than it actually was. But Poulidor certainly gave nothing away in the Dauphiné, and just riding 587 kilometres immediately after that tough race was a super-human effort. Certainly, nobody has attempted anything like it since.

Anquetil's impossible double stunned France into admiration. His reception at the Parc de Princes finish was astounding, and that continued in the press and wherever he went for months after. Anquetil never showed much emotion, he thought it was a weakness and didn't even raise his arm if he won a race, but as Janine drove him away from the track after Bordeaux–Paris he burst into tears. The French public had got him at last.

Anquetil had beaten Poulidor in every respect. 'Poulidor can win the Tour de France now and people will not care,' he told Geminiani with relish. Poulidor started the Tour as the clear favourite, but everyone was still talking about Anquetil. He appeared on the Tour as well, cashing in on his success by riding exhibition races whenever a stage finished on a velodrome, which it often did in those days. Poulidor couldn't break clear of Anquetil's influence, and just to add to his misery, even without Anquetil in the Tour he didn't win it. He was beaten by a lorry driver's son from Bergamo in northern Italy, a 23-year-old who was riding his first Tour de France.

Felice Gimondi was a classy bike rider. He suffered a bit because his career ran alongside that of Eddy Merckx, who would make his Tour debut in 1969 before going on to win nearly every big race on the planet. Gimondi won plenty, but he was often beaten by Merckx and 1965 was his only Tour de France win.

But he won it well, taking the lead by winning stage three into Anquetil's home city of Rouen, then keeping his head while Poulidor steadily cut the lead back. Poulidor won the first time trial and the road stage that finished on top of Mont Ventoux, but Gimondi was never very far behind and on some stages he managed to win a few seconds back.

This see-saw situation continued until stage 18, a time trial up Mont Revard from Aix-les-Bains. Here, with only 39 seconds in hand over Poulidor, Gimondi was generally expected to lose his yellow jersey to the Frenchman, but it didn't happen. Gimondi romped the 27 kilometres in ten seconds under the hour, beating Poulidor by 23 seconds, and that was that. Poulidor's morale dropped, and Gimondi beat him again in the final time trial into Paris to take the Tour from Poulidor by two minutes and 40 seconds.

Second again, no crashes, no excuses – Poulidor couldn't beat Anquetil in the Tour, and now he couldn't win without him. So what Poulidor must have thought when Anquetil announced that he would return to race the Tour de France in 1966 was anyone's guess.

This was to be another classic duel, but with a twist. Anquetil had to ride because Ford, satisfied with the publicity they'd gained from cycling, were pulling out of team sponsorship. This is normal in sports sponsorship now. A company will use a sport to reach a target market, but when they have the penetration they need, they will pull out and perhaps back something else, another sport or the arts maybe. Cycling had traditionally been backed by bike manufacturers who needed the sport to sell their products, or by patronage, businesses where somebody high up had either been a cyclist or just liked the sport. From the 1950s that had slowly changed, and Ford represented a new kind of sponsor, one that had more money, so no one within the sport was complaining.

Anquetil's team needed a new sponsor at the end of the year and Geminiani had to have something to sell. He was forced to take all the team's firepower into the Tour, because even in the sixties it was the biggest marketplace in cycling. Anquetil meanwhile still worried about a man-on-man fight with Poulidor. He would have to out-think Poulidor to get one over on him and preserve his status.

Predictably, Poulidor played into his hands, but he wasn't alone. All the favourites based their race on Anquetil, so when his young team-mate Lucien Aimar got into a break on the first mountain stage, which was in the Pyrenees, he sat back and let the race go. Anquetil was happy; he had no reason to attack, as Aimar had a better track record than anyone else in the escape group with him, so he could be riding to victory.

The attention of Poulidor and the other top riders continued to be fixed on Anquetil, as if they still believed that he would do something as the race went on. The apparent lack of ambition displayed by the Tour's top riders got so bad that some criterium organisers threatened to cancel their races, and the rider's agents had to have a word with their men to get them to make a race of it.

The race finally sparked into life on stage 16 when Tom Simpson, wearing the Rainbow Jersey as the reigning world champion, attacked on the descent of the Col de la Croix de Fer and went off alone up the Maurienne valley towards the Col de Telegraphe. Simpson had broken his leg in a skiing accident and had a lean start to his season. He desperately needed something from the Tour, or his value would go down. He'd been second on two stages so far, but a big day in the Alps might save his year.

The Englishman reached the Telegraphe alone, but behind him the race had exploded. As he began to climb, the only rider gaining on Simpson was Julio Jimenez, a Spanish team-mate of Anquetil and the best climber in the race. Jimenez caught Simpson close to the top of the climb and the pair went over it together.

They descended into Valloire to begin the awesome Col du Galibier, where Simpson made a mistake. He should have climbed at his own pace, but instead he tried to match Jimenez, who was always in a class of his own uphill. In the words of Vin Denson this tiny, balding, frail-looking young man 'seemed to climb by just fluttering his eyelids, you couldn't see where the power came from and he looked effortless.' Jimenez was one of the most gifted climbers never to win the King of the Mountains title, maybe because he used his ability to make big gestures, to win the big mountain stages, like this one on the Galibier, rather than chase down and collect points.

Behind Jimenez and Simpson the race was ripped to shreds, and Poulidor pulled clear of the best of the chasers with Anquetil following directly behind him. Jimenez quickly dropped Simpson, while Anquetil and Poulidor were beginning their final duel. It was just like the Puy de Dôme in '64: Poulidor kept turning the screw, slowly accelerating, while Anquetil took up position by his side and would not give him an inch. Every time Poulidor upped the pace, Anquetil matched it.

Poulidor was making the same mistake again. He should have tried to put everything into one concerted attack; Anquetil didn't like changes of pace, but he could slowly up it forever. But maybe Poulidor was afraid to do it. What if he attacked and it didn't work, and then Anquetil hammered him? To finish close to the master preserved the gallant loser myth, while to be beaten out of hand would make Poulidor simply second rate. Barry Hoban was Poulidor's team-mate for years and he says, 'Some people can be intelligent but still not get the tactics of bike racing, or how to act as a team leader, and Poulidor was one of them. He didn't see the bigger picture like Anquetil did, plus he never had the directeurs that Anquetil did. His first, Antonin Magne, didn't understand modern bike racing, whereas Anquetil's, Raymond Louviot and later Geminiani, were real operators.'

As their pace intensified Anquetil and Poulidor reeled in Simpson, who was suffering a bit by now, and continued together over the Galibier. They then descended to the stage finish in Briançon, where just for old times' sake Anquetil out-sprinted Poulidor for second on the stage behind Jimenez. And that was that, Anquetil caught a chest infection and left the race three days later. Poulidor couldn't do anything about Aimar, or his Pyrenean break-away companion, the Dutchman Jan Janssen, so he finished third in another Tour that on paper he was good enough to win.

The final duel of Anquetil and Poulidor was the story of the 1966 Tour, but there was also trouble brewing between the race organisers, the Tour riders and their teams. The teams wanted the Tour to make changes, but the organisers refused to, and just to put everyone in their place they decided to re-introduce national teams for 1967. Barry Hoban again: 'That was Félix Lévitan. He was a control freak. The teams were getting too demanding, so he thought he'd teach them a lesson. They won in the end, though, because national teams wouldn't work. Top riders wanted their own teams and wouldn't share. Eddy Merckx was already a big name and he said he wouldn't ride the Tour in a national team.'

In a sporting sense this was good news for the strong cycling nations such as France, Italy, Belgium and Spain, but of them only the French could shelve personal pride for the greater good of the team. It was very bad news for the lesser nations, especially for Great Britain and Tom Simpson. By 1967 Simpson had been world champion, he'd won three out of the five single-day 'monuments' of cycling and had finished high up in all the other big races. Even now, when British riders are a force to be reckoned with in pro bike racing, nobody has quite matched Simpson's all-round record.

The Tour de France had never been kind to him. In 1962 he had worn the yellow jersey and was third overall until a crash descending the last mountain of the race dropped him to sixth. He didn't ride the Tour in 1963, was well below his best for 14th place in 1964, then crashed out in 1965 and 1966. Now, in 1967, Simpson felt ready to challenge for the podium.

Winning was going to be a tall order. I'm writing this in 2009, during a Tour de France where Great Britain has been one of the dominant nations. In 2010 a well-funded professional British team (Team Sky) will take part in the Tour de France, something Simpson dreamed about and was working on in the sixties, but in 1967 only five out of the ten riders selected for the Great Britain team were full-time racers on the European pro circuit. The rest raced in the UK. They were good riders but very inexperienced, and the jump to Tour de France level was huge for them.

As ever, though, Simpson had a plan. He intended to use certain key stages to move up the overall standings and have a run on the yellow jersey in the final week. One of the stages he identified as being crucial was stage 13, on 13 July, Marseilles to Carpentras, the stage that climbed Mont Ventoux.

Simpson was on good form early in 1967. He didn't concentrate on the single-day Classics, which was where he was a better rider, but instead won the week-long Paris–Nice stage race and two stages of the Tour of Spain. He went to France really feeling that this was going to be his year, but he also went carrying a lot of financial pressure.

The 1967 Tour de France was the first to start with a prologue time trial. It was a short one, just six kilometres on a circuit lit by hundreds of camping lamps, held the evening before the race started properly. The winner was José Errandonea of Spain, with Poulidor showing he had good legs in second place just five seconds behind. Of the other favourites Jan Janssen was third, Felice Gimondi sixth, Franco Balmamion eighth and Roger Pingeon 11th. Tom Simpson finished 13th.

Simpson then made the break of favourites who gained time on stage four to Roubaix, missed a move that gave the eventual winner, Roger Pingeon of France the lead next day, but did a good ride on the first mountain stage in the Vosges to move into seventh place overall. Things looked good, but next day, on the key stage of the Alps that climbed the Galibier, Simpson fell ill with a stomach bug. He couldn't mount a challenge on that stage and lost time. He stayed seventh but the gap to the others widened.

He was in trouble, and the British team didn't have a doctor, so Simpson called on help from Felice Gimondi, whose trade team he was due to join the following year. Gimondi arranged for the Italian team doctor to give Simpson an intravenous glucose drip each evening so he could get some nourishment. And that is how he got through the next two days.

By the morning of the 13th stage Simpson was still in seventh place but feeling very weak. His Tour de France had gone wrong, and just to add to his problems he'd been visited by his agent, Daniel Dousset, who told Simpson he needed a result from this Tour or it would affect his income. As if he didn't have enough problems that was a big one, as Simpson was heavily committed on a number of building projects that he hoped would provide income for his family when he stopped racing.

July 1967 had seen a heat wave across Europe, and Provence sweltered as the riders trekked towards the region's biggest mountain. Mont Ventoux sat waiting for them like some giant beast waiting to be fed, its rocky white summit shimmering in the distance. It was a simple stage, no tactics, just get to the Ventoux and let the mountain make the decisions.

Vin Denson was on the Great Britain team, working hard as a domestique for Simpson as he had done in his trade teams for Jacques Anquetil and Rik Van Looy. He recalls that Simpson was very nervous about the Ventoux stage:

> He needed to do well even though he was suffering. I'd tried to talk him out of even riding the stage, telling him that there would be other races. I thought that he should quit the Tour and go home to recover, then prepare for the worlds, but he refused.
>
> So I rode alongside him before the Ventoux and tried to stay with him as long as possible on the climb, which wasn't very long. As the road started going upwards Poulidor punctured and some Italians attacked. Tom went after them, and I sprinted after him. I was going flat out because I wanted to tell Tom to wait for Poulidor. He would get back to the front and Tom should have just followed him. The pace would have been steadier, but Tom wasn't listening. With my last bit of strength I pushed Tom forwards as hard as I could and I will never forget my last words to him. They were 'Dai Dai', like Italians shout when they want you to give everything, but they are pronounced die die. The thought that they were maybe the last words Tom ever heard will stay with me forever.

Simpson made his way up the mountain. His slight figure and bobbing style, with his white jersey and a Union Jack on each shoulder, was easy to pick out. He was at the front when things started to split, making a big effort but still in there. The British team car passed rider after rider to get up to Simpson, but as it settled into position behind him he began to slow.

Harry Hall, a bike shop owner from Manchester, was the British team mechanic. It's his jerky black and white home movie film that you can see on YouTube if you Google Simpson's name. Hall is dead now, but for a long time he felt a sense of guilt about what happened next. This is what he told me when the 1967 GB Tour team had a reunion on the 25th anniversary of Simpson's death: 'By the time we got to him Tom had been dropped by the two front runners, Jimenez and Poulidor, and fallen back to a group of chasers, which included the stage winner, Jan Janssen. But instead of riding with them, Tom kept attacking. That's what he was like, he didn't know when he was beaten.'

Simpson wasn't thinking straight. He was an aggressive rider but he had a good head for tactics on his day. For so many reasons, though, this wasn't his day. Instead of getting away from Janssen's group, Tom's attacks cost him his place in it. He slowed quite dramatically and began to struggle. Out of the trees that line the first three-quarters of the climb, at a café called the Chalet Reynard, the riders were met by the full force of the sun and temperatures that were in the forties Celsius.

Three kilometres further up the mountain Simpson faltered badly. He began to weave right and left across the road. Hall, behind him, was worried that Simpson would ride over the edge and shouted at the team car driver to stop. 'I ran towards Tom, but as I did he fell against the steep bank on the right-hand side of the road. I was really worried now and said, "Right, that's it, Tom, it's finished," and I undid his toe straps so I could lift him off his bike, but as I did that he said, "No, Harry, get me up straight." Then he said, "My straps, Harry, do up my straps." What could I do? Tom was coherent, he knew what was happening, and he was the boss. I did up his straps and gave him a great big push,' Hall explained with an undisguised choke of emotion in his voice.

Simpson made a bit of headway but fell once more, and Hall was first to him again. This time, though, he says, 'Tom wasn't breathing. I tried what I knew of mouth to mouth but the medics were quickly there and they took over.'

Simpson was taken by helicopter to the hospital at Avignon, while efforts were made to revive him, but to no avail. At 5.40 that day, 13 July 1967, Simpson was pronounced dead. Naturally, the doctors in charge would not give permission for internment until a post-mortem had been carried out. The French police searched the vehicles, rooms and belongings of the British team. Explanations were needed, although the riders knew what they were. Quantities of amphetamine tablets were found in the pockets of Simpson's race jersey and in his luggage. The autopsy revealed the same in his stomach contents, although I'm told not his blood, a fact that is impossible to corroborate as the relevant files have gone missing.

There's no doubt that Simpson took drugs during the Ventoux stage and at other times during his career. Amphetamines were rife in the pro peloton at the time. I have to declare an interest here as Simpson was my uncle, and since I started as a cycling writer six or so years ago I've spoken to many of his fellow racers about his use of drugs, and I think I now know the extent of it. Of course his friends tried to sugar the pill, telling me Tom wasn't so bad, that he never used injections, just pills, but that's like somebody saying they didn't rob the bank because they were only driving the getaway car. It's an impossible argument in the context of the ethics of sport today.

But those ethics were a long way off in the sixties. Amphetamines were used extensively to pep up the troops in war, and in Europe students could be prescribed amphetamines to help them study longer. They were part of life as well as cycling, and the riders believed, as did parts of the medical profession, that their use was safe. And although drug use had been illegal in sport for a while, there had been no way of policing it because dope tests were not introduced into cycling until 1965.

When they were, they caused an uproar. Jacques Anquetil led a protest against the first tests in the Tour in 1966, and later he actively worked against them, refusing or otherwise dodging any attempts to test him. He was stripped of victory when that happened, but he still carried on racing. It would be a while before suspensions were introduced, and even then they were often tokens that were served during the off-season.

Despite Simpson's death there was a feeling among pro racers that they knew what they were doing, that they should be left to get on with their jobs. They cited other factors in Simpson's death and the fact that the autopsy result didn't conclude that it was entirely caused by drug use, which is true, but they were playing a dangerous game, and one that has continued down the years.

The Tour de France wasn't sure what to do. They managed to avoid Simpson's death reflecting too badly on them, then announced that 1968 would be the 'Tour of Health', even awarding the start to Vittel, where the mineral water comes from. The race was also made easier.

One of Anquetil's, and many other riders', justifications for using drugs was that cycling was too hard to do without, and the 1967 race was a brutal one.

For the 1968 Tour the organisers cut the race distance, they reduced the big climbs to just a couple of days each in the Alps and Pyrenees, and they brought in daily dope tests. In the editorial of *L'Equipe* on the eve of the race, Jacques Goddet wrote about a new start, about how they owed it to Simpson's memory to try and improve things for the riders. This would be a new start for the Tour de France and a new era for cycling. Unfortunately it was the first of many such new starts.

The 1968 race was for national teams again and the battle looked as if it would be between Raymond Poulidor and the previous year's winner, his fellow Frenchman Roger Pingeon. There didn't seem to be anyone in the field to touch the French. The top two Italians, Felice Gimondi and Gianni Motta, both gave the race a miss. The Belgians couldn't get their new revelation, Eddy Merckx, to ride, despite their prime minister getting involved in trying to persuade him. But the reason was that neither Merckx nor the two Italians wanted to ride the Tour in national teams, and they made it clear that they would only ride the Tour if the organisers switched back to trade teams again.

The 1968 Tour de France turned out to be quite interesting and it threw up an unexpected winner. Poulidor and Pingeon had it to lose, but neither seemed willing to really take hold of the race. Poulidor looked the most likely, working his way up to fourth place after stage 14, which took the race out of the Pyrenees. Then Roger Pingeon went on a long lone break next day, which saw him move up to fourth and Poulidor drop down to ninth.

Nobody, not even the riders, seemed to know who was leading the French team, a fact that wasn't lost on the 1966 winner, Lucien Aimar, who was leading the French 'B' team. On stage 16, a tough and quite hilly ride from Albi to Aurillac, Poulidor crashed just before a feed station and Pingeon got in a tangle with his musette, so Aimar attacked.

The French 'A' team took ages to marshal their resources and chase, and when they did they made little impression. Pingeon and Poulidor lost over four minutes each, dropped to 16th and 20th overall and waved good-bye to winning the Tour de France. Aimar became the best Frenchman, but down in 14th.

A few days later a tough stage in the Massif Central saw another big shake-up. Pingeon won and moved to ninth overall, but the main beneficiaries were the Belgians Herman Van Springel and Ferdinand Bracke, who moved up to second and fourth overall, and the Dutchman, Jan Janssen, who ended up between them in third.

Barry Hoban made Tour history next day when he became the first British rider to win a mountain stage. He did it in a long, lone breakaway that saw him cross the Alpine giant climbs of the Col d'Aravis and Col de la Colombière alone in the lead, then climb the steep pitch up to the village of Cordon, near Sallanches and right under Mont Blanc. Hoban scooped up over £1,200 in prize money that day, plus a cow called Estelle which he sold that evening to a local farmer. Hoban still has her bell.

Van Springel took the yellow jersey. Janssen was just behind him in third with Bracke dropping to fourth, but still a threat as he was within two minutes and had by far the best record as a time triallist. That's how it stayed until the end of the first half of the final day, a road stage from

Auxerre to Melun. The final time trial into Paris that after-noon would start with Van Springel in yellow, Janssen in third, 16 seconds behind him, and Bracke in seventh at one minute 56 seconds.

Janssen had been world champion in 1964 and had won Classics; he was an excellent single-day racer, a winner of several Tour stages, the green jersey in 1964, '65 and '67, and he won the 1967 Tour of Spain, but he had never been a great time triallist. On the other hand Van Springel was good at this speciality and would prove to be excellent in the future, and Bracke had been a world pursuit champion, had held the Hour record and had won the time trial Classic, the Grand Prix des Nations. But it was Janssen who won the stage and the Tour from Van Springel. The victory margin was 38 seconds, the narrow-est so far in the Tour, and Janssen was the first Dutchman to win it.

The race ended for the first time on the Municipale track in the Bois de Vincennes after years of finishing in the more prestigious Parc des Princes, where the velodrome had closed over the winter because the track was in the way of the new Paris Périphérique, or ring road. The Municipale didn't have the atmosphere for a race like the Tour, and the organisers were already looking for a better finish location.

Janssen's victory also brought the curtain down on the sixties and the Anquetil era. The Dutchman was a man of his time, from his Buddy Holly glasses to the sharp suits he wore in preference to tracksuits or more casual clothes when travelling to races. Janssen was sixties chic, a smart operator who made money from cycling and invested it well. An example of what could be achieved in a new European society where people achieved things on merit.

12. WIND AND WILDFIRE

Eddy Merckx was born in Flanders, in a village called Meenzel Kiezegem, just to the east of Brussels and on the Flemish side of the language border where Flemish-speaking Belgium becomes French-speaking Belgium. Trivia? Not really, Eddy Merckx is one of the names that put Belgium on the map for the world. In a divided country, the place where their most identifiable celebrity comes from is of core importance.

But just to complicate things, shortly after his first birthday Merckx's family moved to a French-speaking suburb of Brussels. His family history was Flemish, his name is Flemish, but he grew up speaking French at school in a city suburb. To the people of Flanders, where bike racing is really important, Merckx had the whiff of a Walloon, a French-speaking Belgian. Then he married one, Claudine Acou, a true Walloon, and the couple said their marriage vows in French. For a while they hated him in Flanders.

It didn't last long, Merckx was too good at cycling for the Flemish to disown him. Anyway, for all his perceived French affectation he was one of them at heart. For Merckx's part he always stayed neutral. Ask him if he is a Walloon or Flemish and he will say, 'I'm Belgian.' It's a good answer, enabling him to avoid a minefield of class hatred dating from when French was the language of authority in Belgium.

Belgium has always been split in two, but up until the Second World War it was ruled in French. Politics, bureaucracy, the business of the courts – they were all conducted in French. The upper and middle classes looked down on Flemish as the language of factory and field. Official documents were written in French; lessons and army orders were written and spoken the same. Flemish men died on First World War battlefields because they didn't understand their officer's commands. It's not cycling, but this history has a bearing on Eddy Merckx and on his career.

They say that comparisons are odious, but I'm going to make one. Eddy Merckx is the greatest racing cyclist of any generation. Lance Armstrong has won more Tours de France, but that's it. Merckx beats Armstrong in every other field of bike racing. Merckx was a more complete rider than Fausto Coppi, more talented than Louison Bobet, more versatile than Jacques Anquetil, and simply more dominant than any other cyclist before or since.

When Eddy Merckx made his Tour de France debut in 1969 at the age of 24 he had already won four out of the five single-day monuments of cycling, he had won the Tour of Italy, and he'd been the amateur and the professional world road race champion. He would go on to win 445 top-class races during his career, more than anybody else. At his best he had a strike rate of almost 40 per cent. That means he won nearly every other race he rode.

In a sport where people lose far more often than they win, no one has come near to Merckx's batting average. He needed to win. His wife sums it up when she says: 'If Eddy went more than a week without winning he wasn't the same man.' Merckx took that need to the 1969 Tour de France.

It started in Roubaix with a 10.4-kilometre prologue time trial. The 1969 Tour also saw the return of trade teams. Lévitan's two-year experiment was over. The Tour had outgrown national teams, through the sheer interest and exposure it generated, and it was unreasonable for a business that supported a team all year to be deprived of the sport's biggest stage. What is more, the top riders wanted team-mates who were bound to them by money, not national pride. The Tour de France was moving into a new era.

Rudi Altig, the German former world road race champion, won the prologue. Merckx finished second, seven seconds behind. It was a good start but not what he came for. He liked prologue time trials; they played to his character. Merckx never finessed, and there is no finesse about a short solo blast around the streets of a European city. A prologue lays it out there. There are many more hours, minutes and seconds of the Tour to come, but time differences in the prologue are still real.

'I liked to win the prologue because it was a blow to my rivals. Also, I always felt that it was better to race from the front. If I took the leader's jersey early I always tried to keep it. If I lost it I fretted about the seconds that had gone, about how they had to be gained back before I could think about winning. It's better to race from the front,' Merckx explained to me during a long and revealing interview I did with him a few years ago.

Race from the front or, in French, '*la course en tête*' are four words that sum up the Eddy Merckx approach. As well as all of his physical attributes, the biggest of which he says was simple – 'I was very, very strong. No other

explanation' – Merckx was a street-fighting bike racer. 'I
always tried to throw the first punch, to put my rivals on
the defence. If you let them take the initiative, rivals get
confident and become double the danger.'

Next day the race moved on to Brussels, but more
importantly to the suburb of Woluwe-St-Pierre, where
Merckx grew up. It was a split stage, a road race from
Roubaix in the morning and a team time trial around the
streets of Woluwe in the afternoon. Merckx had to get
something from this, and a colleague in his Faema team,
Martin Vandenboscche, remembers the pressure:

> It was always the same. Eddy wanted to win, he wanted to
> win everything, a hand of cards, a charity football match,
> whatever, but in his home town that day he was 100 times
> worse.
>
> He had tried to win the road stage, but the route was
> flat and the others watched him very closely. Still, he was
> up there at the finish, fighting it out with the sprinters. But
> he didn't win, and neither did he get the yellow jersey.
> That was bad news for us, because we knew that Eddy
> wasn't going leave Brussels without it.
>
> That afternoon he ripped us to pieces in the team time
> trial. I had to keep telling him to slow down a little because
> we had to have six finishers together, otherwise he'd have
> gone too hard, left us all maybe, and we wouldn't have
> made a good time. We won, though, Faema won by
> enough for Eddy to have the yellow jersey. Thank heav-
> ens, because he would have been like a bear with a sore
> head if we hadn't done it.

Merckx let the lead go the next day, but he wasn't acting
out of character because it passed to his team-mate, Julien

Stevens. A Frenchman, Désiré Letort, wore it for one day, then Merckx wrenched it back on the first mountain climb, the Ballon d'Alsace, and the die was cast. Over the next few days Roger Pingeon, the French winner in 1967, crept up the overall standings, as did Felice Gimondi, but all the time Merckx was drawing inexorably away from them.

On the eve of the 17th stage, Merckx led Pingeon by over eight minutes and Gimondi by nine. They were the first three and no one else was in with a shout. The race was in the Pyrenees, just over half-way, and so far Merckx had done exactly what a textbook Tour winner should. He had made a good start, won two time trials and taken a mountain stage in the Alps at Digne. Whenever he pressed down harder on the pedals Merckx took a little more time from Pingeon and Gimondi, but when they tried it they could not distance Merckx at all. It was all going very well; it was very controlled, mature and masterful.

That was the textbook way to win a modern Tour de France, but then Merckx ripped up the textbook, set fire to the pages and stamped on their ashes. The first climbs of stage 17 were the Peyresourde and Aspin, where Merckx watched his rivals carefully. They were tired, no one looked as if they wanted to attack, but he felt good. In fact sometimes Merckx's class was too great for him to contain. His excitement with cycling, his desire to race, to go hard and to push was too much. That spirit was about to explode over the Tour de France.

Merckx told his team-mate Vandenboscche to ride hard from the start of the Col du Tourmalet. Vandenboscche was good, too good in fact to stay with Merckx's team. He'd had an offer from a rival during the Tour that he had told Merckx about only the night before. It provided a nice little subplot to what happened next.

Vandenboscche led all the way up, dropping riders until only Pingeon and Poulidor were anywhere near the two Belgians. Then Merckx attacked and dropped Vandenboscche just before the top of the Tourmalet. He shouldn't have done it; in the twisted ethics of pro bike racing it isn't done to humiliate a team-mate like that, but he did. Vandenboscche's new team offer, and the timing of waving it in Merckx's face the night before this stage, had angered him. 'I feel bad about it now, but back then I wanted to teach him a lesson,' Merckx admits.

He's like that, though, ultra-competitive. Merckx surprised me when I commented about how it was nice that his son, Axel, had won a bronze medal at the Athens Olympics. In Merckx's day the Games were amateur only, so he only went to one, Tokyo 1964, and didn't win a thing. I thought it was good that Axel had done something his father hadn't, and said so. Eddy's response was a knee-jerk 'Yes, but I could have won the Olympics in 1964 but for a crash near the end.' He can't help it, you see, he has to be the best, and although he'd deny it, a little bit of that remains, even now.

Back in 1969, Merckx threw himself down the Tourmalet, descending like a maniac. In the Luz valley a group formed that set off to chase Merckx, but they never even saw him. Merckx pounded his pedals, drawing away with every kilometre. He swung left in Argelès-Gazost and roared up the Col d'Aubisque to finish in Mourenx a fraction under eight minutes clear of the chasing group.

I asked Merckx why he went on the attack that day in 1969. Why, with a comfortable lead already and totally in control of the race, did he attack, ride alone for 130 kilometres and take minutes, many minutes more when he didn't really need to? He pondered for a moment. We'd had a good interview, Merckx had tried to answer my questions as fully as possible, and now he tried again. His eyes looked down to see if the answer was on the floor. He looked up, he thought and slowly scanned his hairline from left to right, right to left, trying to come up with a reason, a good reason based on logic and one that I might understand, but he couldn't. Eventually he just shrugged his shoulders, smiled and in his deep voice said, 'I don't know, I guess I must have been crazy.'

Sometimes even Eddy Merckx cannot explain Eddy Merckx. There is no easy answer to him, other than that he was an elemental force, unstoppable like the wind or wildfire. In his first Tour de France Merckx was at his very best. He won by over 20 minutes, he took the green jersey and he won the King of the Mountains as well as yellow. Nobody had done that before, or has done it since. No one has taken hold of the Tour de France and beaten it so hard that there was nothing left for anyone else. It was a rout, and to add insult to injury he says that it didn't even hurt. Cyclists talk a lot about suffering and pain, but Merckx says he didn't suffer in a race until Blois.

Blois is the capital of the Loir et Cher department. It sits on the River Loire between Orleans and Tours. One chilly evening in August 1969 there was a track meeting in Blois, part of the after-Tour criterium circus. The Blois velodrome was an ugly old place, a grey, concrete bowl, and Merckx wasn't enjoying the meeting. He'd travelled to it with Jacques Anquetil and they'd had a car crash. The weather was bad, the track outdoors, and not many spectators turned up.

The last event was a Derny-paced race. Racing behind a Derny is fast, and the Blois track was short and quite narrow. The riders were all very experienced, but some of their pacers that night were not. Having said that, no one would have had much chance with what happened. A pedal on the lead rider's Derny sheared off and he crashed, bringing down his rider. Merckx and his pacer, Fernand Wambst, both hit them and fell. Wambst was killed instantly, and Merckx ended up unconscious and bleeding badly from a head wound.

He recovered consciousness in hospital, where his head wound was stitched and he was found to have cracked a vertebra. At first the injuries didn't look too bad, but Merckx says now that he made a big mistake by getting back into training too quickly. 'I had to do some rehabilitation, which at first was the wrong sort, but once that was sorted out I chose to ride instead, masking the pain with injections. I didn't get to the source of my pain and it steadily worsened. Through 1970, then even more marked in 1971, I suffered until I had to do something.'

He started regular back exercises after 1971, and had acupuncture, but by then the damage was done. 'The pain was less, but I never rode a day without it after Blois. Before, I didn't feel a thing when I pressed on the pedals, everything was light and easy. After Blois I had pain in every race and in every training session. Most of the time I could manage it, but at times the pain was almost too much. Then one day close to the end of my career, I was out training and came to a hill I had climbed a hundred times before. It wasn't particularly hard, but I nearly had to stop. That was the moment I knew the end was in sight,' he says.

That was in the future. Merckx won the Tour de France again in 1970, scoring his first double by winning the Tours of Italy and France in the same year. His back hurt but he could handle it. In 1971, though, Merckx nearly came unstuck. He was OK when training in the winter, but once the racing started his back pain worsened. He began to fiddle with his position on the bike, he says: 'I started taking an Allen key with me on every ride. At first I thought my pain might be due to a slightly incorrect position on my bike, so I changed the saddle height slightly, but the pain came back. I experimented some more and every time I changed the saddle, or the height or angle of the handlebars, the pain eased for a while. Then I realised that the problem was nothing to do with my bike, it was me, and shifting my position slightly just brought temporary relief, not a cure.'

Merckx won races in 1971, good ones too like Milan–San Remo and Liège–Bastogne–Liège, but he was in constant pain and his training for the Tour de France was compromised. He couldn't ride the Giro d'Italia, which was the way Merckx preferred to get ready for the Tour, and instead had a difficult May and June, so he was not at his best going in. It was going to be tough, but a Merckx down on power could still handle most riders in the world. The problem was one outstanding rider who had the ability and the form to give him trouble.

Luis Ocana was born in Spain and brought up in France, and he was nothing like Eddy Merckx except perhaps in his ego. Where Merckx was big for a bike racer, robust, straightforward and capable of racing in any terrain and conditions, Luis Ocana was slim, more fragile and very complicated. He climbed like an angel, like his countrymen Julio Jimenez and Federico Bahamontes before him, and he was blessed with their attacking spirit and killer change of pace. But unlike Bahamontes and Jimenez, Ocana could time trial and that spelled danger, even for Eddy Merckx.

The 1971 Tour started with a team time trial prologue, which Merckx's Molteni squad won, giving Merckx the overall lead. The next day proved just how money driven the organisers had become. Split stages became more common during the sixties. If the race had two finishes in a day, the Tour got two towns to pay for them. So Lévitan and Goddet, or most likely Lévitan on his own, thought why not try three? Stage one in 1971 started with a 59.5-kilometre dash from Mulhouse to Basel, then 90 kilometres from Basel to Freiburg and finally 74 kilometres from Freiburg back to Mulhouse.

OK, the riders got to leave their stuff in one hotel for two nights, but it was still two extra sprints, two extra changes of clothes and a lot of extra bother.

Merckx defended the yellow jersey in the only way he knew how, by going for a win in every stage and keeping at the head of affairs across the north of France and to the Channel coast resort of Le Touquet. Then the race headed towards the centre of the country and its first big test, stage eight from Nevers to the top of the Puy de Dôme.

Luis Ocana was born a few days before Eddy Merckx and it's tempting to say that he didn't develop as quickly, but that is because Merckx's talent was so all-encompassing. In the kind of races that suited him, Ocana built a fearsome reputation. Victory in the 1970 Vuelta a Espana and the Dauphiné Libéré made Ocana think he could contend in the Tour de France. He didn't race much in the spring of 1971, when Merckx had his usual Classics campaign, and threw everything he'd got at getting ready for the Tour, just as the overall contenders do today.

Merckx's pain was no secret, which is why Ocana's manager, a canny Frenchman called Maurice de Muer, didn't over-race his star in the spring and why he told his team that the Tour would be for Ocana. The plan was to hit Merckx hard on the first big climb, which was the Puy, and find out what he'd got. De Muer had a lot of good climbers in his team, more than Merckx had in Molteni, so he decided to use them to attack Merckx and isolate him, ready for Ocana to administer the *coup de grâce*.

It worked. Ocana switched to an extra-light bike on the flat road before Clermont-Ferrand, the city that sits at the foot of the Puy, and then his team-mates Lief Mortensen and Bernard Labourdette set a ferocious pace. The pain in his back brought on by climbing the 20 per cent slopes of the extinct volcanic plug cracked Merckx in the final two kilometres. Ocana was waiting for this and he pounced to steal 15 seconds. Not much, but after all the talk and rumour, Ocana knew that Merckx was indeed vulnerable.

Merckx still had the lead, with Ocana 37 seconds behind in third. The next mountain stage was two days after the Puy de Dôme, through the Chartreuse Massif to Grenoble. Ocana hesitated, not totally confident yet. If he got this wrong, Merckx would eat him, but the day revealed more about Merckx's condition. The Chartreuse is just an outlier of the Alps, but the Belgian lost nearly 90 seconds to a group containing his main rivals, and the overall lead passed to the 1970 runner-up, Joop Zoetemelk.

Ocana was with the leaders, joining in with the attacks but still cautious, his sad eyes taking in every nuance of the stage. The conclusion he came to was that tomorrow would be D-Day, the day he attacked. Allow Merckx time and he might get stronger – it had to be tomorrow.

The hours between Grenoble and the ski station of Orcières-Merlette were among Ocana's finest ever. The stage wasn't long, only 134 kilometres, and he left his attack until the Col de Noyer, about three-quarters of the way through, but when he attacked it was devastating. Ocana ripped the race to shreds. Lucien Van Impe tried to stay with him, but Ocana discarded him without even registering he was there.

Over the 7.5 kilometres of the Noyer, the intervening valley road and the 11-kilometre climb to Orcières-Merlette, Ocana put five and a half minutes into second place Van Impe and over eight into third man Merckx. It was astonishing, almost too good: every rider after 39th place was outside the 15 per cent elimination time limit for the stage. Luckily the Tour rule book has space for exceptions, so where more than one-tenth of the field would be eliminated the time limit is raised. On this stage it would have been two-thirds sent home, so up went the limit, but it didn't save everyone. Three poor souls who finished 40 minutes behind the Spaniard were thrown out.

It was incredible, but Merckx being Merckx didn't take the defeat lying down. Ocana was right when he believed Merckx would get stronger during the Tour. Next day on the rolling road to Marseilles, Merckx launched his counter-attack. He put his team on the front from the start, and they hammered it. He took two minutes back from Ocana, hauled himself back up into second overall and the fight was on.

Next day Merckx won a short time trial at Albi, snatching back more seconds. He wasn't going to give in until Paris. Next day he ran Ocana ragged up and down the Pyrenees in terrible weather that on the Cole de Mente turned into a storm of biblical proportions.

As they reached the summit of the climb, lightning flashed, thunder clashed, rain fell and the road turned into a torrent. Merckx was one of the best descenders in the business. He had an inherent sense of where the limit was on any road and in any conditions. Ocana had many gifts but not that. Merckx dropped down the mountain like an expert skier cutting new lines in fresh snow.

Merckx was on his limit but, miraculously, an inspired Ocana kept with him. Merckx had to push it, take calculated risks that he could maybe get away with but the Spaniard might not. A crash was inevitable and both riders went down on a sharp left hairpin that is edged by a rock wall. Merckx got up quickly, Ocana less so. He was winded but not seriously hurt. Then, as he struggled to his feet, Joop Zoetemelk dragging his shoes along the road because his brakes couldn't slow him enough, cannoned straight into Ocana.

The Spaniard was hurt from two sides. Zoetemelk thudded into him and sent him crashing to the ground. He hit it hard. His back, head, shoulders and ribs were injured, and some reports say that a number of vertebrae in his back were displaced, but nothing was broken. Nevertheless, Ocana couldn't, or wouldn't, get up. He was placed in an ambulance and driven off the mountain heartbroken.

Next day Eddy Merckx refused to wear the yellow jersey out of respect for his rival. He also visited Ocana at his home on Mont de Marsan a few days later when the Tour was in the same area. This was a press stunt because in 1971 there was no friendship between Merckx and Ocana. They had been at each other's throats for over a year, and Merckx had already protested that every Spanish rider in the 1971 Tour had chased him on the stage to Marseilles. There was also a hint from Merckx that he thought Ocana had stayed down after his crash, that the Spaniard was already absolutely shattered and would have lost the Tour eventually. By crashing in yellow Ocana saw himself, as did many fans, as the moral winner.

Whatever the truth, the Belgian and the Spaniard did not like each other. Apart from the occasional snide remark in the press, they ignored each other for much of the next two years. Ocana won the Tour de France without Merckx there in 1973. Merckx wanted to add the Tour of Spain to his victory list that year, and since his sponsor was Italian he had to ride the Tour of Italy. He won both, but not even Merckx could win all three Grand Tours in a single year – no one has, so he didn't even try.

Ocana was magnificent, winning six stages and the overall by nearly 16 minutes. He won in the mountains, he won in the time trials, he was Merckx-like, but Merckx wasn't there and somehow that detracted from Ocana's victory. And it certainly didn't help warm up relations between the two of them. Then, out of the blue, at the end of the season Merckx and Ocana found themselves together in an airport bar. They were alone, with no other friends to talk to, so they had a drink together. They began to talk, then they had another drink, and another, and soon, Merckx says, 'We thought each other to be just about the best two friends in the world.' Their war was over.

When, years later, Ocana's business fell into difficulties, Merckx was one of the few people from the cycling world who lent him a hand. Ocana produced Armagnac but was hit by bad winters just when he'd sunk every penny he had into his business. Ocana couldn't supply his customers, so they dumped him and didn't want to know once conditions improved. On hearing of his problem Merckx persuaded one of Belgium's biggest drinks companies to buy from his ex-rival.

Unfortunately it wasn't enough, and Ocana was ill, suffering from hepatitis C. He tried to negotiate more finance from his bank, he worked at anything he could do to cash in on his cycling fame, but he was slowly going under. It seems that the proud champion, the man who had once brought Eddy Merckx to his knees – although of course Merckx still says that he would have won in 1971 anyway – couldn't cope any more. What exactly happened is surrounded in some mystery, and opinions differ, but the official verdict is that on 19 May 1994 Luis Ocana took his own life.

Other riders beat Merckx during his reign at the top of cycling. They raced so much in those days that it was impossible even for Eddy Merckx to win all the time, but nobody beat him as convincingly as Luis Ocana did at Orcières-Merlette. Ocana could never repeat it, though. Neither did he repeat his steam-rollering of the Tour de France in 1973. By 1974 he was a spent force, the only performance of note before he stopped racing in 1977 was second in the 1976 Tour of Spain. Ocana used up his talent between 1970 and 1973.

Eddy Merckx won his fifth Tour in 1974, equalling Jacques Anquetil, and as the 1975 season progressed there seemed no reason to believe that the Belgian wouldn't win his sixth. He had a very good Spring Classics season, winning four. The only big spring race that escaped him that year was Paris–Roubaix, and he was second in that.

His stage racing record wasn't quite as good in 1975, but you couldn't read much into it. Tenth in the Tour de France's Alpine dry run, the Dauphiné Libéré, was followed up with second in the Tour of Switzerland: two results that show a rider coming into form nicely for the Tour de France.

However, Merckx says now that he could feel the decline. 'I had two gifts, physical strength and robust health. I was as strong in 1975 as ever, but after 11 years of hard racing my health was starting to suffer. I picked up colds and flu, little things like that. It had never happened before, but illness was a factor in my preparation for the 1975 Tour.'

The race started well for Merckx. He was second in the prologue to a young Italian called Francesco Moser, then took the yellow jersey by winning the time trial on stage six. Merckx wasn't brilliant in the Pyrenees, but his rivals didn't seem to have the guts to press him, so he started stage 14 from Aurillac to the top of the Puy de Dôme with a 92-second lead over a Frenchman, Bernard Thévenet.

The Puy de Dôme is not a climb that ever suited Merckx. It's too short and steep for him to set a rhythm and use his strength to burn off the climbers, but it is also too long be a power climb, like the ones in northern Europe where Merckx used his explosiveness to put the hurt on rivals. The Puy is a climber's climb of unrelenting steepness where the laws of physics let men with the highest power-to-weight ratio put in brutal accelerations that can break even the strongest all-rounder.

In 1975 the man already said by many to be the best pure climber ever in the Tour, Lucien Van Impe, made those accelerations. He attacked as the steepest bit started, slowed, then attacked again. Bernard Thévenet wasn't quite in Van Impe's climbing league but he was good, and he was in the form of his life. He was also a huge threat to Merckx, because he was a good time triallist and was strong enough to race for four weeks in a row, never mind the three of the Tour. Thévenet saw Merckx had no answer to Van Impe, so he attacked as well.

Merckx didn't panic, he'd been here before. He stuck to his own constant pace, and after looking as if he was in trouble he slowly began to close the gap that Van Impe and Thévenet had opened. Then disaster struck, or rather a spectator did. Fans push the riders on the climbs, they pat them on the back and they chuck water on them, but even though cycling is open to it, they rarely try to impede a rider. But in 1975 a Clermont-Ferrand local, Nello Breton, punched Eddy Merckx in the stomach as he heaved himself by him.

Merckx was at his maximum, suffering. His back hurt, as it always did, and he was struggling with his breathing. But the blow nearly finished him off. 'I was in a sea of pain. I slowed, but then something inside took over and carried me to the line,' he says. Once he recovered, Merckx went down the Puy with some police officers and identified Breton, who had been arrested and held by the crowd. Breton was French, the crowd were largely French, and it was a Frenchman, Bernard Thévenet, who had profited in the Tour de France, but the fans' sense of fair play was offended.

Breton was prosecuted but claimed he was pushed. However, the court still found against him. Merckx didn't ask for damages but was awarded one franc. 'No damages could replace what I lost. That punch cost me my sixth Tour de France,' Merckx says now.

Maybe the story might have been different if there had been a flat stage for Merckx to recover, and he certainly thinks it would have been if his doctor hadn't administered blood-thinning medicine to lessen Merckx's bruising. 'It robbed me of my strength. I don't think my blood was as good at transporting oxygen for the rest of the Tour, and that is why I ran out of strength when I did,' he says.

Recovery was impossible because the next stage was from Nice to Pra Loup, a tough 217 kilometres with five mountain climbs along the way. Merckx still had the yellow jersey with a 58-second lead over Thévenet, and anyone else but Merckx might have been tempted to watch and wait and let others take the initiative, but he couldn't.

Just like the bar-room fighter he always was, he decided to get in the first punch and attacked on the Col des Champs with quite a long way to go. He sailed over the huge Col d'Allos and began the climb to the ski station at Pra Loup in good form and with a healthy lead. Then it happened.

If Merckx was Superman, Pra Loup was his Kryptonite. It's not a steep climb, or very dramatic, the drama was all on the road as Merckx slowed as though someone had switched his life film into slow motion. In French cycling they call it being visited by the 'man with the hammer'. Brits and Americans call it the 'bonk', but Merckx simply ran out of power. He'd been eating and drinking, but he thinks that his blood wasn't carrying the fuel he needed to his muscles. They'd been working in the red for too long and gave out a few kilometres short of the line.

Behind Merckx, Thévenet launched an attack which splintered the chasing group. He caught Merckx and rode straight by, not even looking at him. Next up was Felice Gimondi, Merckx's oldest rival in so many races as well as the Tour. How he would have loved to have beaten Merckx in a straight fight, but now he looked across at a man who over the years had also become his friend, whom he admired, and who was now in trouble. Gimondi rode alongside Merckx for a while, seemingly trying to rally him, but it didn't work and the Italian had to press on.

And that was that, Merckx lost the yellow jersey, and he was humbled by Thévenet again next day when the Frenchman won alone in yellow on Bastille Day by climbing the legendary Col d'Izoard. For French cycling this was like Geoff Hurst's goals at Wembley in the 1966 World Cup final. Louison Bobet had done the same in 1954, and ever since 1975 the image of Thévenet has hung subliminally over every promising French rider.

Merckx crashed early next day, fracturing his cheekbone in a silly accident just before the stage start in Valloire. It would have been the perfect reason to stop, but Eddy Merckx didn't stop. Fans and journalists thought that Merckx wanted to give Thevenet the satisfaction of beating him, something he didn't disabuse them of because it gained him a lot of admiration, but it wasn't the real reason.

'The team depended on the Tour de France for a lot of their earnings. If I had pulled out then my second place prize would have been lost from the pot of money we shared at the end. It cost me, though. Today I think that if I had stopped, taken some time off to recover, I might have won the Tour again next year. Instead I had to dig really deep to finish, and because of my cheekbone and jaw I couldn't eat solids for the final five days. I lost a lot of strength in those days and coupled with my back they brought the end of my career a year or so nearer,' he says today.

The 1975 Tour ended on the Champs-Elysées, something for which Lévitan had been lobbying for several years.

Merckx didn't ride the Tour in 1976, when Lucien Van Impe continued Belgian domination by winning a mountainous race. Van Impe was without doubt the best climber ever in the Tour de France. Six King of the Mountains titles, a figure he says he stopped at because it was the same number as his hero, Bahamontes, and an overall victory, are the history book evidence of his Tours de France, but for those who saw him race and raced against him, Van Impe leaves a bigger impression.

Nobody, not even Bahamontes and Charly Gaul, the Eagle and the Angel, made dancing up mountains on a bike look as easy as Van Impe did. It seemed effortless, although of course it wasn't. Van Impe's secret, apart from being only 1.67 metres tall, so quite light, and blessed with the kind of muscles that supported prolonged efforts and leg-snapping accelerations, was a rhythm he calls '*coupe de pédale*'.

'I always began a climb on a lower gear than I needed, then I matched my breathing to the rhythm of my legs. That way I was in control. If you start a climb in too big a gear you never get enough oxygen into your legs. Once I had a good rhythm, then I would think of the race. Then I might click up a gear or two and attack, but always sit back, regain my composure, then go again. A climber who does that two or three climbs out can break the rest and win the Tour in one day in the mountains,' he explains.

In 1977 Van Impe tried to win with a magnificent performance on a single mountain stage, overreached himself, almost collapsed before the stage finish and lost his chance of a repeat victory. Eddy Merckx rode the 1977 Tour as well. In pain, and a shadow of his former self, he struggled along to sixth overall, but typically combative he says, 'They wish in Belgium now that they could have a rider finish sixth.'

And that was Eddy Merckx and the Tour de France. He began the 1978 season but stopped racing in March. He switched from riding bikes to making them and built a brand to be proud of, although he went through some tricky times along the way. He was his best salesman, doing the rounds of cycle shows, races and other functions. Glad-handing, back-slapping, all the people he met were meeting Eddy Merckx, the cycling legend, and it was all they wanted to talk about.

But reliving the past over and over can distance a celebrity from who he is now. Merckx revealed something about that when he told me: 'Sometimes it's strange being me. I travel the world meeting people, I'm surrounded with friends and my life is full, but all the time I am confronted by a young man I have nothing in common with. He is me, but he is not me now. In fact I have been me now for longer than I was him, but no one wants to know about me.'

13. THE BADGER

Somehow it doesn't sound right in English. The name Badger speaks of *The Wind in the Willows* and animals' tea parties, but in French it works: Le Blaireau. They still call Bernard Hinault 'Le Blaireau' and he's still as combative and feisty as ever that animal was. Hinault ruled the Tour as a racer until half-way through the eighties, and now he rules the podium on the Tour de France like a blazered bouncer. You wouldn't want him as an enemy, trust me.

The badger is a dangerous animal when cornered. Powerful of tooth and claw, it's not a creature to provoke, and neither was, nor is, Bernard Hinault. He was the last true '*Patron*' of the Tour de France, and because the race was coming out of the times when the best rider of his generation ruled it, Hinault's rule had to be iron hard and would be enforced with his fists if necessary.

Bike riders who dared to go against him quickly regretted it. Hinault could be vengeful in the extreme. On more than one occasion, protesters who used the Tour to demonstrate had Hinault wade through them with his fists flying. He's still the same. During the 2009 Tour some joker made the mistake of invading 'his' podium and was rugby tackled off it by Hinault. He's also still opinionated, still controversial. During one short conversation I had with him I made the mistake of contradicting him. He didn't deign to argue, but just looked at me as though I had come from another planet.

Hinault was a fearsome competitor who wanted to win everything, from the Tour de France down to an argument. His wife, like Eddy Merckx's, knew him best, and she says, 'He couldn't take failure, he wouldn't have been able to handle it,' which is why he was an instant success. In his first racing season as a 16-year-old novice he won 12 out of the 20 races he entered.

That was 1971, and the following year he burst on to the French national scene. He was 17 but looked about 25, an old head on a young body that had already worked out what cycling was all about. By 1975, with his military service behind him, Hinault was a professional racer with the Gitane-Campagnolo team, under the management of Cyrille Guimard.

Guimard had been a good Tour rider. He had a reputation as a sprinter, so pundits didn't think of him as a Tour contender, but in 1972 he took the fight to Eddy Merckx. He was one of the few riders who had the ability and the will to do it, but as the race wore on he suffered injuries to both knees and was forced out of the race.

And that was that. Guimard never rediscovered the form he had in 1972 because his knees never really got better. He won races, but not as many or as big as he should have done. In 1976 Guimard drew an end to his racing career when he was still young, still ambitious and still very unfulfilled.

He transfused his desire into Lucien Van Impe, who for the first time in his career decided to chase the overall classification in the Tour rather than the King of the Mountains, and he won. Van Impe won the 1976 Tour de France because he had amazing form and also the confidence that Guimard had given him. A pure climber like Van Impe has one card to play if he is to win overall, and that is to attack early on a mountain stage and win the Tour in one big day. He tried the same thing next year and it backfired, but by then Guimard had a rider who wouldn't have to go for one big day in the mountains to win the Tour. Bernard Hinault was a classic Tour de France rider, an impregnable fortress who could climb and time trial, and keep on doing it.

In 1977, and still only 23, he hit the big time by winning two Classics, Ghent–Wevelgem and Liège–Bastogne–Liège. He then won the Dauphiné Libéré stage race, and rounded off the year by taking the Grand Prix des Nations. The following year was his Tour de France debut, but in a move typical of Hinault's swashbuckling style he won the Tour of Spain, which in those days was held in April and May, before the Tour.

There was huge anticipation. Hinault came to the Tour as Eddy Merckx had done, already a Classics winner, a super time triallist who had proved himself in the mountains, and over the distance of a Grand Tour. He had some tough opposition: the previous year's winner, Bernard Thévenet, Hennie Kuiper and the super strong TI-Raleigh team, Lucien Van Impe, Joop Zoetemelk, and the usual gaggle of talented Spanish climbers that made up the KAS team. Plus a strange-looking Belgian from the coastal dunes of West Flanders. Michel Pollentier looked like a monkey on a stick when he rode his bike, but he could climb and time trial like the wind.

It was also the Tour de France debut for two English-speaking riders, Irishman Sean Kelly, who would win the green jersey four times, and a British rider called Paul

Sherwen, who in recent years along with fellow commen-
tator Phil Liggett has formed the Tour soundtrack for
hundreds of thousands of English-speaking bike fans.

Looking back now, Sherwen remembers how the enor-
mity of his first Tour was brought home to him by an old
hand at the race:

> Not only was it my first Tour but my first three-week stage
> race, but when you are young you can't wait to get stuck
> in. The prologue was on Friday night and next day we had
> a split stage. I finished quite well up in the morning, so
> was jumping around like a cat on a hot tin roof trying to
> get into a break that afternoon. But then Barry Hoban rode
> up alongside me and said, 'What are you are doing, Paul?
> There are three more Saturdays to go, you know.' That
> calmed me down. We were on our third stage in two days
> when Barry told me that, and there was still three weeks
> to go. I wasn't going to last the way I was carrying on.

Hoban was 38, coming back from an injury that had
dogged him for two years. He was trying to add to the
eight stage victories he'd taken since 1964, a British record
that was only beaten by Mark Cavendish in 2009. He
came close in the 1978 Tour on a couple of occasions, but
this wasn't the Hoban of old, and he later had cause to
regret riding the race at all. While he'd been injured he'd
turned down the directeur sportif job of his Miko-Mercier
team, which had gone instead to Jean-Pierre
Danguillaume, who wasn't a Hoban fan. Danguillaume
refused to select Hoban for the Miko Tour team the following year, when he was on better form, so the terrific Tour
career of one of Britain's pioneers, a man who was often
the only Brit in the race, ended with a whisper rather than

a shout. And at the end of it he found that the Miko management doors were firmly closed to him.

Hinault laid bare his intent by winning the first time trial on stage eight of the 1978 Tour, but Joseph Bruyère, the man who had served his whole cycling life as Eddy Merckx's most powerful and most loyal domestique, took over the race lead. Bruyère stepped up to the plate after Merckx stopped racing in 1978. Merckx had secured a good deal for his loyal team from the clothing chain C&A, and he had every intention of racing this season, but he was running on empty and had to call it a day in March. The team had Lucien Van Impe to fall back on, and when he had the chance Bruyère had won some tough races in the past. They would have to look after themselves without Merckx, and they did.

Bruyère kept the lead through the Pyrenees, with Hinault in second, but then something happened at Valence d'Agen which showed that nobody in the peloton believed that situation would continue to Paris. The riders were fed up with split stages, because they required early starts, they upset their rhythm, they meant long days and they did nobody any good but the organiser's bank balance. This was a split stage day, so the riders went on strike. They dawdled along in the sun at 20 kilometres an hour, then 100 metres short of the line they all got off and walked the rest of the way. All the top riders marched at the front, but their shop steward wasn't the yellow jersey; it wasn't Joseph Bruyère. It was Bernard Hinault.

It was also Hinault who put the riders' case to Felix Lévitan, right on the finish line in Valence d'Agen. No one questioned his authority to do it either, not even Lévitan. There were no split stages the following year, and whenever they appeared in the future they were kept short.

Bruyère clung on to the jersey through some torrid stages in the Massif Central, and then came the big day, 240 kilometres between St Etienne and L'Alpe d'Huez. At the end of it there would be a new race leader and a huge scandal. The Belgian Michel Pollentier won the stage. He danced up L'Alpe d'Huez wearing the polka-dot jersey of the King of the Mountains, with all the appearance of writing another epic page in Tour de France history.

He won by one minute and 50 seconds and took over the race lead. Then, after disappearing who knows where for a length of time, he presented himself to the doping control in his yellow jersey. Two Spanish riders were also there, José Nazabal and Antoine Gutierrez, both picked at random for testing. The riders were required to pee in a flask, whereupon their urine would be divided in their presence between two further flasks, which would be sealed by the doctor administering the test, also in their presence, and signed by them and the doctor.

This day, however, the doctor was unusually attentive. To preserve their modesty riders pulled out the front of their shorts, slipped the flask down inside, and let fly. Gutierrez went first but he was ages fumbling about down the front of his shorts and the doctor grew suspicious. He pulled up the Spaniard's jersey and found a tube secured to the rider's body with surgical tape. One end led to a rubber bulb strapped beneath his armpit, and the other ran beneath his penis. That end had come adrift, which was why Gutierrez took so long fishing about in his shorts. Inside the bulb was a third party's urine. The idea was to insert the bottom end of the tube into the flask and squeeze the bulb with the upper arm. Its armpit location kept the urine warm, as a cold sample was sure to provoke suspicion.

Once he discovered what was going on, the doctor turned to Pollentier, asked him to lift his jersey, and found a similar set-up. The Belgian was thrown out of the Tour, his trickery denounced in the papers and on TV, but interestingly he received thousands of letters from fans in support. Pollentier was later given two months' suspension, which was incredibly lenient, but he was badly affected by the whole affair. Was that because he'd cheated? Not necessarily; it was more because he lost a Tour he should have won and all because he'd been found doing something that, in his own words, 'half the riders in the race were doing'.

That doesn't make it right, but a lot of people think Pollentier was singled out. One pro who rode the 1978 Tour, but asked me not to attribute this to him, told me, 'What Pollentier did was the standard way of cheating the dope test. The only difference was that the doctor was inside when they tested with him. With other riders the doctors would stand outside. Once I even saw a doctor knocking on the door of the dope control asking the rider inside if he had finished and if so could he come in.'

Gutierrez was thrown off the race with Pollentier, and of the three picked for testing the only one who gave his own urine, Nazabal, was found positive for drugs. The inconvenient truth was out once again. Of three riders tested, two were caught cheating the dope control and one was caught taking drugs. The underlying message was that a lot more were doing the same, but with that the race moved on.

Joop Zoetemelk was given the yellow jersey, but with Hinault just 14 seconds behind him it was only a loan. Zoetemelk clung on where he was strong, in the mountains, but Hinault was waiting for the final time trial, where he beat the Dutchman by over four minutes to win his first-ever Tour de France.

Hinault dominated again in 1979 in a race that started very unusually at the foot of the Pyrenees. Stage two, a 24-kilometre time trial, all uphill from Luchon to the ski station at Superbagnères, gave Hinault the yellow jersey from Zoetemelk and a Portuguese rider called Joachim Agostinho.

Agostinho was a late starter who had been a soldier before he was a pro racer, one who'd seen active service in the Angolan jungle while Portugal tried to hang on to its colony there. Agostinho was discovered by a Frenchman famous as a talent scout called Jean de Gribaldy. He styled himself as the Baron de Gribaldy, although no one is sure whether the title was really his. In fact De Gribaldy was a former pro racer who was better at business and owned a big furniture store in Grenoble. He part-sponsored teams but was particularly interested in riders from non-mainstream cycling countries. It was De Gribaldy who offered Sean Kelly his first pro contract after flying to Ireland in his private plane and tracking Kelly down to his father's farm.

The result of the 1979 Tour shows Hinault winning from Zoetemelk by 13 minutes and Agostinho by 26, but it might have been closer had Agostinho not spent the week before the race tramping the hills around his farm near Lisbon to round up his stray cattle. And had he not crashed so badly on stage six to St Brieuc that he was still feeling the effects on the crucial Amiens to Roubaix stage three days later, where he lost 15 minutes.

Agostinho was tough and bounced back to win the Alpe d'Huez stage. Then, even though he was already 38, he continued racing for a number of years. By 1984 he restricted himself to races in his home country as his farm had grown, but he enjoyed racing so much that he said he intended competing until he was at least 50. Then fate struck in the form of a dog that ran out in front of Agostinho and brought him down during a stage of the Tour of the Algarve. He suffered severe head injuries and died later the same day.

As the curtain fell on the seventies, Bernard Hinault was the number one cyclist in the world. Just as Eddy Merckx had done, Hinault won single-day Classics and stage races, and that continued into 1980 with an astonishing victory through terrible conditions in the Liège–Bastogne–Liège, then overall success in his first Giro d'Italia.

Hinault was winning but he was playing with fire. He was working closely with Claude Genzling, who had studied bike ergonomics. Genzling looked at the cadences involved in cycling, then compared them with other sports, particularly those where artificial levers were involved, like rowing. He concluded that cyclists pedalled too fast and that they could benefit from using higher gears by spending longer in the power phase of each pedal stroke. This led to Hinault not only using higher top gears for something like a time trial, but using higher gears when climbing as well.

To help cope with this slower pedalling style, Genzling advised Hinault to move his saddle backwards, the idea being to fully recruit his lower back, gluteal and quadriceps muscles in pedalling. He went along with it, slowly changing his position incrementally over a number of months, and at the same time increasing the length of the pedal cranks he used and raising the height of his saddle, which Genzling also thought would bring more muscles into play.

Unfortunately, pro bike riders are like the princess who could feel a pea under her mattress, so accustomed do their bodies become to pedalling within the parameters fixed by their bikes. And this was particularly so in Hinault's day because they did little else for training other than ride their bikes, although later on in his career he did a great deal to change that. No matter how carefully it's done, any change in position can put unaccustomed strain on a rider's ligaments and tendons, and if a lot of things are changed at once then the result can be disastrous.

This is what happened to Hinault during the 1980 Tour de France. Everything started well, and after the second long time trial on stage 11 Hinault had the yellow jersey, although only by 21 seconds from Joop Zoetemelk. Something was wrong and it got worse on the next stage to Pau. Hinault's knee hurt badly, and after working on it with his soigneurs that evening it was decided that the injury would not take the strain of a stage in the Pyrenees next day.

Without Hinault, Joop Zoetemelk won the Tour, fulfilling his own ambition – and after five second places and being in the first ten every year since 1970 that ambition was getting fairly desperate – but also fulfilling the ambition of a British bicycle company to win the Tour de France. Raleigh had set out on this road in 1971, linking with parent company TI to sponsor a team of mostly British racers taking on a limited European campaign. They built up slowly, making their Tour de France debut in 1976, by which time none of their squad was British, and 1980 was the peak of their Tour de France career.

It was Zoetemelk's peak too. Hinault returned the following year with a vengeance, winning by nearly 15 minutes from Lucien Van Impe, but the 1981 race was just as famous for another comeback. Freddy Maertens of Belgium was the fastest sprinter the Tour has ever seen. In 1976 he won eight stages in a single Tour. But Maertens wasn't just fast, he was durable too, with a top ten Tour finish, several single-day Classics and two world titles to his name.

Mark Cavendish is a similar rider to Freddy Maertens. He's already doing some of the things Maertens did and will do more, but despite being quite outspoken, Cavendish is nowhere near as volatile as Maertens was. Living in Flanders for a top bike racer is like living in a pressure cooker, and for a once-in-a-generation star like Maertens it requires iron discipline. Everyone wants to be your friend, to help you celebrate and help you spend.

After 1976 Maertens made some bad investments, got injured then got depressed. He pulled himself together just long enough to win four stages in the 1981 Tour, plus the green jersey, and later that year his second world title. Unfortunately it did little to fill a growing hole in his finances, and the following year Maertens began a long, sorry and agonising slide out of cycling. Today he has his life back together and works happily as a guide in the Tour of Flanders museum in Oudenaarde, but it can't have been where he saw himself in his fifties during his glory days at the Tour de France.

By 1982 there were five native English speakers in the Tour de France. Paul Sherwen and Sean Kelly were getting to be old hands at the race, and Kelly, who by now was a big star in Europe, led one of the teams. Sherwen and Kelly were joined in the Tour by an American, Jonathan Boyer, a New Zealander, Eric McKenzie, and an Australian, Phil Anderson, who had won the Commonwealth Games and then dominated French amateur racing.

After a good ride for fourth place behind Hinault in the prologue, Anderson won stage two and took over the race lead. He was the first Australian ever to wear the yellow jersey, and only the second English-speaker after Tom Simpson. Anderson stayed in yellow until stage 11, with Kelly by then wearing the green. The 57-kilometre time trial proved the Australian's undoing, and was where Bernard Hinault took over the race lead. And that was that: Hinault dominated the rest of the race, even winning the last stage in a sprint on the Champs-Elysées to win the Tour. Anderson finished fifth, the best Australian result ever until Cadel Evans's second in 2008. Sean Kelly won the green jersey, the first classification victory by any English-speaker in the Tour. And the blue touch paper on a cycling revolution had been lit.

Cyrille Guimard and Bernard Hinault recognised that this revolution was about happen. With the 1982 racing season behind them, the Frenchmen travelled to America to meet a young man who had been coming to Europe and winning regularly as a junior, Greg Lemond. The press went with them, and pictures of the teenager with Guimard and Hinault on horseback in cowboy hats adorned the pages of bike magazines for months afterwards. But there was serious business too. Guimard wanted Lemond to make his professional debut for his Renault-sponsored team, and when the deal was done it wasn't negotiated between a manager and the rider's unqualified agent in the usual way, but between Renault as a company and Lemond's highly paid lawyer. That was something new too.

Hinault kicked off 1983 by winning several top races including the Tour of Spain, but ended that race with knee problems, and again they refused to go away. An operation was the only answer, but it meant Hinault would miss the Tour de France. He had to leave his team's hopes in the legs of a young studious-looking man from Paris called

Laurent Fignon, who had gained the nickname 'Professor' for no other reason than that he wore glasses.

The 1983 Tour was billed as the first-ever open Tour de France, meaning that amateur national teams, if they were good enough, could theoretically take part. There was still a strict divide between amateurs and professionals in sport in the eighties, at least in cycling, with pros barred from competition in the Olympic Games, and there were separate amateur and professional world championships.

However, state-sponsored amateurs from the Soviet bloc dominated the amateur world, particularly in cycling, and the situation was ludicrous. So the Tour threw open their race in the hope of maybe attracting the Russian national team. Instead they got a team of Colombian climbers who had been waiting for a stage like the Tour de France to perform on, and they had much more of an effect on Tour history than the Russians ever would.

The Tour welcoming amateurs wasn't an altogether altruistic move. Europe was going through a recession, and sponsors were finding their sports budgets harder to justify. The race needed the stronger amateur nations to keep the size and quality of its field up.

The English-speaking Tour army was augmented in 1983 by Ireland's Stephen Roche, Scotland's Robert Millar and a Manchester lad, Graham Jones. They all did well, and the old hand Phil Anderson challenged for the lead again early on. Sean Kelly won the points competition and got a day in the yellow jersey. And Robert Millar was the best of the newcomers, winning a big mountain stage in the Pyrenees and wearing the polka-dot jersey as King of the Mountains leader for a while. Millar also finished 14th overall, one place behind Stephen Roche, and he was eventually third in the mountains competition.

The Tour winner in 1983 was Laurent Fignon, and he won again in 1984 with a returning Bernard Hinault in second place, and Greg Lemond making his Tour de France debut in third. British cycling history was made when Robert Millar finished fourth and took the King of the Mountains classification. His finish was the highest by a British rider until Bradley Wiggins equalled it in 2009, and Millar is still the only Briton to win one of the jerseys of the Tour de France.

Hinault's Tour comeback had been a long and very thorough one, and it was achieved by using a lot of techniques that had come out of the revolution going on in the way cyclists trained during the early to mid eighties. An Italian professor of sports science, Francesco Conconi, had discovered there was a threshold of effort beyond which an athlete could get but then would be forced to slow down. More importantly – because the threshold was known intuitively by anyone involved in endurance sport anyway – Conconi also found a way of predicting where that threshold occurred through examining heart rate under effort. He also discovered that the threshold could be raised by specific training, and at the same time portable heart rate monitors were invented so that the specific training required could be done with pinpoint accuracy.

Hinault used these techniques for his on-the-bike training, but he also did a huge amount of training in gymnastics and callisthenics, even jogging, and what would now be called core training. His new ambition for the mid eighties was 'to be a cycling athlete, rather than just a cyclist'. Hinault had learned through bitter experience that a strong cyclist could be brought down by a weak link, and he was determined not to have any.

He used all his new ideas to prepare for the 1985 Tour de France, when he was joined by Greg Lemond in the La Vie Claire team. La Vie Claire was a health food chain owned by a French business tycoon and media star called Bernard Tapie. There had been sponsors in cycling similar to Tapie before, rich businessmen with an eye for self-promotion who liked to be seen with top sports stars and celebrities, but Tapie made them look like wallflowers because he was infinitely more ambitious.

Hinault was the hottest property in world cycling and Greg Lemond would be the next. Tapie needed them because he had political ambitions and he saw his best way to office was by being a socialist. He already had the self-made man credentials, because that is what he was, but by aligning himself with cycling, which was still very much a working-class sport, Tapie would have more credibility with his target voters.

Tapie later cemented his man of the people image by buying the Olympique Marseille football club, and in due course he became a government minister. However, the Tapie train was halted when he got indicted for match fixing and corruption. He eventually served a prison sentence, but you can't help feeling that France's ruling class, the career politicians and graduates of the Ecoles Polytechnique and Supérieur, did not and still do not like Tapie.

He was no Teflon-coated smoothie who could ride out a scandal. Tapie liked money, as demonstrated by his huge, clipper-like yacht – now owned by Club Med – and he liked talking about money, which is not a trait approved of by the French establishment. Tapie made a big deal out of the first million-dollar contract in cycling that he signed with Lemond, while Hinault, about whose money nothing was said, surely couldn't have been getting any less. But it was all still too 'in your face' to win Tapie enough friends to stay out of jail.

Laurent Fignon was ruled out of the 1985 Tour by tendonitis. Stephen Roche was shaping to be a Tour contender, although he was still young and had left the strong Peugeot team, which had Robert Millar as its leader. Sean Kelly was at the height of his career, but despite winning the Tour of Spain it was thought that the Tour de France was just beyond him. Looking back, the two clear Tour favourites in 1985 were in the same team, Bernard Hinault and Greg Lemond.

La Vie Claire was a bit like the Astana team in the 2009 Tour. They had two riders with the potential to win, and a lot has been spoken about the morals of what happened within both the teams in 1985 and 2009, but the unwritten law in cycling teams is clear: the highest rider in the overall, so long as he is a bona fide candidate for team leader, always gets total commitment from the rest.

Bernard Hinault knew that for certain, Greg Lemond must have known it too, and in the style of a Mafia boss scenting the whiff of an uprising, Hinault struck first to stake his claim for total team support. His preparation was timed to perfection and Hinault came roaring into the Tour, taking the prologue in his native Brittany and winning the 75-kilometre time trial stage eight to take the yellow jersey by two and a half minutes from Lemond.

Hinault threw everything at that time trial. Part of the technical revolution in cycling had been a study of the forces that hold bike riders back and how to beat them. The biggest is wind resistance, the drag of the air which a cyclist has to ride through. The solution to the problem is to reduce the frontal area of both bike and rider, so making the hole they need to penetrate in the air as small as possible, then allowing the air to flow smoothly over and around them.

By 1985 track riders had been using bikes that were low at the front and had a smaller front wheel, plus tear-drop helmets and one-piece suits made from super-slippery materials, but the take-up by road racers had been slow. Hinault used all of those things in the time trial, plus another piece of cycling kit that is normal today, the clip-less pedal. The ski-binding company Look was owned by Bernard Tapie, and Hinault helped the company perfect the pedals. Not only was Hinault a great champion, he was open to innovation too, but when you look back through cycling history those two things nearly always go together. Jacques Anquetil used a wind tunnel to perfect his riding position and had an ultra-light, uphill-only bike which he used to switch to at the bottom of some important long mountain climbs. Eddy Merckx trained in an oxygen tent for his successful hour record attempt in Mexico City, and there are many other similar examples.

Hinault won a stage in the Alps at Morzine and was second in a shorter time trial at Villard-de-Lans. On the eve of a tough stage to St Etienne, Hinault was in the lead and now more than five minutes ahead of Lemond. Then Lemond got in a breakaway and gained two minutes back, but a bigger problem occurred for Hinault when he crashed after colliding with Phil Anderson in the final kilo-metre along St Etienne's Cours Fauriel. Hinault flew over the handlebars and his face made first contact with the road. He ended up dazed, with a broken nose and deep cuts to his face caused by the stylish and very French Ray-Ban sunglasses he wore.

Two flat stages gave Hinault some time to recover, but his overall Tour strategy also began to add to his problems.

Hinault won the Giro d'Italia just before the Tour and had come into the race on top form, which was exactly what he needed to get his team behind him, but now that form was beginning to ebb away, and Lemond's was building up.

Hinault suffered badly on the first day in the Pyrenees, when Lemond was flying. He had difficulty breathing on the Col du Tourmalet and was dropped from the lead group that Lemond was with, and there is still controversy about what happened next. Lemond reckons he was strong enough to attack, but that the La Vie Claire team manager, Paul Koechli, directed him from the team car to take it easy, saying according to Lemond that Hinault was only 40 seconds behind and catching him, whereas he was over one minute behind and losing ground.

Hinault limped in four minutes behind stage winner Pedro Delgado and just over a minute behind Lemond. Lemond's fans think that Koechli did the equivalent of getting his man to throw a fight, and Hinault's think he should have stayed to help the wounded yellow jersey. Despite a somewhat strained show of unity at the time, both riders probably agreed with their fans then and they certainly do now.

The rest of the Pyrenees weren't tough enough to be decisive, and although Lemond won the final time trial, he only snatched back five seconds from Hinault, who claimed his fifth and final Tour victory to equal the records of Jacques Anquetil and Eddy Merckx. Hinault wasn't finished with the Tour de France, though. He had always said he would retire at the age of 32, and that was going to be in 1986. Hinault had one more Tour to do, and what a battle that would turn out to be.

14. BORN IN THE USA

The 1986 Tour had a record number of starters, 210 spread across 21 teams with riders from all over the world. Lemond lined up in the La Vie Claire team with Bernard Hinault, Canada's Steve Bauer and another American, Andy Hampsten. Stephen Roche was leader of the Carrera Jeans team. Robert Millar was Panasonic's big hope, backed by Phil Anderson. Another Brit, Sean Yates, was in the Peugeot team. Two more Irishmen, Martin Early and Paul Kimmage, were there, plus two full teams from Colombia, but the big story was American.

A whole team of them, sponsored by the 7-Eleven chain of convenience stores, got a last-minute entry to the Tour after fierce lobbying by their manager, Jim Ochowicz, who began the project in 1981. 'The Los Angeles Olympics helped. American cyclists pretty well cleared up the medals, and that brought us sponsorship from an Italian electrical goods manufacturer, which got us into the 1985 Giro d'Italia,' says Ochowicz.

Pro racing in Europe was a huge step up but the Americans adapted quickly, winning two stages in the Giro and getting Félix Lévitan to take them seriously for the 1986 Tour de France. 'We weren't a shoe-in, though,' says

Ochowicz. 'I had to keep nagging at Lévitan and our entry wasn't confirmed until one month before the Tour. But I had the guys prepare like they were riding, so that wasn't too much of a problem.'

It can't have been. 7-Eleven came straight out of their corner punching hard. The prologue was won by Frenchman Thierry Marie, riding a bike that took aerodynamic development to another level with disc wheels front and back, super-thin handlebars and a tail-fin behind its saddle. But the next day was all about America.

Their fellow pro riders treated the 7-Eleven team as a bit of a novelty. They accepted Lemond, who had served an apprenticeship in Europe, and his ability forced their admiration too. Andy Hampsten had won a stage in the Giro when with 7-Eleven, and with La Vie Claire had become the first American to win a big European stage race when he took the Tour of Switzerland, which ran just before the Tour de France.

Those two were good riders, everyone in the peloton accepted that, but this team, 7-Eleven – were they serious? What cycling background did they have? These awkward Americans weren't schooled in the Euro-pro way. Look at this one now, for example, he's turned up at the start of a road stage in a one-piece time trial skinsuit ...

That's what Canada's Alex Stieda wore at the start of stage one, an 85-kilometre dash that was the prelude to a team time trial in the afternoon, and he wore the skinsuit because although this was a road stage, *he* was going to ride a time trial. 'I was going after winning the first points sprint of the day. I figured that if I got that it would bring the team some publicity. I also figured why not wear the skinsuit? It was a short stage, so I didn't need jersey pockets to carry food, and it would help me ride faster to stay away to get the points,' he says.

What Stieda didn't figure on was getting caught by a small group, staying with it and gaining enough time by the stage finish to take the yellow jersey, the first ever by anyone from the American continent. The race was one and a half days old and a racer from 7-Eleven led the Tour – no one was laughing now. Well, some did later that day when the team were third last in the team time trial and lost the jersey, but even the biggest doubters were silenced when Davis Phinney won the third stage. The Yanks weren't just coming, they had landed.

Ochowicz, who is still deeply involved in American cycling, says looking back now: 'I was really proud of what we did in 1986. I was proud of Alex and Davis making the headlines, yes, but the thing that gave me most satisfaction was getting five riders, half of the team, to the finish. The Tour is huge, the demands are incredible, so just keeping it together for three weeks and getting to Paris is an awesome achievement. I think that is what made us a real team, getting through made us as good as the rest.'

The main story of the 1986 Tour de France, though, was the battle between Bernard Hinault and Greg Lemond. A rumour persists in cycling that a deal was done in 1985 whereby Lemond would support Hinault that year for his fifth win, then Hinault would support Lemond the following year to help him take his first Tour. Greg Lemond believes this to be true, but Bernard Hinault doesn't, at least not the bit about Lemond helping him win in 1985. Hinault claims that he won in 1985 on his own merit with no help from Lemond, although he says that he did give help to Lemond in 1986, but he made him work for it.

One thing is certain though: the two of them were head and shoulders above the rest. Hinault won the time trial stage nine, with Lemond 44 seconds behind in second. Hinault widened the gap with a superb display in the Pyrenees to Pau, where he was second to Pedro Delgado, with Lemond third at more than four minutes.

The Frenchman led the Tour at Pau by five minutes from Lemond. The next stage was another tough one to the mountain-top finish at Superbagnères, and it was the turning point of the race. Hinault attacked on the descent of the Tourmalet. He powered up the Col d'Aspin, building up a good lead, but on the Peyresourde climb he began to slow down. Then on the descent Hinault was caught by a group that contained some rivals: Urs Zimmerman, Robert Millar and Luis Herrera, plus Hinault's team-mates Andy Hampsten and Greg Lemond. On the climb to Superbagnères, Hampsten attacked, pulling Lemond clear, and Lemond won the stage.

Was Hinault's attack in yellow aimed at winning his sixth Tour? He says not. He says that he was trying to draw Lemond's rivals, trying to tier them by making them chase him. Lemond is sure that it was an attempt to win the Tour.

Hinault still had the yellow jersey, but only by 40 seconds. Then, on the first big day in the Alps, Hinault lost contact with Lemond on the Col d'Izoard. He then struggled to the finish on top of the Col de Granon, still the highest ever stage finish of the Tour, losing the lead of the Tour de France to Lemond.

I think the Hinault and Lemond rivalry has been built up over the years, not least by the two concerned themselves. Lemond didn't attack Hinault on the Izoard, he followed Zimmerman, who was having a brilliant day and who moved into second overall. Next day Hinault attacked repeatedly on the first two climbs. Some said that was against Lemond, but it was to get rid of Zimmerman, and when that was done he joined forces with Lemond to give us one of the iconic moments of the Tour de France.

The pair hit the bottom of the final climb to L'Alpe d'Huez together and everyone watching held their breath. Were the team-mates going to slug it out on the climb? Maybe Hinault would have liked to; no one had won six Tours. Maybe he would have liked to ride Lemond off his wheel – it would have been true to his nature – but Lemond was too strong for the Frenchman even to try. Towards the top they began to talk and began to smile. Then, as the finish approached, Hinault grabbed Lemond's arm and raised it as though he was saluting the new champion. I'm sure Hinault would rather have been grinding Lemond into the dust, but that wasn't going to happen, not now. They crossed the line together, except that Hinault made sure his wheel was slightly ahead.

Hinault won on the Alpe, but Lemond had won the Tour. He had a brief scare when he crashed in the time trial, but the American survived to be the victor in Paris. On the podium all was smiles, but afterwards war broke out. Lemond said that he felt burned by a man who had been his hero, and he's stuck by that ever since. In reply Hinault says: 'I gave my word to Greg that I would help him in 1986, and that is what I did. I attacked, but it was to wear out our rivals. It wasn't my fault that Greg didn't understand that. However, when I think of some of the things he has said since, I wonder whether I was right not to attack him.'

And so their relationship festered, but what happened first, following the star-spangled scene in Paris with

Lemond in yellow and Andy Hampsten taking the best young rider's white jersey, was that America fell in love with cycling. There was huge publicity for the victory in what for most Americans was a totally foreign sport played out in a foreign country, but they caught on to it quickly. President Reagan received Lemond at the White House. American companies approached the Tour organisers with sponsor deals. There was even talk of a feature film based on an American winning the race.

Félix Lévitan loved it. Perrier lost the job as official drink of the Tour, to be replaced by Coca-Cola, and there was talk of holding the Tour prologue in New York, possibly franchising the race. There's been no feature film, the New York prologue has yet to happen, but the Tour went global in 1986 and hasn't looked back since, in commercial terms; although a large body would disagree with me, many of them French, it hasn't been the poorer in sporting terms either.

Lemond looked set to win for the rest of the eighties. He had multi-Tour winning ability, even if his American ways used to wind up the old school. He was outspoken, he did other sports, and was even pictured playing golf in the evening during a stage race. He puts on weight quite easily, and when he started the 1987 European season a little thicker around the middle than a whippet-like Euro-pro was expected to be, he provoked a headline in a French bike magazine that asked if Lemond lived on Big Macs, fries and Coke all winter.

The American way was all new, but it looked as if the Tour de France would have to get used to it. Then disaster struck Lemond on 20 April 1987, when he was accidentally shot during a hunting trip. A helicopter diverted from a traffic accident saved his life, but he lost pints of blood and despite undergoing operations he still has pellets lodged close to his heart that were in too dangerous a position to be removed.

It was two years before Lemond returned to the Tour, and although he'd win again he was never as good as he was in 1986. That's a fact that must be difficult to deal with, especially in the light of the steam-roller success of Lance Armstrong. Meanwhile, though, Lemond's absence made the 1987 Tour very open, and very exciting.

It started in Berlin, right up close to where the symbolic Berlin Wall had separated East from West since just after the Second World War. Freedom was coming to the Soviet bloc countries, and one of the competitors who lined up for that Tour de France has proved since what a big difference that freedom made to the opportunities available for ordinary people.

Czeslaw Lang is Polish, a former member of their national cycling team who with the Russians and East Germans dominated amateur bike racing before the Olympics went open in 1992. Of the former Soviet countries Poland was the one that fought hardest for freedom, and their cyclists were some of the first who were allowed to turn professional for western teams. This is how Lang, along with Lech Piasecki, got pro contracts from the Italian Del Tongo pro team, but his racing career isn't Lang's story. After it he went into business, promoting races, building a huge media group, the Lang Team, and is now one of the richest men in Poland.

The other interesting entrants among the 229 starters were a team backed by British money; well, theoretically it was backed, and it had four British riders in it. They were the ANC-Halfords team, and unknown to their riders they were going into the world's biggest bike race on a wing and a prayer and the say-so of a dodgy dealer who disappeared half-way through the race, just when the money ran out.

The native English-speaker list had grown to 20, nearly ten per cent of the field, and they provided the winner again after a see-saw battle with a Frenchman and a Spaniard. The Tour was won by Stephen Roche, the talented yet so far not quite fulfilled Irishman. The Frenchman was his country's new great hope, Jean-François Bernard, and the Spaniard was Pedro Delgado.

Roche was an amazing talent, but one who had good years followed by bad. Some said this was bad planning, but injuries played a part too. It sometimes felt as though Roche's body couldn't support his talent, and a crash in the 1985 Paris six-day track race didn't help either. Roche had a terrible year in 1986, and towards the end of it a doctor told him that problems with his knees might limit his potential from then on. Luckily Roche sought a second opinion.

What he was then told encouraged him to throw everything into 1987. He built up very slowly, with no track meetings or even many late nights over the winter, just work, rest and a slow build-up to the racing year. And when it started he hit the ground running.

Good performances in early-season stage races and the hilly Classics were followed by a hard-fought Giro d'Italia, where Roche suffered the wrath of the home fans because he attacked his team-mate, Robert Visentini, when Visentini was leading overall. It was a professional no-no, but there was no love lost between Roche and Visentini, and Roche found out during the Giro that the Italian wouldn't be riding the Tour de France as he had promised, so if Roche helped Visentini in Italy he couldn't pay him back in France. That upset Roche, who thought Visentini was high-handed and spoiled, and nowhere near as talented as he was.

Roche had one team-mate in the Carrera team that he could trust, a Dutchman called Eddy Schepers, so between them they plotted a way of staging a coup. They decided to attack when Visentini wouldn't expect it, on an innocuous stage, and when Roche did it the remaining members of his team chased him. They didn't catch him, though; the element of surprise, strong riding by Roche and some allies in the breakaway meant Roche took the lead from Visentini.

For the rest of the race the Irishman was spat at, booed and threatened by irate Italian fans. To shield the Irishman, Eddy Schepers rode on one side of him and Robert Millar, a man from a rival team but who had lost two Tours of Spain because home racers had all ridden against him, rode on the other. Roche won the Giro, but I've included this story not so much for that, as to demonstrate who Stephen Roche was: a confident, self-assured, brave and very talented bike racer. It also shows the selfless side of the enigmatic and often puzzling Robert Millar, who added the Tour of Italy King of the Mountains in 1987 to complete his clean sweep of climber's titles from all three Grand Tours.

Stephen Roche says now that he went to the Tour de France 'hoping but not expecting. I had ridden well in Italy but the circumstances of the race made it very tiring. The first few stages didn't help. Central Europe has hot, humid summers and 1987 was especially so.' It was true: a long hot trek out of Germany and across the north of France took the Tour to its first big rendezvous, an 87-kilometre time trial in the Loire valley from Saumur to the space-age holiday park of Futurscope.

Roche won the time trial with Charly Mottet in second place, but Laurent Fignon was way back in 20th at over four minutes. It looked as if Mottet, a talented climber from the edge of the Alps, and the new French hope, Jean-François Bernard, would be Roche's main rivals. The Pyrenees reinforced that impression and the Tour left there with Mottet leading, Bernard second and Roche in third place. Then Bernard went for it.

They say that the length of a racer's career isn't decided by years or number of miles ridden, or even by the number of races they take part in, but by the number of times they go into the red. It's a graphic phrase that describes when a rider goes beyond his capabilities. Jean-François Bernard did that on stage 18, a time trial from Carpentras to the top of Mont Ventoux.

As the new leader of La Vie Claire now that Hinault had retired and Lemond was out, Bernard felt nervous. 'It was the best team in bike racing with the best support riders, ones that were used to their leader winning. I felt I had to do something special to gain their respect,' says Bernard. He did, he won the stage by one minute and 39 seconds from a pure climber in the Colombian mountain ace Lucho Herrera, but he dug very deep to do it. Bernard swapped his time trial bike for a road bike after the first flat part of the test, then launched himself up the Ventoux, sometimes turning the 50-tooth outer chainring fitted specially for the occasion. It was a huge gear for a huge performance. Bernard took the lead, lost it next day and was never the same rider again. It was as though he blew his entire Tour career on that one stage – an amazing and crazy thing to do, but an indication of the pressure French cycling felt under with the influx of English speakers.

Roche took the lead for a day, but a Spanish rider, Pedro Delgado, had been doing a stealth attack up the overall standings and he took over after the next stage to L'Alpe d'Huez. That was OK by Roche, because there was a time trial left and he could beat the Spaniard there. Still, he couldn't let Delgado get too far ahead in the remaining mountains, and that led to one of the most dramatic moments ever in the Tour de France.

The race was still in the Alps and Roche needed to peg Delgado's lead to a minute at most, and Delgado was a formidable climber. Stage 21 finished at La Plagne, a ski station at just over 2,000 metres, and it was shrouded by fog. It was too thick even for the TV cameras to penetrate, but reports came that Delgado had dropped Roche and gained a minute. With one more day in the mountains to go, a minute was too much.

But if the world couldn't see what was happening, Stephen Roche could. This is what he remembers: 'Delgado was a true climber and capable of killer changes of pace uphill. When he attacked I didn't even think of following him. His acceleration was too brutal for that. I decided to ride at my own rhythm until five kilometres to go, then give it everything.'

As a strong time triallist Roche knew that he had five kilometres of constant-paced, all-out effort in his legs, but living with the accelerations of Delgado would have wrecked him. The fog would also play into the Irishman's hands, as neither Delgado nor his team manager sitting in the car right behind him would know where Roche was.

There was confusion on the mountain and confusion for those watching at home. The only TV camera relaying anything was just beyond the line. We saw Laurent Fignon out-sprint Anselmo Fuerte for the stage, then Fabio Parra finish alone behind him. Next across the line was Delgado, pushing all the way to take as much time out of the foe he couldn't see but he knew was behind him – but how far behind him? The English-speaking world's voice of cycling, Phil Liggett, was left guessing in his TV commentary. 'That's Delgado alone,' he said as the Spaniard appeared out of the gloom. Then there was silence, a silence that seemed to go on for ages but actually only lasted a handful of seconds. Another rider appeared out of the gloom, close behind Delgado. Liggett again: 'Just who is that coming up behind? Because that looks like Stephen Roche! That looks like Stephen Roche! It *is* Stephen Roche!'

Liggett's voice broke up with emotion as he said those words. Roche had saved the Tour de France. Delgado had only taken four seconds from him. The effort the Irishman made in the last five kilometres was enormous. When he crossed the line he collapsed. 'I put my hand out but no one was there. I fell, they caught me and lifted me off my bike but I had no strength and I fell to the floor,' he says.

The Tour doctor, Gerard Porte, rushed up with oxygen and clamped the mask to Roche's face. 'I came round immediately.' But, ever the pro, Roche says: 'When they lifted the mask off I pulled it back again. I was thinking about tomorrow. I'd saved the Tour but still had to win it and was worried about recovering after the effort I'd just made. I thought that getting as much oxygen as I could would help me recover, so I held it on my face until I felt quite giddy.'

Roche did recover. He took time off Delgado next day and in the remaining time trial to win the Tour de France. A few days later he was driven though Dublin with his family and his yellow jersey in an open-top bus. Then a few weeks later Roche won the World Championships in Austria to become only the second man in history to win cycling's triple crown: the Tour of Italy, Tour de France and world title in the same year. Eddy Merckx is the other. That is how good Stephen Roche was. Unfortunately his agonising good year, bad year cycle continued, and Roche had a terrible year in 1988. In fact he was never as good again, nowhere near. He had the ability but not the body.

The Tour winner in 1988 was Pedro Delgado, and what a controversial winner he was. He fairly dominated the race, taking the lead on L'Alpe d'Huez and cementing it next day by winning a largely uphill time trial between Grenoble and Villard-de-Lans. He extended his lead in the Pyrenees, but when the race hit Bordeaux a rumour began to circulate that Delgado had failed a dope test. This was confirmed a few days later, and the substance he tested positive for was Probenicid.

There is absolutely no performance gain to be had from Probenicid, but it was used in sport as a masking agent, and what it masked was anabolic steroids. But this was still in the early days of the authorities getting seriously to grips with doping in sport, they'd only been playing at it before, and although Probenicid was on the banned list of the Olympic Games, it wasn't on that of the authority that governs cycling, the Union Cycliste Internationale. That is the body that runs cycling at all times other than the Olympics, and the UCI's rules govern the Tour, so Delgado had no case to answer.

But there were mumblings of discontent in the peloton. On the same day as the Probenicid story broke, a Dutchman, Gert-Jan Theunisse, was penalised ten minutes in the race for testing positive for steroids. Next day at the Clermont-Ferrand start the riders went on strike. It was a confusing affair, officially recorded at the time as a protest at what were seen as fudged rules, but there was also some division among the riders on the subject of drugs. Where there had been solidarity with and even support for those who were caught, now some riders thought differently, and a few spoke out. A number of riders told journalists that they were unhappy with the leniency being shown to dopers. That had hardly ever happened before.

To this day, though, Delgado says he did nothing wrong. He cites the fact that Probenicid wasn't found in any samples taken before or after the positive one, which, if he was using it as a masking agent, does give food for thought. Riders have often mumbled darkly about the safety of samples, the possibility of contamination, and a number of positive tests have been thrown out because a clear chain of evidence between the rider and the sample he was supposed to have provided could not be proved.

Delgado kicked off the following year's Tour in the news again. He was the favourite, but a series of mix-ups meant he missed his start time in the prologue time trial, losing nearly three minutes before the race had even started. He panicked and tried to gain time back on the morning portion of next day's split stage, but only succeeded in tiring himself. That afternoon he had a disastrous team time trial and lost even more time. He was last overall at seven minutes but would eventually finish third at just over three.

Delgado's amazing climb back through the field would have had everyone on the edge of their seats in another year, but the headlines in 1989 were made by Greg Lemond and Laurent Fignon and the battle between them that seesawed this way and that before eventually coming down to eight seconds gained on the Champs-Elysées on the final day for the closest ever finish of a Tour de France.

Lemond returned to racing in 1988 but he rode so badly that it hurt to watch him. He had a big contract with the Dutch PDM team, but by the end of the year nobody wanted him, at least not at his old price. Lemond had to sign with a Belgian team for a contract that was relatively low on salary but high on bonuses. The team, ADR, would pay Lemond 150,000 Euros as wages, then another 150,000 if he became the world number one ranked cyclist, another 150,000 for winning the world title in 1989 and another 150,000 if he won the Tour de France. And they can't really have thought that they would have to pay out on any one of these outcomes, never mind all three.

The 1989 season didn't start well for Lemond. Even just before the Tour de France he was riding so badly in the Giro d'Italia that he thought he was staring at the end of his racing career. Then he was diagnosed as being anaemic, but this was treated with the appropriate medicine, and he began to get stronger.

Laurent Fignon was on a comeback too. After sorting out his persistent knee problems he slowly built up to his 1983 and 1984 Tour-winning form, and won the 1989 Giro d'Italia where Lemond struggled so much. Fignon started the Tour de France as joint favourite with Pedro Delgado, and no one gave Lemond much of a chance. Plus the Tour's final stage had special resonance for Fignon. It would be a time trial tracing in reverse the route taken 200 years before by Parisian revolutionaries when they marched out of the city to Versailles, after which the royal family were imprisoned and France became a republic.

The French republic was now celebrating its bi-centenary, Fignon was from Paris, where it all happened, and proud of it too. He had to win. But who would have predicted that the race would come down to that time trial and a bent piece of aluminium tubing that set race bike technology on another level?

Boone Lennon was an American inventor who worked in the ski industry and who made a connection between the tuck position of a downhill skier and that of a cyclist. Skiers held their arms up towards and a little ahead of their chests, this kept their arms in line with their bodies so they didn't create any drag of their own. To mimic this position on a bike, Lennon came up with a U-shaped extension that cyclists could bolt to their handlebars. When they grabbed the forward part of the U and rested their forearms on two pads, their position on the bike was exactly like the downhill ski tuck, and for the same effort they could ride faster.

Lennon found some triathletes who took up his new idea, so he called the handlebars tri-bars, but European pros wouldn't look at them. Early in 1989, however, when Lemond raced in an American stage race, Lennon gave him a pair, and Lemond not only looked, he tested them out. Lemond's tests showed that the handlebars gave a definite advantage. They reduced the rider's frontal area by bringing his arms in line with his body, and they locked a cyclist into position so that his upper body required less energy to support it and more could go to the legs.

The manager of the ADR team was a canny Flemish called Jose De Cauwer. Like many of his countrymen De Cauwer is a bit of an operator – there is a lot of Del-Boy in the Flemish psyche. De Cauwer decided to let Lemond use the tri-bars in the first long time trial of the Tour de France.

He didn't want other teams to see them early and copy them, but he also needed permission from cycling's governing body to use something new. He left it as late as possible, applying the day before the time trial, and even thought up a cover story to justify their use on medical grounds because Lemond had a bad back, which he didn't.

De Cauwer got the nod from the UCI and Lemond won the 73-kilometre time trial, taking over the yellow jersey just ahead of Laurent Fignon. With Delgado still a long way distant, and fighting back from his self-imposed time penalty, the Tour de France that was to celebrate the bicentenary of the French revolution had come down to a match between America and France.

The lead swung one way then the other. It was like a boxing match: Fignon would have Lemond on the ropes in one stage, only for Lemond to come out next day and punch him right in the face. Sometimes Lemond would look gone, almost cracking when Fignon attacked. Lemond would rock back into his saddle, grinding a big gear. Then minutes later he'd find something and pull his French rival back, only to let go again.

It was fascinating to watch, and the American's vulnerability, while still never being totally out of it, endeared Lemond to the French in a way they never took to Lance Armstrong. Lemond won having looked all the time as though he could lose. Armstrong won and then rubbed his rivals' noses in it.

The duel came down to the final stage. Fignon led Lemond by 50 seconds and there was just under 25 kilometres left to ride. Fignon couldn't lose. Or could he? Lemond had his tri-bars plus a massive top gear to take advantage of what was mostly a slightly downhill route. Fignon had a low-profile Raleigh time trial bike with disc wheels. No tri-bars, though, and no aerodynamic helmet. That was another innovation Lemond worked to perfect, the tear-drop aero helmet that acts as a fairing to smooth airflow over a racer's head and back.

If Fignon was down on technology, his health was going too. He was suffering with a huge boil on his backside, and once he started the time trial you could see him sitting to one side of his saddle, and he could rarely sit in one position for very long. He couldn't get the power into the pedals, and his constant shifting around into and out of the saddle created extra drag. In contrast, once Lemond got started he was locked solidly on to his bike. His upper body was perfectly still as his legs churned away, and he slipped through the air like a bird in flight. Slowly but surely Fignon's lead ebbed away until eight seconds short of the finish line on the Champs-Elysées, with the Arc de Triomphe back-lit behind him, he lost the Tour de France. Lemond had won; the comeback was complete.

Lemond won the world title and became world number one later that year, and then with a team behind him that was built around him and sponsored by Z, a big French baby clothes chain owned by Robert Zannier, the American won the Tour de France again in 1990.

He came in with more innovations. He wore Oakley sunglasses looking like the ones racers use today and not like the welding goggle lookalikes that Oakley first produced for cycling. He also brought even stranger Boone Lennon handlebar creations, both for the time trials and for normal road stages. But the biggest revelation of the 1991 race was the man who won on the top of the Luz Ardiden climb in the Pyrenees, a tall Spanish rider called Miguel Indurain.

15. THE FIRST TO FIVE IN A ROW

Like many of the best Spanish cyclists Miguel Indurain was a Basque. This hilly region of north-west Spain has a huge sense of its own identity, and cycling is a popular sport among the hard-working people who live there. Indurain is from Villava, a small town in the Basque region of Navarra, which over the years has become joined to and a suburb of the bull-running city, Pamplona.

The son of a farmer, Indurain grew up tall and strong, and was a natural athlete. Once he started cycling he won races as a matter of course and was a pro rider by the time he was 20. Indurain was powerful, a good man to have in a team, strong as a horse and a hard worker. He was the kind of rider who could have made a good career from helping others as a super-domestique, but his team manager, José Echavarri, saw that there was more.

Indurain was strong but he was heavy, and not all his weight was muscle. His team's trainers told Echavarri that Indurain had a huge physical engine, powered by enormous lungs and a heart so big that it only had to beat 28 times a minute to pump blood around his body, whereas 60 to 80 beats is normal for an untrained but healthy adult at rest.

His extra weight meant that the mountains defeated Indurain in his first Tour de France, but when he slimmed down from 85.5 to 79 kilos during the winter of 1986 he began to approach his potential. Indurain spent the next three Tours working hard for team-mate Pedro Delgado and was an integral part of his compatriot's victory in 1988. Then in 1989 Indurain began winning big races for himself, including Paris–Nice. He also won a stage of the Tour de France.

He started the 1990 Tour de France in the role of a luxury helper for Delgado, but when his leader faltered in the Pyrenees, Indurain took over and won at Luz Ardiden, dropping everyone on a mountain stage. He finished tenth overall and his apprenticeship was over.

Indurain and his Banesto team were not on it at the start of the 1991 Tour and came in for a lot of flak from the Spanish press, but then something happened that the Tour de France would have to get used to. Stage eight was a time trial, 73 kilometres of rolling Normandy roads, and Indurain won it. Lemond took second and the race lead. He wasn't far behind Indurain either, but it was cycling's first real sight of Indurain at his most devastating.

Indurain was a beast on a bike in a time trial. Everyone used tri-bars by 1991, plus every other aerodynamic aid available to make them slip through the air quicker. The time trial mantra of 'stay low, go fast' was the blueprint for every rider's time trial position. But amid the flat backs and skier's crouches, Indurain rode like a Spanish galleon. His huge lungs pushed at his lower ribs, pressing them and his stomach outwards. He couldn't get low, so he relied on his huge power to push him through the air. Miguel Indurain was the Bugatti Veyron of cycling – his engine was so big that aerodynamic subtlety didn't matter so much.

Indurain moved into contention after the time trial, but he was not yet an obvious choice for victory. It seemed likely that Lemond would win his fourth Tour, but on the first day in the mountains he looked vulnerable and on the second he cracked completely.

Stage 13 of the 1991 Tour was a huge one by today's standards, 232 kilometres from Jaca to Val Louron that included the climbs of the Pourtalet, Aubisque, Tourmalet, Aspin and a tough climb up to Val Louron itself. Lemond cracked on the Tourmalet, so Indurain went down the other side like the wind. He pushed so hard on the Aspin and up to Val Louron that only a climber like Claudio Chiappucci could stay with him.

Chiappucci took the stage, but Indurain took the yellow jersey. Now he had to defend it. It wasn't easy; with Lemond out of the way a lot of riders who hadn't been able to beat the American stepped up to try and seize the race. Chiappucci and Gianni Bugno went on the attack, but Indurain countered everything they did, then was content to let it lie.

That was typical of him. Indurain beat rivals but he never humiliated or tried to crush them; he never played the mind games of Jacques Anquetil or Lance Armstrong; neither did he go for the 'win everything just because I can' attitude of Eddy Merckx. That is partly why Miguel Indurain was extremely popular with fellow racers, and hardly anyone anywhere has a bad word for him, except maybe for some journalists. Most of them found that getting a juicy quote from the quiet Spaniard was like prizing a pearl from an oyster with a piece of string.

He was the quietest, most modest and level-headed of all the great Tour riders, and just a little bit of an enigma. Many Tour winners wanted to win so badly that it took over their lives, but when Indurain was asked in Paris if winning the Tour de France was the greatest day of his life, he replied, 'It's a big day in my sporting life, but even in that I have had other very happy days that were important to me. Not in big races maybe, but races that were important to me.' That perspective is why, when Indurain retired from racing, he didn't have the sense of loss other Tour champions have had. He didn't continue racing beyond his sell-by date, and he never once considered a comeback. The Tour de France was part of Miguel Indurain's life, not the be-all and end-all of it.

Another Indurain feature was his sense of place. He loved Villava and it loved him. He'd had a big following in the town ever since he started racing. The media discovered it during the 1991 Tour de France, and it fascinated them. TV crews and journalists from all over Europe were sent to the Jaizki bar in town where the Indurain fans that didn't go to Paris – and there were two busloads that did – met to watch the stages each day. TV coverage of Indurain's triumphal ride into Paris on the final day was regularly interrupted with cuts to the bar for interviews with fans who had supported Indurain since he was a teenager. And when he returned home next day the celebrations were even bigger.

Miguel Indurain rocketed to the number one slot in world cycling. He won the Giro d'Italia in 1992, and as a celebration of Basque cycling the Tour de France that year started in the Basque coastal city of San Sebastian. As the defending champion Indurain wore the yellow jersey in the prologue, and in a display that was ominous for his rivals he powered around the short course to win the stage by a good margin.

He lost the jersey next day, but stage nine was one of Miguel Indurain's career glories. He won the 65-kilometre time trial in Luxembourg with a time of one hour and 19 minutes, three minutes ahead of the French time trial specialist Armand de las Cuevas, and nearly four minutes in front of the third placed rider, the man who most thought would be Indurain's closest rival in the Tour, Gianni Bugno. *L'Equipe*'s headline was simple: 'Indurain the Rocket'. He tracked around the principality's hilly roads like a guided missile to blow the race apart and close right down on the yellow jersey. Yeah, rocket, that's just about right.

It was one of the best performances in a modern-day Tour de France, pure athleticism that left the field gasping. Allan Peiper, an engaging and articulate Australian who was 16 when he escaped to Europe with a suitcase and racing bike so he wouldn't have to witness his drunken father hit his mother any more, was riding his last Tour de France in 1992. He will never forget Indurain that day.

Peiper was a good pro, especially in the tough single-day races of northern Europe, but he was a sensitive person who lacked the protective shell that would have allowed him to really flourish. His career had been a tough one, and by 1992 he was at the end of his tether with pro racing. 'I was struggling and quite afraid of the time trial. It was a long way and the possibility of elimination was real. I warmed up, psyched myself with what was left of my morale and raced every one of those 65 kilometres as hard as I could, but I was still last,' Peiper remembers. He finished nearly 19 minutes down on Indurain. Indurain's Luxembourg time trial was huge and it broke everyone, from Peiper right up to Gianni Bugno.

Indurain's time trial supremacy was the highlight of the 1992 Tour. Nothing troubled his majestic ride to victory, but there were still some very good performances during the race. The most spectacular was Claudio Chiappucci on a gigantic Alpine stage from St Gervais to Sestrières.

Chiappucci grew up listening to tales of Fausto Coppi. His father had wanted to be a bike racer but family circumstances and the Second World War put paid to that. Signor Chiappucci was a Coppi fan before the conflict broke out, so he was delighted to find himself in the same prisoner of war camp as the great Italian champion. Chiappucci senior's efforts on a bike were way below the league Coppi played in, but he was a tough soldier who survived internment better than Coppi. He befriended Coppi and even gave him some of his food, so the champion could keep a semblance of his strength for when the normality they both hoped for returned.

Claudio Chiappucci started out life as a pro working for riders such as Stephen Roche and Roberto Visentini, but he progressed well and when Roche left the Carrera team, Chiappucci became its leader. He was a good climber with a really combative attitude to racing. His attacking had brought him the yellow jersey in earlier Tours, and in 1992 he became a King of the Mountains.

The stage to Sestrières was Chiappucci's greatest day. It was Coppi who won the first-ever Tour stage to the ski station of Sestrières, and with the Col des Saisies, Cormet de Roselend, Col d'Iseran and Mont Cenis all to be climbed in 254 kilometres, it was a day that Coppi would have liked. Chiappucci attacked on the first climb and led over all of the others before riding in solitary splendour to Sestrières. As a spectacle it seemed Coppi-esque, but Chiappucci only gained one minute and 45 seconds on

Indurain, who did just enough to keep him in check. At the end of the stage Indurain took over the yellow jersey, with Chiappucci's effort gaining him second overall. His exploit had failed as an attempt to win the Tour in the way Coppi would have, but it was Coppi enough for Chiappucci.

No one else gave Indurain any trouble, and he won the second long time trial, where incidentally Peiper rode a lot better, but by then Indurain had won the Tour because everybody else had virtually given up. In Paris the margin was four minutes 35 seconds to Chiappucci and over ten minutes to Bugno. It was a rout.

Indurain won the Tour of Italy again in 1993 and was the obvious favourite for the Tour de France. His main challenge would come from Tony Rominger, a Danish-born Swiss who is fluent in seven languages. Rominger was an intelligent, careful rider who could climb and time trial. He suffered early in his career with allergies, so a Grand Tour in July didn't suit him, but by 1993 he had overcome that.

Their battle was fascinating. Indurain took the lead early through another good time trial, but Rominger got better as Indurain began to feel the Giro in his legs. The Swiss challenger won two mountain stages in the Alps and even beat Indurain in the last time trial, but he ran out of stages to take back enough time and Indurain scored his Tour hat-trick.

The other story of the 1993 Tour, and it's a big one now looking back, was the first participation of a young Texan who in his own words was still little more than 'a bone triathlete finding his way' – Lance Armstrong. He was already a sensation who didn't know when to attack, or rather when not to, who had been last in his first big pro race and second in his next. A quick learner, Armstrong's full-on hammer style won him a stage in his first Tour before he was pulled out. He was still only 21 and the people behind him had big plans, although maybe even they could not have foreseen how big he would become in the Tour de France.

In 1994 Indurain decided not to go for victory in the Giro. Winning the Tours of both Italy and France in the same year had been the seal of a Grand Tour champion, but racing had evolved to the point where doing it was close to impossible. Miguel Indurain was the fifth and final rider ever to do it. In 1994 he did ride the Italian Tour, but said that it was only in preparation for France.

The 1994 Tour de France started in Lille, and what also started was the third coming of the British to the Tour de France. Chris Boardman, fresh from his 1992 Olympic triumph in Barcelona and from beating Francesco Moser's long-standing world hour record, won the prologue time trial in a record average speed for the Tour that still stands today.

Boardman represented a new era of Britain cycling. The country had produced a few good racers in the past, but they were talented and driven individuals who went to Europe with nothing more behind them than the belief that they could make it. There was no system in Britain for picking up talent and guiding riders upwards in consistent numbers. When there were coaches at all they were willing, and sometimes knowledgeable, amateurs. But at the beginning of the nineties there was a big change within the governing body, British Cycling. The new blood attracted funding and with it professional coaches. Boardman was the first, if partial, product of the new system British Cycling created.

Winning in Lille gave Boardman the first British yellow jersey since Tom Simpson back in 1962, and it was doubly exciting because the Tour was to visit Britain in 1994. It did so first in 1973, when a token stage was ridden up and down a stretch of the newly made Plympton bypass in Devon. It wasn't a huge success, but this was a much bigger plan to have two stages in south-east England.

In the perfect scenario Boardman would have retained the yellow jersey for these two stages, but his Gan team did a disjointed team time trial to the Eurotunnel terminal in Calais, so a Belgian, Johan Museeuw, wore the yellow jersey from Dover to Brighton. Then an Italian, Claudio Vanzella, took over for a big circuit that started and finished in Portsmouth. The trip was a huge success with millions out to watch the race pass by. And it gave the newly opened Channel Tunnel some great publicity, although Alex Zulle memorably asked why he couldn't see any fish on the journey through it. Nobody was sure if he meant it; he's Swiss, you see.

Back in Europe on the next stage it appeared that British yellow jerseys were like buses – you wait 32 years for one, then two come along at once – when Sean Yates took over the lead. Yates was a second-wave Brit, a talented young bike rider who made pro the Simpson-Hoban way and decamped to Europe as an amateur and made a name for himself. He was a big unit, a super-domestique who could work all day, and was highly valued for it. A good time triallist, Yates won one of the time trial stages of the 1988 Tour, the first British rider to do so.

When Yates took over the yellow jersey it was an emotional day. He is now a directeur sportif with Team Sky, the only Brit ever to direct a Tour de France winner,

in Alberto Contador, and is very well respected both inside
cycling and with bike racing fans. Yates is quiet but has
strong views, and was really looked up to by Lance
Armstrong when he was young and a team-mate of Yates.
Armstrong still loves telling a story about Yates from his
first Tour. 'A few of us in the team were loafing at the
back, trying to avoid any work. The Tour was a shock, far
harder than I thought it would be. The stage was lined out
but we were trying to coast a bit and catch our breath.
Then Sean drops back down the line, looks at us and says,
"Gentlemen, the race is at the front. Get your asses up
there." And we got our asses up there. You didn't argue
with Yates.'

The Tour had started well, and the British stages and
yellow jerseys were particularly memorable, but it was still
the warm-up act. Miguel Indurain was the main show and
he hit the roads between Périgueux and Bergerac hard,
winning the first long time trial by two minutes from
Rominger. The defending champion had taken control of
the Tour in 64 kilometres of skill, speed and concentration. Next day *L'Equipe* said Indurain was an extra-terres-
trial and carried a cartoon showing one of the Tour
organisers dangling by his neck from a noose, with a plac-
ard around his neck which read, 'The Tour is finished'.

It wasn't, though. Certainly, Indurain's form was enough
to more or less ensure victory again, but the 1994 Tour
threw up some future stars, including a future winner. He
was Marco Pantani, a slightly built climber from the
Adriatic coast of Italy. Pantani finished third overall but he
had excited in the mountains, where he fluttered uphill
like Charly Gaul and Julio Jimenez before him.

The big story was undoubtedly the fact that Indurain
had now won four Tours in succession for the first time in

Tour history – and the 1994 race had not been made with him in mind at all. Six mountain stages, with five of them finishing at altitude, was a Tour made for the climbers, but Indurain had simply taken them in his stride.

He was at his zenith, his absolute career best, and was the centre of the cycling world. But those around him wanted more, and despite being almost a track novice he was talked into risking it all by attacking the world hour record. It was a big ask. One hour alone lapping a velo-drome might sound simple, but it requires a huge amount of technique. Also, the record he had to beat was set by a specialist, Scotsman Graeme O'Bree, on a revolutionary bike that Indurain had no time to copy and get used to.

Indurain had enough to do in learning to ride on the track. He got his normal bike position as low as possible, and with his Tour-winning form rapidly disappearing he went for it just five weeks after the finish in Paris. That he succeeded with 53.040 kilometres in one hour to O'Bree's 52.713 was a case of brute force overcoming elegance. Like Eddy Merckx when he set his hour record, Indurain said he'd never suffered so much in his life. 'It wasn't just that my legs and back ached, but I also had no feeling at all down the right side of my body, and I had a tingling sensation in my arms and hands,' he told the press who witnessed the record in Bordeaux.

Indurain sailed into 1995 as undisputed favourite to win the Tour de France again. More history was within his grasp. Three other racers had won five Tours, but no one had won five in a row, not that Miguel Indurain got anything like excited about the prospect. He followed his tried and tested preparation. He had a quiet winter, mostly at home in Villava, where he relaxed and let things go a bit. By Christmas he was seven kilos overweight, as he was at the start of every year he won the Tour. He'd been active, done some mountain biking, walked and worked in the fields; but he also ate what he wanted, which Indurain always regarded as a safety valve. Then, on 1 January, as he had done every year, he started training in earnest.

Indurain's younger brother, Prudencio, was his teammate and training partner. To start each new training year they did three hours together on their bikes. Not too hard, that would come later, but then they did a little more each day until it was time for a test. Villava is at the foot of two climbs that go up into the western Pyrenees. One of them, the long pull to Roncesvalles, was where Indurain gauged his progress each year. The date he felt able to ride up there, and how he went on the climb, would set the scene for his year. In 1995 Indurain climbed to Roncesvalles earlier, quicker and feeling stronger than ever before. It was going to be an excellent year.

The first time trial of the Tour de France was stage eight, 54 kilometres from Huy to Seraing in Belgium, and all the favourites had psyched themselves up for it. They had to just keep Indurain in check that day. They knew that the Tour would really start then – except Indurain decided to start it the day before.

Prophets are seldom honoured in their own country; or something like that. Well, cycling champions are seldom valued in their own era. Eddy Merckx is lauded now because he won nearly every race there was, but during his career he was accused of stifling bike racing because he won everything. It was the same with Miguel Indurain. His Tour formula of winning time trials then not losing time in the mountains, but seldom winning there, is viewed now as very even-handed and noble of him. At the time he was accused of not attacking enough, of not being spectacular, or having no sense of drama.

Well, on stage seven of the 1995 Tour, Indurain was dramatic enough for anyone. It wasn't a mountain stage, but a lumpy one nonetheless, in the Ardennes hills of Belgium. It was a hard stage, but one for the favourites to get through rather than attack on. Except that 20 kilometres from the end Miguel Indurain did attack.

This was serious. Indurain had a face for when he was going hard. It wasn't a face screwed up in pain or an open-mouthed gasp for air; it was a sort of smile. Maybe a baring of his teeth describes it better. His eyes would shine a bit more; his face betrayed nothing, but his lips would pull back to reveal two rows of white teeth glowing against a deep Spanish tan. On the Ardennes stage Indurain switched on his face and shot off down the road.

He quickly got a gap on everyone but a canny Belgian rider called Johan Bruyneel. Bruyneel is famous now as a manager, the architect behind Lance Armstrong's seven Tour de France wins and Alberto Contador's two. Nobody has directed more Grand Tour winners than Bruyneel, and that is no coincidence. The man is a supreme tactician with a gift for seeing through situations and a profound understanding of what makes bike racers tick. He certainly sensed what Indurain was thinking that day.

I've interviewed Bruyneel several times, usually about Lance Armstrong, but once we spoke about Johan's own racing career. 'I was in the right place at the right time that day for sure,' he explained. 'But before the attack I felt Indurain's presence. I felt a surge was coming. I moved on to his wheel in the peloton, and when he went I was ready. I stayed behind him too. He was trying to win the Tour de France and I was trying to win a stage in Belgium.

I didn't help him make the pace at all, because it wasn't for me to help. I couldn't anyway, and he never asked. Riding behind Indurain that day was like riding behind a motor-bike. It was an honour, and I felt a pang of guilt as we came into the finish, knowing what I had to do.'

What Bruyneel had to do was stay behind the great Tour champion until the last minute, then sprint past to win the stage. Which is what he did, taking the second stage of his Tour de France racing career – and he got a day in the yellow jersey as well. But just in case Bruyneel comes across as something like a cold-hearted killer, let him tell you how he won his first Tour stage. It was 1993, stage six to Amiens in northern France, and Bruyneel's father had died a few days before the Tour started.

My dad was crazy about the bike. I grew up riding with him and his friends. He was a businessman and he was young at a time in Belgium where if you had a good education you didn't become a bike racer. He had a good education so he never raced, but he would have loved to have done and he was very proud of me. Cycling was something we shared; it was an extra bond between a father and son. When I lost my dad I lost someone and something very, very special. But on the stage to Amiens I felt him with me. I attacked and my dad was with me for every kilometre, and that allowed me to do something that was impossible. I wasn't a good enough racer to do what I did that day, but I did it nonetheless because my father was with me.

What he did was hold off the entire peloton on flat, open roads when all the sprinters' teams were chasing after him. And to do it he set a record average speed for the Tour. It was impossible, but Bruyneel did it nevertheless, with a little help from his father.

Predictably Indurain won the time trial the day after his exploit, not by as much as he had won them in the past, but it was enough to take over the yellow jersey. The stage was set for Indurain's fifth victory. He slipped into Tour-winning mode and took second place on both Alpine stages.

Max Sciandri, a rider who was born in Britain, brought up in Italy and the US and started racing as an Italian but swapped to being British, won a tough stage to St Etienne. Then the race headed for the Pyrenees and for a dreadful accident on the descent from the Portet d'Aspet.

Fabio Casartelli was the reigning Olympic road race champion, a talented young Italian rider in the American Motorola team with a great future ahead of him. The Portet d'Aspet is a wicked climb, especially from the west. It's in the middle of the Pyrenees and it's one of those mid-stage mountains that the Tour can climb in either direction. In 1995 it was climbed from the east, so the wickedly steep section formed part of the descent.

This twisty piece of downhill tarmac is dark and over-shadowed by trees. Casartelli wasn't the best climber in the world so he was trying hard to make up lost time on the descent. The steep section comes abruptly and the Italian was doing 70 to 80 kilometres per hour when he entered it. He was in a line of riders, all going as fast as they could, when the two in front of him fell on a bend. Casartelli could do nothing to avoid them and he was cata-pulted across the road surface to its edge where his head struck a concrete block. You find these on remote moun-tain roads, where they serve as cheap Armco to prevent motor vehicles crashing over the edge. Casartelli was airlifted quickly from the scene but he died on the way to hospital, the third fatality of the Tour de France.

Next day the peloton rode quietly out of the Pyrenees as a mark of respect in a stage that wasn't contested. The Motorola team car drove directly behind the riders carrying one of Casartelli's bikes on its roof rack with his race number still on it. The bike he'd ridden in the crash was placed in the Madonna di Ghisallo chapel above Lake Como in Italy, and one year after the fateful day a memorial was erected on the spot where Casartelli died. It's a beautiful tribute in white marble quarried in his home region. At the exact time and day when Casartelli died the sun illuminates a hole in the base of the monument, and deep inside you can read an inscription that records three dates: Casartelli's birth date, the date he won Olympic gold and the date on which he died.

Casartelli's death brought down the curtain on the Pyrenees. Some said that the organisers should have stopped the stage when they knew the full extent of the tragedy, but they didn't and Richard Virenque won on an epic route that was designed for a climber like him. Indurain stayed with those closest to him in the overall standings, Alex Zulle and Bjarne Rijs.

A time trial around the Lac de Vassivière on the penultimate day would be the final showdown for the favourites, but before that was a stage on the heavy roads of Limousin to Limoges. Lance Armstrong won it and dedicated his victory to Casartelli.

Indurain won the remaining time trial, and with it his fifth Tour. He had equalled Anquetil, Merckx and Hinault in total Tour victories, and the latter two were in Paris to shake his hand, but Indurain had also beaten them by winning five in a row. As well as his wife, Marisa, his family and friends from Villava and many Spanish dignatories, even Spanish royalty in the form of Princess Elena, were there to greet the man dubbed in the *Journal de Dimanche*'s headline next day 'Miguel V of Spain'.

I bet not one of them thought they wouldn't be crowning him Miguel VI the following year, but even as he celebrated in Paris, Indurain's five-year domination of the Tour de France was over. His reign would end in shivering conditions the following year, and the Tour de France would enter its darkest era.

16. THE DAY THE TOUR NEARLY ENDED

Miguel Indurain's grip on the Tour de France was finally broken in 1996 – by the weather. It was a cold, wet and confusing race. Indurain went in with good form, appearing as invincible as ever in the run-up to the Tour, but freak weather would expose his one weakness. The lizard Indurain, who soaked up heat and used it to solar-power his legs, was susceptible to the cold. This is not normally a problem in France in July, so it had never been a factor before, but it was in 1996.

It rained for the whole of the first week, and it wasn't balmy, tropical rain. It was cold rain on the flat stages of the north that turned to sleet and snow when the race hit the mountains, and Indurain began to take on water, literally. Not from outside but inside. Some people are like that. In cold weather they retain water in their body tissues. And when they do they get heavier and heavier. Seven, eight or nine kilograms can be gained. It affects them on the flat, not so much through the actual weight gain but more because their swollen muscles don't work properly; but in the mountains it is a big problem. Climbing is about power-to-weight ratio. Add on enough weight and even someone with the power of Miguel Indurain can't climb any more.

Research into this problem since 1996 has identified that controlling sodium intake can help racers who suffer from it, but that was too late to help Indurain. On the first stage in the Alps his swollen body creaked and groaned as he desperately hauled himself up the early climbs, but on the stage that climbed the tough Cormet de Roselend he cracked and had to dig very deep just to get over the top. He lost a hat full of time from that point and any chance of winning the Tour. Losing and suffering the ignominy of finishing many minutes behind riders he had previously beaten with ease sapped Indurain's taste for the Tour and for racing, and towards the end of the year he announced his retirement.

While Indurain suffered on the Cormet de Roselend, a Belgian racer was having his best-ever Tour de France. Well, that is until he met near disaster on the descent. As I've said before, Johan Bruyneel wasn't a super Tour de France rider, but he was having his best race in 1996, reaching the top of the Cormet de Roselend close to the front of the race. With one climb left to do he looked about to move right up the overall standings. This is how he recalls what happened next:

> I was beginning to congratulate myself. I had done a good climb but I knew I couldn't relax. I still had to race, to descend as fast as possible and stay in contact for the final climb. It isn't easy coming down mountains, but that day it was slippery and very risky. I skidded on a corner and took off. Yes, took off. I saw the retaining wall at the side of the road pass underneath me, and then there was nothing. That happened in a moment but then, while I was in mid-air, everything began to go slow. I had time to think. I remember the process clearly; thinking, I have gone over

the edge, there is nothing below me, and I am going to die, in that order. Then, after what seemed ages, my fall stopped and I slithered to a halt.

Bruyneel had fallen 20 or 30 metres down a ravine, then got caught up in some shrubs. Their branches were stout and they held his weight. The slope below the road wasn't vertical and the Belgian managed to climb back up. He was full of adrenaline, and a mass of mixed emotions. His reflexes took over as he grabbed a new bike from his team mechanic and set off in pursuit. Then the shock of what had just happened hit him, and all the strength left his legs. He crawled up the final climb, finishing many minutes behind the target he had looked set to achieve. Any chance of a high overall position had gone.

The weather then went from bad to worse. Snow caused the abandonment of one stage and another to be seriously curtailed as the whole peloton were bussed around impassable mountains before being kicked out for a 50-kilometre drag race to the finish of the stage. But eventually the Tour made it through to Paris, where it was won by Bjarne Riis, the first and so far only Danish rider to win, but his victory caused some ripples of disquiet, even within the peloton.

Riis sealed his victory with an amazing ride on the slopes of Hautacam, a ski station above Lourdes in the Pyrenees. He was with the front group, riding at the front of it and looking well in charge, when Riis slowed dramatically and dropped to the back of the group. As he did so he looked at every rider in the line behind him, looked right into their faces as though he was weighing up who might be stronger than him. The answer was simple, no one was, so Riis shifted up not one gear but several, and attacked. He left the rest for dead. They looked impotent. Riis looked mighty. And the whole thing looked too easy.

Anyone who knew pro cycling knew that there was doping in it, and it had been there almost from day one. Some knew that it was rife and regarded it as a fact of life. It evolved slowly and the products used changed, but in the early nineties doping had developed into an arms race.

A Dutchman, Peter Winnen, was a pro in the eighties and until 1991. He was good too, winning two mountain stages, including one on L'Alpe d'Huez, and he was third overall in the 1983 Tour. He's now an award-winning author and journalist, but he was always a deep thinker. This is his insider take on doping in cycling. 'Up until the nineties it wasn't really a secret because there was nothing to hide, because the products used didn't really make a rider any faster. For example, amphetamines gave the feeling of being better but they didn't make a big physical difference. Then in the early nineties EPO came into cycling and for the first time this was a drug that made riders a lot faster. I can remember the first year it came. I was a climber and in the first races there were guys who couldn't climb to save their lives who just left me behind. Now that was a reason to keep quiet, to keep things secret,' he says.

There's a lot of truth in what Winnen is saying, although he oversimplifies things to make his point. Steroids and hormones had been used in cycling for years before the nineties and they did make a rider faster, but not by ten per cent, which is what EPO could do. So what is EPO? The initials stand for Erythroprotein, a naturally occurring substance in the body that stimulates the production of red blood cells. Synthetic EPO was developed to help cancer patients produce red blood cells when natural mechanisms are too stressed.

Red blood cells carry inhaled oxygen to the muscles where it is used with glucose to produce energy in a similar way to a car's engine using oxygen to ignite its fuel. Deliver more oxygen, with a turbocharger for example, and the car's engine is more powerful. EPO is a human turbocharger. If you inject synthetic EPO into a healthy human being you can boost their red blood cells so that they can deliver ten per cent more oxygen to their muscles. Ten per cent more oxygen roughly translates into ten per cent more power. EPO is the dictionary definition of a performance-enhancing drug.

That is the subtle difference Winnen was trying to stress. He says other drugs only helped to maintain performance. That's not entirely true, as I've said: steroids, testosterone and their like improve recovery and help deliver a little more power, although nowhere near the ten per cent that EPO can do. EPO is a definite, direct and quantum boost, and the feeling I have from talking to pro riders over the years is that for some – maybe only a few at first, but their numbers slowly increased – EPO went against the group code. As a former Belgian national champion once told me: 'Guys took stuff. They weren't forced to do it, but it happened. The thing was that the same guys won anyway, the top guys, the ones who were best. But EPO was different. That could make a racehorse from a donkey, and when donkeys start winning that is wrong.'

Pro bike riders are, broadly speaking, a type. They like to present themselves as tough, street-savvy Jack the lads. They wheel and they deal. It's less true now, but it was once common for races to be sold, favours to be given and taken between individuals and teams. The argument they used was that they were pros. It's a sport, yes, but primarily they were there to entertain and make a living. Drugs?

Yes, don't shout about it, but if you need help – well, it's a tough game. They shared the bond of a tough job and developed an unwritten code to cope. EPO upset that code; it wasn't coping, it was cheating, although as we'll see that didn't stop the drug's use spreading.

But how did drug use in cycling come about? I read something recently where a journalist blamed doping on the riders, on their unwillingness to play on a level playing field, but is it that straightforward? In my opinion doping existed before each generation of pros, leaving them with the perception of having to use it to get on to the playing field. Some didn't, quite a few probably, but many did.

Of course a racer could say no, but this is what the first British leader of the Tour de France, Tom Simpson, told his sister, my mother, during the winter of 1966, the year after he'd been world champion: 'What we do looks glamorous but it's not, it's Hell. I have to take stuff, I don't want to and it scares me. I don't do it all the time, but when guys beat me who I know are not as good as me, what else can I do? All I want now is to make enough money so my family are secure, and get out, and to do that I have to do a good Tour de France next year.'

I'm not saying that Simpson was morally correct; he could have come home, brought his family with him and settled for less. I don't condone any level of doping. If it's against the rules it's cheating, and everything has to be done to eradicate doping from the sport, not just in the name of fair play but to protect young, often naive, driven individuals from hurting themselves. Also, again, I'm not saying that every pro doped, even when things began to really hot up in the nineties. There's clear evidence that many did, but a lot didn't, and they weren't ostracised either, so long as they didn't bleat about it to the press. I'm just trying to say how it was and that the choice, although essentially yes or no, didn't always seem so clear to those making it.

The conditions Simpson encountered continued through the seventies and into the eighties, but then along came EPO, and it was rocket fuel. Going back to Winnen's argument, before EPO arrived, doping kept riders going, helped them recover and gave marginal gains; EPO made racehorses out of donkeys. Bjarne Riis wasn't exactly a donkey, but he wasn't a natural winner either and his victory shocked a lot of people. He didn't set the world alight when he turned pro, although he had fearsome ambition and drive, and he is very intelligent too. He slowly turned himself year by year into a better rider, winning bigger and bigger races until he eventually won the Tour de France.

Riis studied cycling until he was a master practitioner. After his racing career he became a team manager and today is one of the most successful and respected in the business. But a few years ago Riis was forced to tell the truth about his 1996 victory. He'd been named by others involved with the team he raced for, T-Mobile, who had admitted doping. Riis's position became untenable and he admitted using EPO to win the 1996 Tour de France, underlining what most people suspected. There was even a black joke inside cycling that referred to Riis as Mr 60 Percent.

That name came about because there was no test for the presence of artificial EPO in the body until 2000, so when its use was first suspected by the cycling authorities they began to test the rider's red blood cell count, which is expressed as a percentage reading called a Heamatocrit. If the tested rider's Heamatocrit was over 50 per cent, then they were prevented from racing until it fell. It's obvious then why Riis was called Mr 60 Percent.

I should stress though that a 50 per cent result didn't necessarily indicate drug use; normal readings can be that high in certain circumstances, which is why the tests were euphemistically referred to as 'health checks'. Nowadays each Tour rider has a blood passport, with the results of Heamatocrit and other tests taken at regular intervals entered in it. The result is a profile of their blood values over an extended period, and if anomalies turn up on a test the rider is investigated thoroughly until an explanation is established.

The reason that authorities took Heamatocrit readings underlines another problem with EPO. Not only was its use cheating, it could be dangerous. The normal Heamatocrit range lies between the high thirties and high forties per cent. At over 50 per cent the blood becomes thicker. Factor in dehydration from heavy exercise, which lowers the plasma volume, and red blood cell concentration rises even more and there is a danger of blood clots and heart failure. There's no evidence that Riis ever actually did have a reading as high as 60 per cent, but anyone boosting to that level would be taking a huge risk with their health and could die.

Some riders did die, although not big-time pros. But this is another danger of doping: if done by experts it can be relatively safe, but EPO could be bought on the internet and self-administered. In the nineties a number of good amateur racers and second-level pros simply died in their sleep. Maybe it wasn't the reason for every death, but the suspicion was that some were due to EPO. It is dynamite that in the wrong hands can explode on the user, who must keep his or her blood diluted enough to cope with the extra cells. This requires expert help or advice and specialist equipment like mobile centrifuges to monitor red cell concentration. To be absolutely safe it requires a doctor, and the number of medical practitioners who began to oversee the training and preparation of pro bike riders increased during the nineties. That was no coincidence.

A doctor who knows his stuff can make big money from doping in sport, which must be a temptation in itself, but the former Tour racer and current directeur sportif with Team Columbia, Allan Peiper, reckons that there's more to it:

> I think some doctors get a bit of a God complex. It's like with surgeons; they come up with procedures that can defy nature. You know, where you get a patient who is so ill that it looks impossible for them to survive, but the surgeon says, 'Now hang on, if I do this and this,' and they save their life. That must be a buzz, must be addictive, and in a way when doctors get involved in doping I think they get the same kick by saying: 'OK, nature says you can go this fast, and do this and this. But I can change that, I can make you go that fast and do more.' I think they get into that and get a kick from it.

Whatever the motivation of the people advising Riis, his reign was short. The following year his young team-mate Jan Ullrich won the Tour de France. Ullrich was 23 and extraordinarily talented. He was born in Rostock in the old East Germany and learned his cycling under their nationally controlled regime. When the Berlin wall fell in 1989 he moved to Hamburg, becoming amateur world road race champion in 1993 at Oslo the day before Lance Armstrong won the pro title.

Ullrich was a super-strong all-rounder without a chink in his physical armour, and was literally quite glorious to watch on a bike. Uphill or on the flat he would sit rock solid in the saddle and power his pedals around, hardly ever moving his upper body. If Ullrich had a flaw it was in his head. He didn't have the tactical savvy and, it later emerged, the dedication of some of his rivals, but by the way he won in 1997 it didn't look as if Ullrich would need tactics to win the Tour de France for many years to come. That prediction didn't turn out right, and Ullrich too would see his career ruined by doping.

On the surface pro cycling and the Tour de France didn't look at all in trouble as 1997 passed into 1998, but underneath it was. The show was going along and a lot of vested interests were helping it to do so. Some young racers and other campaigners had tried to draw attention to the fact that doping had got out of control, but in the main nobody was listening, or at least wanted to listen. Then something happened to take pro cycling and the policing of doping in the Tour de France temporarily out of the hands of the usual authorities. No one is absolutely sure why it happened, although my suspicion is that Tour outsiders thought that doping in the race had become so out of hand that a higher authority needed to sort it out.

Willy Voet, a Belgian who lived in France, was a soigneur who had worked in cycling for a very long time. He had good hands and a deep understanding of the sport, so he'd worked with some of the best, and he knew every trick in the book. He was also a good man to have on your side in a murky world; trustworthy and dependable, with a Machiavellian belief in ends justifying the means.

A few days before the start of the 1998 Tour de France in Dublin, Ireland, Voet travelled from his home in the Alps to Paris to pick up the car supplied by the Tour organisers that he would drive to get him around the race. He then set off on a looping journey to Belgium that included a visit to Switzerland, calling at various places to pick up supplies for his team, a Spanish outfit called Festina. In Belgium he ended up at the house of the team's doctor, Dr Rijckaert, to collect some medical drips. The plan was to set off next day for the French port of Calais, then drive across England and Wales and take another ferry to Ireland. Rijckaert, knowing exactly what Voet had in his car, advised him not to cross into France by the E17 coastal motorway, but to take a less well travelled route.

Theoretically there are no borders in Europe any more, but customs officers still patrol, still stop people and regularly turn up loads of smuggled cigarettes or booze or recreational drugs, or even people being trafficked in from outside the EEC. Customs carry out some random stop-and-checks, but mostly they work on intelligence, trading information with officials from other countries and choosing the right moment to stop someone, when the goods or whatever are on board.

Voet knew the back roads of Flanders like the back of his own hand, and decided to cross at Neuville-en-Ferrin. Normally you would never even see a customs vehicle at such a crossing, but on 8 July the place was swarming with them, and they stopped Voet. They didn't even look at him, they just asked him to pop the boot, give them the keys and stay put, and placed an armed officer to watch him. His car was full of drugs, enough to stock a pharmacist: 234 doses of EPO, 160 of testosterone, 80 bottles of growth hormone, and lots of blood-thinning tablets. Voet was arrested, the secret was out and when news reached Dublin a lot of people began to panic.

The riders and management were already in Ireland. The Tour started without Voet, Rijckaert was arrested almost immediately and rumours were bouncing around Dublin like explosive tennis balls. Britain's Chris Boardman won the prologue, then crashed out of the race. But what happened in Ireland was totally overshadowed by what was happening in mainland Europe.

Voet spilled the beans. He'd been involved in doping riders for many years, he said, and he wasn't alone. At Festina he was part of an internal doping system to which the riders chipped in part of their salaries, and it was all done under the expert supervision of Dr Rijckaert.

As the race dragged on the cat was slowly dragged kicking and screaming out of the bag. There were more raids, more teams were quizzed by the police, and at the end of the first week the organisation threw the Festina team out. At first the riders protested. They talked about the dignity of their profession being violated. But as more revelations came out, as more riders were questioned, products seized and teams put under investigation, their protestations sounded increasingly hollow. The riders went on a go-slow, then on strikes, and only a fractious peace brokered by Bjarne Riis got the Tour rolling again – it was won by Marco Pantani.

That is another point about doping. Pantani's victory was the first by an Italian for over 30 years, it was brave and it was classy, but because of doping it is an aside to the story of the 1998 Tour. It was almost an aside to Pantani's career too, as he would soon be connected with doping and slip into a career and personal tailspin that would see him die alone in a hotel room of an apparent cocaine overdose.

Doping nearly killed the Tour de France in 1998, and at one point it looked unlikely even to reach Paris. The race director Jean-Marie Leblanc gave up his brave face and simply broke down in tears when it looked as if the Tour would die on his watch. Leblanc is a nice guy – intelligent, good company, at one time a very good sports journalist and before that a less good pro rider who had raced the Tour – but just who was he crying for? Did Leblanc not see this coming? Didn't the shocked journalists see it? Didn't the UCI? A doping arms race had been going on right under their noses and they didn't know, despite being repeatedly told by some brave whistle-blowing pros like the Frenchman Gilles Delion.

Nobody listened to Delion; he spoke out too early, at the beginning of the nineties. No one was ready to listen then. Delion was a good rider, who won the Tour of Lombardy Classic, but who got labelled as soft. People said the reason he talked so much about drugs was that he simply wasn't good enough. His fellow riders did that to him, and journalists and the cycling authorities let them.

They listened to Christophe Bassons, though. He was a French pro with Festina. He wasn't racing in the Tour, partly because as a first-year pro he didn't have the form or experience to be selected, but possibly also because he wouldn't join Dr Rijckaert's programme. He just said no, but during the 1998 Tour he said yes to every interview he could. He became something of a hero, although his racing career was virtually over because the professional *omertà*, their vow of silence about drugs, still existed, although it was beginning to sit uncomfortably on the shoulders of some.

There are many things that are difficult to understand about doping in the Tour de France, but the one that is most unfathomable for an outsider must be the unspoken vow that pros took about doping, even those that never used the stuff. It happens less now, but countless journalists have come away from interviews with reputedly clean riders frustrated at their refusal to speak out against riders who've been proven to have taken drugs.

As recently as 2006 I asked a Tour top-ten finisher, who I knew quite well and had interviewed a number of times, to go on record with what he would say to an impressionable teenager in order to assure him it was possible to finish in the top ten overall without using performance-enhancing drugs. He did so, reluctantly, then a few days later he called me and retracted everything he said. He agreed that it was still true, but he just didn't want to say it. I told him that someone had to make a stand, which he accepted, but then asked, 'Why me?'

Why indeed. Pro cycling is a sport in which, no matter how strong you are, you don't need enemies. The rider in question thought that by saying he was clean the others would think he was implying that they were dirty. He envisaged the whole peloton chasing him down whenever he attacked. It could have happened, and it has. Why him? I agree. Well, I agreed then.

Now that same rider does speak out about doping, and so do many others. There has been a sea change in the treatment the peloton gives its members who get caught taking drugs. The 'hard luck, mate, tough break' attitude that existed when dope testing was first introduced has slowly disappeared, and there is genuine antipathy towards anyone caught now. A lot of racers still don't like talking about it, though. They deflect the question, saying that other sports use dope and they aren't policed half as well as cycling, which is true. Or they just state that they have never failed the many tests they are given. They are right, that should be enough, but given cycling's past it isn't. Testing is tight nowadays – some whose opinion is important say watertight – but cycling's doping past is bad, and riders have to expect that there is going to be suspicion from outsiders for a long time to come. Maybe more of them need to address that.

But on a more positive note, cycling does lead the way in detecting performance-enhancing drugs today. As doping methods became more sophisticated, so did the testing. Pro cyclists are the most tested athletes on the planet, and the majority of testing is done out of competition, where it is the more effective. Also, the tests they are subjected to are the most rigorous in sport, where surprisingly there isn't a uniform standard of testing. Cycling still takes urine tests, but the effort is concentrated on blood samples and comparing those samples from test to test for each athlete in a personal blood passport. This will throw up any anomalies, and if this happens the rider is tested more often. It's the same if a rider has a run of good form, or if he improves dramatically, or if the testers get intelligence on changes of habit. On top of this the doctors who work in cycling, like the masseurs, soigneurs and other practitioners, are rigorously vetted. It's got so strict that one team manager told me recently: 'You could try and dope, but the lengths that you'd have to go to and the risks involved would be so much that just the worry of it would probably negate the effect. And you couldn't really boost anything dramatically, or it would show.'

So is there doping in the Tour de France today? To be honest I don't know. Someone will always take the risk, and there will always be practitioners offering the ultimate product or regime. I'd like to say that the balance has shifted from 1998, when it seemed as though non-dopers were a minority, but I still can't, no matter how tempting the lack of a positive test from the 2009 race makes it to do so. Journalists have been guilty of knee-jerk reactions in the past. After Tom Simpson's death in 1967 the following year's Tour was dubbed the 'Tour of Health' by the press, and they've kept doing that every year after there has been a scandal. I won't do it, not even now when teams talk openly about their desire to race clean.

The fact is that there are possible performance-enhancing procedures out there that are undetectable at the moment, and it would be flying in the face of history to suggest that they are not being used. However, there is one extra factor to consider that might give hope for the future.

Aldo Sassi, an Italian coach with a good reputation, says: 'People are hard wired to take drugs. When we are tired we reach for the coffee pot; when we have a headache we reach for the aspirin. Taking performance-enhancing drugs is logical when looked at in that light, but we have to each decide on our own ethical stance, which is what I have always done.'

And that may be the key. It's fashionable in the cycling press now to really have a go whenever someone tests positive for drugs and make them a scapegoat for everything that is wrong in cycling. I've even heard dopers called scum, but dopers in sport are not scum. I've been a police officer and I've met scum, real scum. People who are scum don't get into sport. Riders who use drugs start out good kids, not saints maybe, but good kids. Dopers get lost along the way when their morals get kidnapped and held hostage by their own ambition, needs, greed some-times, or by fear of failure. However, I feel that there has been a change in the whole peloton's ethical stance recently, a subtle change in the way in which the game is played now. Also, there are fewer people in cycling to show young ambitious racers the path of doping, and more like Sassi who have decided on a high ethical stance and stick by it.

So the way forward for the Tour de France, and for the cycling authorities as a whole, in their fight against doping is to keep up the vigilance, keep up the policing intensity, but rejoice and invest in a new generation of athletes and team staff who talk openly about playing within the rules. I suppose what I'm saying is that the Tour de France should adopt the sporting equivalent of walking softly but carrying a big stick.

17. SEVEN FOR TEXAS

I'm in Madrid at the home of Johan Bruyneel, the man who wrote the blueprint for Lance Armstrong's unprecedented seven straight Tour victories. It's 2005 and Armstrong has just signed off his winning streak. We've known all year that this was his final Tour and I'm writing about Armstrong for a magazine, but I want to do it from the perspective of the man who maybe knew him better than he knew himself.

'It's quite simple,' says Bruyneel when I ask him to sum Armstrong up in a sentence. 'Every year, since we worked together, he did something to impress me. I saw a lot of things with Lance, but every year, even in this his final Tour, he showed me something that impressed me.' Was it a superficial answer? No, not really. Bruyneel was the first person ever to speak the words win, Tour de France and Lance Armstrong in the same sentence. Bruyneel's vision was the path they chose to do it. The specific training, the hour upon hour spent riding key parts of the Tour's route again and again until they were hardwired into Armstrong's head and legs, were all Bruyneel's idea.

He supervised all the projects, the special time trial bikes, bike and body weight control, and things like that.

Bruyneel was in the wind tunnels with Armstrong, in the testing labs, and he was there, driving behind Armstrong on all those interminable training sessions in the Alps and Pyrenees. Bruyneel knew all the numbers, but from time to time even he was amazed. No matter where the bar was set, Armstrong jumped it, and every year he would throw in a triple salko, just to make his manager's jaw drop.

Their intense, controversial, but at the same time ground-breaking relationship began in 1998. Armstrong had returned to racing almost from death. Two years earlier he had been diagnosed with multiple cancers, and although he and those who know have never put a number on them, his chances of survival had been slim. But he beat the disease, returned to health and eventually returned to pro racing. It was a rocky ride, and even in 1998 Armstrong had a crisis about racing, but by the end of the year he was not just back in the sport, but back to win.

He didn't ride the 1998 Tour de France, but fourth place in the Tour of Spain and in both the world road race and time trial championships got Armstrong believing again. He believed he could get back to the top, perhaps win some of the single-day Classics he had won before his illness, and to do well in Grand Tours, maybe. But first his team, a fledgeling American outfit sponsored by the US Postal Service, needed a new manager, someone who knew European racing. That's where Johan Bruyneel came in.

Bruyneel had just retired from racing, and he'd been a capable pro. He wasn't the most physically talented, but he'd made the most of his ability. What Bruyneel had done was study cycling down to molecular level, and Armstrong knew it. He offered the Belgian the US Postal management job, but Bruyneel characteristically didn't say yes straight away. He needed some advice from outside the sport about running a team, and, as he told me, he needed Armstrong to buy into an idea:

> I'd always been impressed by Lance. He was a special talent, you don't become world champion at 21 by not being very special, but the 1998 Tour of Spain got me really thinking. If he could come back from near death to fourth in a Grand Tour, with no racing the year before and no special training – I mean, he just went and did the Tour of Spain and finished fourth – I thought there must be so much this guy can improve on, and it made me think that he could maybe win the Tour de France.
>
> What I needed him to do, though, was buy into my ideas of how to do it, because they were a bit crazy for cycling at that time. He had the ability and the desire, but I had the rest. Lance and I spoke, and I thought long and hard, and in the end I believed I could get him to see it my way. I took the job and we began to talk about him winning the Tour. We were going to do it, so I said to him we might as well win.

Those words 'we might as well win' became the title of a book that Bruyneel wrote about their Tour de France journey together. A bit trite perhaps, a bit management-speak, but the words were a turning point in cycling history. US Postal weren't a big budget team, Armstrong was a blank canvas, in the sense that his recent near-death experience meant that anything he achieved in cycling was a bonus, so the two of them might as well try and win the Tour de France. But to make certain they did it, they had to prepare in a different way from any previous winner. 'It was the way I would have liked to prepare as a rider, if there had been no sponsor obligations,' says Bruyneel.

Now every Tour favourite uses the template that Armstrong and Bruyneel laid down to prepare for the 1999 Tour, and the six after that. To kick it off the two of them met during the winter of 1998. 'We sat and talked about it and put it all down on paper. I wanted Lance to change a lot, but talking about it was one thing, doing it was another,' says Bruyneel.

Doing it meant getting the logistics, the staff, riders and infrastructure of US Postal honed to the project, which was fairly straightforward, just good business practice, for a marketing graduate and the son of a successful businessman. 'I asked for help too. For example, I asked for advice from a friend of my father's who ran a big business, and he told me that running a professional team was no different to a company. I had to find good people to do specific jobs and delegate that responsibility to them,' he says.

The hard work, though, the work that Bruyneel undertook personally and couldn't delegate, was one to one with Lance Armstrong. 'I wanted to change the way he raced, or even more fundamentally the way he rode his bike. When he won before his cancer he did so with huge bursts of power – everything with Lance was horsepower. Horsepower was his natural gift, but he used it too much. I wanted him to save it by pedalling faster in lower gears and save his power for key attacks. That way Lance would be pedalling aerobically and not building up fatigue while his rivals were lunging and grinding in bigger gears,' says Bruyneel.

Riders had raced like that before, but only gifted climbers such as Charly Gaul. For power riders like

Armstrong, this way of racing was counterintuitive. Jacques Anquetil never raced that way, neither did Eddy Merckx or Bernard Hinault. Miguel Indurain did a bit, especially on climbs, but not in a time trial. Bruyneel wanted Armstrong to up his cadence in both, and not just by a bit; he wanted Armstrong to take his pedalling from a rate that was generally considered in cycling as optimal of 90 revs per minute, up into the 100 to 120 revs range, higher even than the twinkling feet of a mountain Angel like Charly Gaul.

Work began as soon as Armstrong returned to his European base in early 1999, and Bruyneel regarded the new way of pedalling as so core to their goal that he accompanied Armstrong on almost every training ride he did, driving behind him in a car. Sometimes he and Armstrong were linked by radio, sometimes not, but in this initial stage of training their communication was simple. 'Every time Lance got out of the saddle I would tell him to sit, using the same words – sit, spin, high cadence – using those same words all the time,' he says.

It was tough. As a cyclist gets fitter there is a natural tendency to push on the climbs, get out of the saddle and enjoy the surge of power from their legs. But every time Armstrong did that he heard Bruyneel's voice and the sit, spin, high cadence mantra repeated time and again. Once or twice Armstrong got irritated and ripped out his radio earpiece, but Bruyneel wasn't put off. 'If he did that I just leaned on the horn until he sat down again to spin,' he says.

Their work continued when the winter snows started to melt and the Tour's high passes opened. Bruyneel and Armstrong travelled to all the mountains that would feature in the 1999 Tour, not just to recce them but to learn them. It was spring, the weather is often wet in Europe then, and when rain falls in the mountains it's cold rain. Armstrong would ride a climb, and if he wasn't happy that he knew it, turn around and ride it again. 'One time he went three times up a climb. It was getting dark, really wet and cold, and I was ready to go to the hotel, but at the top Lance said, "No, I don't get it yet," and went down to climb it once more,' Bruyneel remembers.

This went on day after day. No one had prepared like this before. Other riders had looked at key parts of the route, and Jacques Anquetil had a system all his own. He sometimes rode a Tour time trial course well before the race with a load of stamped, self-addressed postcards in his pocket. He'd stop every few kilometres and write down direction and terrain comments, then post them, so that when he got home a description of the route was waiting for him. Some climbers, like Lucien Van Impe, would spend a month in the mountains in May or June, but in general races got in the way of doing too much of this specific preparation.

Anyway, it was thought that racing was the best way to train. Armstrong missed so many races in the spring of 1999 that nobody believed he'd be ready. Even Armstrong had his doubts. One day, fed up with training day after day and missing the buzz of competition that he enjoyed so much, Armstrong told Bruyneel, 'OK, I'm going to see this through, but if it doesn't work this year I'm not doing it again.'

But it did work. Armstrong was best in the time trials in 1999, and the best in the mountains.

The result might have been a bit closer had Armstrong's nearest rider, Alex Zulle, not been delayed behind a crash on the seaweed-slick Passage du Gois in Brittany. But even that was partly due to Armstrong and his US Postal team. The Passage is a notorious stretch of coastal road which is submerged twice a day by the tide. US Postal hammered the approach to the Passage, lining out the whole Tour behind them, where crosswinds ripped the peloton to bits. Riders take risks to hang on in conditions like that, and a risk taken down the pace line on a slippery road can soon become a crash. It was a moment when a contender had to be at the front. Armstrong was and Zulle wasn't.

Winning the Tour de France is never easy. During the race Armstrong told his then wife, Kristen, that he was tired, more tired than he'd ever been in a bike race, but he looked good, too good some said afterwards. Given the revelations of 1998, it was inevitable that the winner in 1999, a winner who made winning look relatively easy, would be suspected.

Battle lines were drawn. The sceptics on one side, who no matter how much Armstrong protested his innocence, refused to believe in him. The believers on the other, who pointed to Armstrong's exceptional talent before cancer, to the weight he lost fighting it and how that improved his power-to-weight ratio, to the extraordinary lengths he went to in preparing for the Tour, and to all the marginal gains that Armstrong and Bruyneel accrued through relentless study. The battle has raged ever since, and books have been written arguing each side.

The conclusion that Bruyneel and Armstrong took from 1999 was that their template worked, but they couldn't rest and were determined to refine it in the coming years. They still made mistakes, and one of the biggest occurred in the 2000 Tour. Armstrong's closest rival then was Jan Ullrich, the German rider who won the Tour in 1997 and who would get closest to the American in the future.

When asked once if Ullrich kept him awake at night, Armstrong said, 'No, but he's the reason I get up in the morning and ride my bike every day.'

That's something the German didn't do. In the winter he let things slide, put on weight and had to play catch-up during the early part of the racing season. He was good, hugely talented. In fact Bruyneel reckons that if he had been Ullrich's manger, and if Ullrich had worked as hard as Armstrong did in that relationship, then he could have been closer to Armstrong. 'Ullrich was the only one who could physically match Armstrong,' he reckons.

Bruyneel makes no secret of the fact that he thinks Ullrich was badly advised. 'Each year he was our number one rival, but it used to make me smile that each year his team would race with the same tactic. You know, if it hasn't worked one year, why try the same thing again next year?' he asks.

But back to the 2000 Tour: one criticism I would lay at Armstrong's door is that he can be, if not insensitive, then undiplomatic. He suffers for it, both in terms of his image and because it winds some people up, and in 2000 it nearly cost him the Tour. He was very undiplomatic on the stage that finished on top of Mont Ventoux. Armstrong had the yellow jersey, but he and Marco Pantani were both way better than the rest, so they romped away from the other favourites. At the top it appeared that Armstrong, happy with his gains in the overall stakes, gifted the stage victory to Pantani. But Pantani didn't like that. He wanted to sprint it out with Armstrong, and he felt that by not contesting the sprint Armstrong had insulted him.

A few days later Pantani, who had come into the Tour under-prepared, won a big Alpine stage without any gifts.

He was clearly coming into superb form and had moved into sixth place overall, nine minutes behind Armstrong. Maybe if Pantani attacked early enough – and if he did so US Postal as the team with the yellow jersey would have to chase – maybe Pantani could cause an upset. At least he would cause Armstrong a lot of grief, and that alone might be worth it.

Whatever his motivation, Pantani took off early, attacking on the first climb of the day, the Col des Saisies, and a race was on. Back in the US Postal team car Johan Bruyneel watched his worst nightmare unfold. He began asking himself questions and didn't like the answers. 'Could Pantani stay away all day and upset the Tour? Could he win? Surely not, but you never knew with him. I didn't want to do it, not that early in the stage, but I had to get the team to chase. Not hard, but just enough,' he says. He also had to do it in a way that wouldn't panic the team, as if Pantani's attack was something that Bruyneel expected. 'I spoke very softly into the microphone and said, "OK, we'll do a little chasing." But later I saw that we'd have to chase harder,' Bruyneel adds.

Eventually, as the race approached the final climb of the day, the Col de Joux-Plane, US Postal caught Pantani, but the chase had cost them. One of the features of the 1999 and 2000 Tours was how Armstrong had strong team-mates to make the pace for him early on each climb. The tactic was to ride at a constant hard pace and cook the legs of the true climbers. They rely on brutal accelerations, so spit-roasting them with constant hard riding draws their sting.

Armstrong didn't have that now: as soon as the riders hit the Joux-Plane's fearsome nine per cent average slopes, his blue-jerseyed team-mates disappeared like melting snow on the flanks of Mont Blanc that dominates the south side of the climb. Armstrong was alone – and he was in trouble. In the panic to rein in Pantani he'd not eaten enough, and he felt it immediately in his legs. 'The radio crackled, it was Lance. "Johan, I don't feel so good," was all he said, but I knew we had a problem,' Bruyneel remembers.

Endurance athletes burn glucose to produce energy when they are going hard. Their bodies can carry about two hours' worth of this fuel, which is why pro bike racers need to eat during a race. They spare their glucose supplies when they are riding in the peloton, because they are sheltered and it's easier. Going steady they burn fat as fuel, but on a mountain or in a breakaway group they ride full-on and their bodies work like racing cars, burning glucose like mad. If they run out of glucose they have to slow down. They can still burn fat and keep moving, but nowhere near as fast.

That is what happened to Armstrong. His head began to roll as he used his shoulders and arms to help his legs, but slowly and surely the others in the front group began to ride away from him. Then, just at the wrong time, he came to the steep part of the Joux-Plane, nearly five kilometres of climbing a 12 per cent wall of tarmac. Jan Ullrich was now the big danger. Armstrong had a big gap on him in the overall, but he was running on empty and had to spread his effort perfectly to the top, otherwise he would blow completely. It must have been incredibly painful, pushing on with his body telling him to slow down, but he did it, only losing two minutes on Ullrich by the top of the climb. His second Tour victory was assured.

There were no scares in 2001 and 2002. Johan Bruyneel has often been referred to as a master tactician, but he plays that down. 'Tactics are not so complicated if you have the best racers to carry them out. Really, the only time we used them was in 2003, when Lance was not so strong. Then we had to use tactics. One day, for example, we had Beltran go away in a breakaway in the mountains. He was just in or just outside of the top ten overall, I can't remember which, but he was close and a threat to other riders hoping for a high overall position. I told Beltran not to help in the break, and the team to stop chasing. Eventually Beltran was the leader on the road, so the other teams had to chase, which gave us an easy day. But there again, you have to have the riders. I had to have Beltran in a high overall position,' he says.

Jan Ullrich pushed Armstrong the hardest in 2003, and he and Bruyneel always point to it being their toughest Tour. Ullrich never had the ability that Lance Armstrong had to focus entirely on bike racing. He could do it for short stretches, but he needed time away from his bike. Armstrong's first autobiography is called *It's Not About the Bike*, but in his Tour-winning years it was, it was all about the bike, 365 days a year, and it governed everything he did. Even working for his cancer charity Livestrong, and on the many public appearances that entails, Armstrong would want to know where and when he could sneak in a bike ride. He trained all the time, and then in the run-up to a Tour he trained manically, even to the point of weighing out his food.

Jan Ullrich never did that. In May 2002 his private life went totally off the rails and he was arrested for drunk driving. A month later he was busted for ecstasy and amphetamine use after he'd been partying on the stuff in a nightclub. His team, Team Telekom, sacked him, and he was given a six-month suspension by the cycling authorities, who drew the distinction that he'd not been using the drugs in a race, or he would have got much longer.

However, Ullrich came out of that with more focus. He started a team with his agent and advisor, Rudi Pevenage, who seemed to have more empathy with, and get more from, the German than the Telekom boss, Walter Godefroot. Their initial team sponsor folded before the Tour started, but the bike manufacturer Bianchi took their place, so Ullrich went into the 2003 race wearing the colours and jersey design of Fausto Coppi, who had his best years with Bianchi.

Ullrich started shakily, but put 90 seconds into Armstrong during the first time trial stage, which was run off in terrible heat. Armstrong led with Ullrich less than a minute behind going into the second mountain section, the Pyrenees. There the German clawed back 19 seconds on the first day and moved to just 15 seconds behind Armstrong.

Next day Ullrich looked even stronger when he dropped Armstrong half-way up the Tourmalet, but Armstrong fought back. Then Armstrong's handlebars clipped a baseball cap being held by a young spectator, who was stood on the inside of a bend, and he fell. Amazingly, Ullrich waited, and somehow contrived to lose 40 seconds to a rejuvenated Armstrong on the final climb to Luz Ardiden. Would Armstrong have waited, though?

Another big difference came in the final time trial between Pornic and Nantes. Ullrich was still only just over one minute behind Armstrong, the closest he or anyone had been to him at this stage of a Tour since his comeback. Armstrong was struggling, Ullrich was in better form, and on this flat route he was maybe, just maybe, the better time triallist. But Ullrich crashed on a wet roundabout.

Armstrong didn't and won the Tour. Armstrong had ridden this time trial weeks before. Ullrich hadn't. Armstrong rode the time trial course twice that morning, just to make sure it was in his head. Ullrich drove it once in the Bianchi team car. For Lance Armstrong cycling was 24/7. For Jan Ullrich it wasn't.

Neither did Ullrich inspire dedication from his team. In fact Johan Bruyneel thinks that they often undermined him:

> I think the way they went into the Tour with Ullrich, Kloden and Vinokourov displayed a lack of confidence in Ullrich. It's not a bad tactic to have other good riders attack, but in my mind that tactic undermined Jan. OK, one year Vinokourov attacked, and then Kloden, and we suffered, but Ullrich was also suffering.
>
> The good riders should have remained with Ullrich to help him. That is what we did mostly in our team. OK, we liked ambitious riders, but when we were in the Tour there was no room for personal ambitions, especially in the last three or four years for Lance. We had to win those Tours, second place would have been a disaster.

Armstrong dominated again in 2004, winning his sixth consecutive Tour to shatter the glass ceiling that had pegged the top Tour winners, Anquetil, Merckx, Hinault and Indurain at five. In terms of victories he was the number one Tour de France rider of all time, and he had become its most famous winner, and maybe the most controversial, at least in the way he divided those who followed cycling.

Suspicion that he took performance-enhancing drugs dogged each one of Armstrong's victories. Given that some riders who finished behind him were caught doing just that, the Tour's history with doping, and rumours that the testing protocols in use at the time could be sidestepped, it wasn't too hard a suspicion to hold.

The journalists David Walsh and Pierre Ballester certainly believed so. Just before the 2004 Tour they published a book in France called *LA Confidential*. It was scheduled to come out in English later in the year and Walsh, who was a senior sports writer for the *Sunday Times*, wrote an article in that paper implying that Armstrong had taken drugs to enhance his performance. Or at least that is what Mr Justice Gray said he'd done when Armstrong sued the *Sunday Times*. Gray rejected the paper's argument that the words used by Walsh conveyed no more than the existence of reasonable grounds to suspect. The *Sunday Times* issued an apology to Armstrong, stating that it never intended to accuse him of taking any performance-enhancing drugs. The book was never printed in English.

However, it was the big talking point at the start of the 2004 Tour, and it got to Armstrong. He is very competitive, like every other great sportsman or woman, competitive to the point of being a pain in the arse. That's normal, but Armstrong relishes it and he'll take on anyone, whether they are riding a bike or not. Maybe he doesn't go as far as looking for a fight, but if someone wants one – well, bring it on. A fight seems to inspire him, to give him the energy to surpass his physical ability. At least that is one of my pet theories, so in 2005 I put it to Bruyneel.

I asked him if Armstrong needs a problem to bring out his best racing. It was no secret that he called those who'd written bad things about him 'Trolls'. He implied that they were trying to bring him down, that whatever he did he could do no right for them. So I asked Bruyneel if Armstrong actually needed the Trolls to bring out his best.

He recognised what I was saying immediately, because he smiled and said: 'I could see something different to normal in him in 2004. He wanted to win everything in the Tour, and that was because he was angry at people. There was a quote in a paper just before the Tour about *LA Confidential*. It said something like "Armstrong is not even going to be able to get on his bike and ride, never mind win the Tour." That made him really angry, and when he is really angry he can do more.'

But Armstrong's battles were also wearing, with too much collateral damage on all sides to go into here. Despite his detractors, by 2005 Lance Armstrong was huge, a giant global brand and very influential, especially in the fight against cancer. On a personal level his first marriage had ended and he was in a relationship with the rock singer Sheryl Crow. 'Two people with big lives,' he was fond of saying, intimating that he had a soul mate who could understand him and his world and was part of it.

Still, bike racing was tough for Armstrong at the beginning of 2005. He was a world celebrity, admirers fawned on one side, and a lesser but noisier number of detractors snapped at him from the other. There was talk of him running for public office, even the presidency one day. But Armstrong was contracted to ride another Tour within the next two years, and a lot of people he cared about depended on him doing that for their living. What is more, he couldn't lose the Tour. Not only would that have damaged the Armstrong brand but, I suspect more important to Armstrong himself, it would have taken the shine off the Armstrong story. If he was going to win in 2005 or

2006 he had to pay his training and racing dues, and that meant, when the 2005 racing season began, lining up in a grey and glacial Paris suburb on a Sunday in March for the start of Paris–Nice.

Those first racing kilometres of 2005 were a huge shock. He was fit, training was still the number one priority, even in his new jet-set life with Sheryl Crow, but this was different. This was reality. A reality made up of fast racing with ambitious young pros who were up to 12 or 13 years younger and knew no fear. Win-hungry Belgians, proud French and Italians, Eastern Europeans who had been brought up in little more than a shed and were hungry for money. It was like Muhammad Ali taking on allcomers in bare-knuckle fights at the county fair.

After a few days Armstrong succumbed to a cold, which was his ticket out of Paris–Nice, but the experience was enough to show him that this year was going to be tough, and his taste for tough had gone, albeit, as time has proved, only temporarily. At home in Texas, Armstrong considered his options. The contract his team had with Discovery Channel, who had replaced US Postal, specified that he had to race the 2005 or 2006 Tour. 'There were options,' Bruyneel reveals. 'We talked about missing the Tour in 2005 and going for the Classics and the world hour record, then doing the Tour in 2006.' But after thinking long and hard, Armstrong decided to get it over with and do the Tour in 2005.

Johan Bruyneel had a big input in that decision. 'For me it was impossible to imagine Lance in a season without the Tour de France. He would go crazy. So in the end we said, "Look, you have to do one Tour de France and so many things can happen between now and 2006. It's just crazy to plan like that. Why not do the Tour de France this year, try to win it and finish?" That is what I wanted from the start. We had been through a lot of things, and it wasn't the races any more that were hard, it was the other things. I think that Lance had become too big for cycling.'

Jan Ullrich was again Armstrong's biggest rival on paper for 2005, but a freak crash 24 hours before the start, which unusually was a 19-kilometre time trial, left the German injured and below his best. As the runner-up in 2004 Ullrich started a minute in front of Armstrong, and the Texan, realising that he could land a good punch on his big rival on the opening day, rode like a man possessed. He finished second in the stage and caught Ullrich. Then he set about his other rivals.

'Our tactic was always to focus on our rivals,' Bruyneel explains. 'A lot happens in three weeks so you have to be adaptable, but you know who the best are so it makes sense to focus on them. For 2005 the best were Lance, Ullrich, Ivan Basso and Vinokourov. If you see one of those in trouble, you go to eliminate them. Of course you take stronger action if you see Ullrich with problems than Vinokourov.'

That plan was inexorably put into action in 2005 and Armstrong slowly but inevitably emerged as the best, capping his performance by winning the last time trial of the race. It was an emotional end in Paris, the end of an era for Armstrong and for all the people who were involved in the sport, but Armstrong looked glad to be getting out.

18. ANOTHER TOUR, ANOTHER CONTROVERSY

When he was 12 years old Floyd Landis told his fishing buddies in Famersville, Lancaster County, Pennsylvania, that he was going to win the Tour de France. In 2006 he did just that, and then became the first Tour winner since Maurice Garin back in 1903 to have the title stripped from him.

Landis was raised as a Menonnite. His upbringing was good, holy even, but totally unworldly. That's not a problem; I think that the world could use some more unworldly people. The problem for Landis started when something reached into the psyche of this unworldly kid and called him to be a professional bike racer, because that was a clash of cultures if ever there was one.

Nothing could stop him. Landis lined up for his first race wearing sweat pants because his religion forbade him to show his legs. The other kids couldn't stop laughing, until the flag dropped to start. Landis killed them, winning by many minutes, his sweaty red face wreathed in a smile. He was on his way.

Landis was good, his friends knew that, and you might have thought that his father would be very happy that his teenage son had found a healthy outlet for his excess energy, but that was not Paul Landis's way. He believed in exercise, yes, but exercise as a means to an end, and that meant work that produced something. Cycling was play, frivolous and pointless. If it was exercise his son wanted then he could do extra jobs on the farm.

But that didn't work either. Landis obeyed his father and did the jobs, and when their house was quiet at night he climbed out of the window, slid down a drainpipe and went riding alone in the dark. Sometimes he was out from ten until two o'clock in the morning. Then one day someone told Paul Landis that he'd seen his son riding at night, but instead of confronting him, Mr Landis was intrigued and wanted to find out more. He waited for him and followed his son at a discreet distance, suspecting that alcohol or undesirable friends, maybe even a girl, were at the root of his son's nocturnal rides. But they weren't; Floyd just rode and rode and rode alone for hours in the dark. His father was impressed, and relaxed a little about what was obviously his son's passion.

Paul Landis dropped the extra chores. Floyd trained more and became the American junior mountain bike champion. Then, when he was 20, Landis moved to Southern California to train with other mountain bikers. But California is a centre for road racers too, and Landis was soon giving them a hard time. He started winning road races and turned professional for an American team that raced partly there and partly in Europe. Eventually Landis was recruited into the US Postal squad of Lance Armstrong.

His first Tour de France was in 2002, when Landis became a crucial part of the 'blue train' that set the pace for Lance Armstrong. He speciality was climbing, but Landis was good everywhere, so good that he began thinking of going for the Tour on his own. He did one last one for Armstrong in 2004, when he proved to be his strongest team-mate, and then accepted an offer from the Phonak team to lead their squad.

Landis finished ninth in the 2005 Tour, and with Armstrong out of the way set about training for 2006 with a vengeance. Early in the year he won the Tour of California and was so good that he prompted no less an authority that Eddy Merckx to predict that Landis would win the 2006 Tour de France.

Landis did win, but a few days later he entered a world of controversy that he has no head for. Before I go into that, however, consider what a physically tough guy Floyd Landis is. Training for three or four hours every night, pulling extra jobs in the day because all he wanted to do was race his bike – for a teenager not to rail against that kind of life, not to question it even, indicates a remarkable character. Then there was Landis's hip. An old fracture to the head of his femur that didn't heal properly had caused osteonecrosis in the joint, making a hip replacement inevitable sooner or later. By the 2006 Tour bone was rubbing on bone, but Landis didn't tell anyone until the race was well under way because he didn't want to appear weak. He described his symptoms then as 'pain, constant pain. It's better in a morning and gets worse during the day. By evening it hurts from my hip to my knee, some-times stabbing, sometimes more of an arthritis pain. It hurts when I walk and it hurts when I ride.'

Pain or not, by stage 16 Landis led the Tour but then had an incredibly bad day in the heat, losing eight minutes and seemingly any chance of winning the race. Stage 17 was from St-Jean-de-Maurienne to Morzine and Landis had a plan, or rather he'd been given one by the physiol-ogist who helped to train him, Dr Alan Lim. 'The key in endurance sport is getting oxygen to the muscles,' Lim explains.

> Oxygen is transported by the blood, but when the air temperature around the athlete is high, blood is used to carry heat away from the body by radiation through the skin. This means that less blood, so less oxygen goes to the working muscles and the rider's power output drops. What I said Floyd should do was attack and ride hard on his own, but his team would keep getting cooled bottles of water to him. Some he'd drink to keep hydrated, but the rest he'd pour over himself. That would help him lose heat through the evaporation of the water instead of radiation by blood, so more blood would go to his muscles. The riders chasing behind wouldn't get access to as much water, so where Floyd could stay thermoneutral and keep his power output up, the others would struggle to do that and their power would drop.

And that is what Landis did. He raced alone, drinking or showering the contents of 55 bottles of water that his team car supplied over his head and body. He won the stage and took back almost all of the time he lost the previous day. It looked incredible, unbelievable even, but according to a report in the *New York Times* afterwards Lim revealed that Landis averaged 280 watts as his power output for the stage, where he had averaged higher than that for an effort of similar length in training.

Landis was now less than half a minute behind the race leader Oscar Pereiro, and he took back that and more in the final time trial to win the Tour. The race finished on 23 July, and four days later news broke that Landis had provided a positive dope test for testosterone on stage 17, when he had performed his incredible comeback. He said he would be exonerated and asked for the B sample to be tested. All urine tests are separated into two identical phials and the rider concerned decides which sample is labelled A or B. If following a positive result the athlete asks for the B sample to be tested, then both samples have to be positive for any sanctions to be applied.

Unfortunately for his case, and making it difficult for anyone to take what he subsequently said seriously, Landis then came out with a ludicrous explanation for the high testosterone reading, saying that he had been dehydrated due to drinking whisky on the night of stage 16. He later recanted that story, saying that the Spanish lawyers acting for him had told him to say it. What did I say about being unworldly?

Still, Landis fought like a tiger to defend his case. Testosterone is a natural substance in the body, a male hormone that controls, among other things, muscle repair. It can be naturally high, and often is in top sports people as quick muscle repair is a big natural advantage for them to have. The critical figure to measure in a dope test is the ratio of testosterone to epitestosterone. Four to one is the maximum allowable; Landis's ratio in the stage 17 sample was 11 to one. Further investigation revealed that some of the testosterone was exogenous, or from an external source. He was banned from cycling for two years and eventually stripped of the 2006 Tour title, Oscar Pereiro being declared the winner.

The case has died down now, most fans are bored with it, but Landis still won't admit that he took drugs. He's appeared on TV chat shows to explain his innocence, cast doubt on testing procedures and appealed to every arbitration body in sport, without success. And because of that it is hard to bring the case to an end. You would think that with his upbringing Landis would find it difficult to maintain a lie for as long as, and to the extent that, he has. However, he's so uncomfortable when he talks about his doping case that he looks as if he's lying, or is that his unworldliness again? Then there is his family; they haven't lost faith in him, and Paul Landis is still his son's biggest fan, encouraging his return to the sport once Landis's ban ended, even though his worst fears of his son being led into drugs look to have come true. The Landis case is a salutary lesson in what happens when the unworldly get involved with something as worldly as the Tour de France.

And so to 2007 and to another intense athlete who was hell-bent on winning the Tour de France. Michael Rasmussen was a world mountain bike champion who, unhappy that his branch of cycling had an earnings ceiling, switched to road racing in 2001, taking an initial pay cut in the hope of gaining much more.

Rasmussen has scary eyes that are capable of looking right through you, but they don't seem to have a colour or substance themselves. I've known a number of people with eyes like that, and they've all been trouble! He is Mr Intense, not given to smiling, who lived and breathed cycling. When he realised that winning the Tour de France was within his grasp he turned all his intensity into doing just that.

He is painfully skinny. It's a natural skinniness that some people just have, but Rasmussen worked on it too. In top form he weighed just 59 kilograms for his one metre 74 height. He was so skeletal that doctors wouldn't need an X-ray to check him for a suspected broken bone, they could just hold him up to the light. He even applied his weight-saving focus to his bike, peeling off excess stickers and only having one bottle cage on it. Rasmussen wouldn't even wear one of the rubber wristbands that were fashionable for promoting various causes in the pro peloton in 2007, and he shaved off all of his hair.

Not surprisingly, Rasmussen was a gifted climber, and because of the bike handling skills he learned as a mountain biker he could descend mountains too. Floyd Landis was the same, and so is another former mountain bike world champion and Tour podium placer, Cadel Evans.

Rasmussen first raced in the Tour in 2004, when he finished third in the King of the Mountains competition. In 2005 he won the competition and a stage, and might have been third overall but for a disastrous time trial. He was King of the Mountains again in 2006, winning another epic mountain stage and succumbing to mountain madness by having polka-dots on every stitch of clothing he wore, and even on his bike.

He won stage eight of the 2007 Tour from Le Grand Bornand to Tignes, taking the yellow and polka-dot jerseys. As the race progressed from there it emerged that Rasmussen and a young Spanish racer called Alberto Contador, who was coming back from a life-threatening cerebral vascular disorder that required delicate and very risky surgery in 2004, were the best two riders in the race.

They were both climbers, and battles between climbers are spectacular. On one stage they ripped into each other to such effect that they were the only two together on the road, and were almost coming to a standstill between taking it in turns to mount the sort of ferocious uphill attacks that only true climbers can do.

Contador tried but he couldn't break Rasmussen that day, and with four stages to go the Dane led his Spanish rival by just over three minutes. But just when Rasmussen's narrow-minded obsession looked like paying off, his past caught up with him. Athletes who want to be considered for the Olympic Games, and all cyclists now at top level, have to adhere to a strict 'whereabouts' policy. They have to inform the doping authorities of where they will be for a certain number of hours on every single day of their lives, so that they can be visited in surprise, out-of-competition dope tests, which everyone agrees is the best way to police doping.

This arose because it was discovered that as testing at races grew more sophisticated, EPO, growth hormones, testosterone and other drugs were being used less in competition and more in training, where their effect is to allow athletes to train harder and recover quickly so they can train hard again, and so do a greater volume of work. And in endurance sports work equals results.

Anyway, it slowly emerged during the Tour that Rasmussen had been struck off the Danish Olympic list because of missed out-of-competition dope tests. That means the testers were where he said he'd be at a time and place he specified, but he wasn't or was otherwise unavailable to them. Then came the news that one of his missed dope tests had occurred when he was supposed to be training in Mexico. One person who read that, David Cassani, an Italian TV reporter who had been a top pro racer, thought it odd because he had seen Rasmussen training in Italy on the date when he'd missed the Mexican test.

Rasmussen's answer was to deny everything. He said that the missed dope tests were an administrative mistake and that Cassani was wrong, he hadn't seen Rasmussen in Italy at all. The Tour de France had a go at the UCI for leaking this story during the race, which they said was done because they and the UCI were in dispute about a number of matters at the time. And nobody could work out whether Rasmussen's team, Rabobank, knew about the problem or not, and whether they were just hoping to get to Paris before the whole thing blew up in their faces. Although I don't know what difference it would have made if the news had broken after Rasmussen had won, except that a second consecutive Tour winner could have been stripped of his title. But this race does turn people's heads and they do the craziest things.

It was a mess. Once the story was out, Rasmussen was withdrawn from the Tour by Rabobank, then fired. His in-laws, who lived in Mexico, weighed in to say that they had been visited by him during the time he said he was there, but they couldn't give him an alibi for the date when Cassani saw him in Italy. Rabobank's directeur sportif, Theo De Rooy, nearly had a nervous breakdown because he told the press that Rasmussen had admitted to him that he'd been in Italy when Cassani said he was, but then Rasmussen denied it. There was even a story going around that Rasmussen had tried to get someone to smuggle a product into Europe for him that could have been used in doping in 2002, which he denied and continues to do so.

Then in November 2007, after months of speculation, Rasmussen made this statement in a press conference. 'First of all I would like to clearly state that I was not in Mexico in June. I have therefore misinformed both the UCI and the public. It is, however, important for me to stress that at no point did I lie to team Rabobank.' He went on to explain that it was for marital and private reasons that he didn't tell the truth, although he wouldn't expand on what they were. Rasmussen continues to deny taking or importing banned performance-enhancing substances.

He was suspended by the UCI for breaches of the 'whereabouts' procedure, but he also sued Rabobank for unfair dismissal. In 2008 he was awarded two months' salary by a judge in Utrecht, who stated that while Rabobank were entitled to sack Rasmussen, they should have given him two months' notice.

If the affair hadn't been so sad it would have been funny, at least a Dutch comedy show thought so. They did a sketch in which a skinny bald guy was cycling along a road in Italy wearing Rabobank team kit and followed by a Rabobank team car. The phone rings in the car and the driver leans out and shouts, 'Michael, it's the UCI.' At this point everyone stops in the road and a full Mariachi band gets out of the car, crowds around the cyclist and begins to play. Then you hear the skinny guy say, 'Yes, this is Michael Rasmussen. Yes, I am in Mexico.' Some aspects of the Tour de France had become a bad a joke.

With Rasmussen out of the way the 2007 race was won by Alberto Contador, who at 24 was the youngest winner for a long time. He was racing for Lance Armstrong's old team, Discovery Channel, and was their team manager Johan Bruyneel's sixth Tour success, and the first without Armstrong. Bruyneel had known Contador for a while, and he knew he had the talent to win the Tour one day, but this was early.

Sean Yates was impressed too. He was the directeur sportif under Bruyneel for the 2007 Tour and couldn't believe how much pressure Contador absorbed. 'I followed him on the morning of the final time trial. He was 24, he had the yellow jersey and there was all this stuff going on around the Tour. You can't imagine the pressure that was on his shoulders. It would have got to me when I was a mature pro, but it didn't worry Alberto at all. The Tour victory was just down the road, all he had to do was his best ever time trial, and that is exactly what he did,' says Yates, who was professionally impressed.

The 1998 Tour was the worst, and it was bad when Landis was stripped in 2006, but in 2007 the Tour de France appeared to be as close to meltdown as at any time in its history. Alexandre Vinokourov was found to have used blood doping during the race, which involves taking blood from the body some time before the race and pumping it back in when it was needed to carry extra oxygen. Ivan Basso, the runner-up in 2005, had been implicated in Operation Puerto, a blood-doping ring run by a doctor in Spain, as had Jan Ullrich and a number of other Tour racers, so they weren't there. Nearly everywhere you looked there was bad news, but then something clicked and pro cycling woke up to the fact that it could not continue as it was.

Sean Yates again: 'There was a meeting of the teams at the end of the season, lots of things were discussed and for the first time there was agreement about everything. In the past it was all posturing, like "I'm not doing this because he did that in 1986" and stuff like that. Most of the directeurs sportifs are ex-pros and some even carried grudges from their racing days. Finally, though, in that meeting, they saw that the end of pro racing was in sight. I mean, our team had come to the end of its contract with Discovery Channel and we had the Tour winner in it, and we couldn't find a sponsor, so what did that tell you?'

It had long been said that the policing of doping was one thing, and that had to be kept up and intensified, but you would only rid cycling of doping if the riders changed the way they played the game. What Yates is suggesting is that at the end of 2007 pro bike racing realised that it couldn't carry on as it had done and it had to put its own house in order, it had to make a group effort to clean up its act. Several teams signed up to internal doping controls to monitor their own men, as well as willingly accepting every measure the authorities wanted.

Not everyone was ready to do it in 2008, as Bernard Kohl, Stefan Schumacher, Ricardo Ricco, Leonardo Piepoli, Moises Duenas and Manuel Beltran proved, but their doping was so in-your-face, reckless almost, that the sport is well rid of them. They were never going to get away with what they were doing under current testing procedures. Let's hope they were the last of the old 'we are pros leave us alone' resistance against dope-free cycling.

In that light maybe the 2008 Tour de France was a turning point. A lot of stars were absent again, some through no direct fault of their own. It was an interesting race nonetheless that boiled down to a battle between the Australian ex-mountain biker Cadel Evans, Frank Schleck from Luxembourg and a Spaniard, Carlos Sastre. The extra problem Evans faced was that his two big competitors were from the same team, CSC, while his, a Belgian outfit called Predictor-Lotto, was hopeless at helping him in this Tour.

Evans is a bit of a one-off in cycling. You don't get to be a pro if you are thick, but in the main a pro bike rider's intelligence is down at the cunning end of the spectrum. Evans's is at the thoughtful and artistic end. He's well read, his wife, Chiara, isn't an ex-model as many pro racers' WAGS tend to be, but an Italian concert pianist. He's quiet, with a thin, piping voice, and he gets dewy-eyed when he talks about his dog, Molly, who comes with Chiara to visit him on Tour de France rest days. Evans was born in the Australian outback, but this is no Crocodile Dundee, although underneath he is a bit of a toughie.

The race was still close by the final day in the mountains, by the final mountain in fact, and that was L'Alpe d'Huez. Evans was there in third behind Frank Schleck, who had the yellow jersey, and Carlos Sastre was lying fourth. Any one of them could win, but Evans more than anyone else knew what was coming. He was in a Team CSC sandwich and was going to get attacked by them in turn. If he answered the attacks, he'd get beaten; if he didn't, he'd get beaten. Evans was going to get beaten, and that must have crossed Carlos Sastre's mind when he went first.

Sastre is a good climber but not so good in a time trial. If he was going to win the Tour he needed a big lead going into the time trial that was left. Is that why he went early, or was he playing the good team man? I ask because when Evans didn't react Schleck couldn't, because Sastre was his team-mate, and hauling Evans back up to him would have been a professional no-no. It was a canny move, and Sastre put in a virtuoso performance on the Alpe to leapfrog into the yellow jersey and virtually win the Tour with one ascent of L'Alpe d'Huez.

If you look at the 2008 Tour in the light of Kohl and Schumacher et al, then the race was a failure, but the mood coming out of it didn't feel like that. The Tour, instead of wringing its hands in agonised apology over the positive tests, patted itself on the back. The Tour director, Christian Prudhomme, who took over from Jean-Marie Leblanc in 2005, stated that the positive results were evidence that they were winning the war against doping.

There was no sympathy from any of the many Tour racers I know for Kohl and his mates. A year later, with no positive dope test results at all from the 2009 race, there is reason to believe that the war is being won, but these are early days.

You have to admit, though, the Tour is never dull. Warts and all, it's been over 100 years of intrigue, bravery, death, triumph, beauty and disgrace. To coin a phrase, you couldn't make up the Tour's 100-year script if you tried.

19. ARMSTRONG'S COMEBACK AND BEYOND

Even though Carlos Sastre won the 2008 Tour de France, Alberto Contador was still the biggest name in cycling. Sastre was a worthy and very popular winner, but a big factor in the 2008 Tour was who was missing. There was no Ivan Basso, no Jan Ullrich, no Michael Rasmussen and no Astana team – so no Alberto Contador, who had gone to the team after Discovery Channel ended their cycling sponsorship. Contador did the only thing left to him and won the Giro and Vuelta, two Grand Tours in the same year, taking his total to three in two years, and he was still only 26.

But then a rumour began to rattle around cycling: Lance Armstrong was coming back. At first no one believed it, even those close to him, including Johan Bruyneel. Once he'd made up his mind, Armstrong contacted Bruyneel, who was now in charge at Astana and busy trying to rehabilitate its reputation after Alexandre Vinokourov's expulsion from the 2007 Tour. The team were persona non grata to the 2008 Tour, but it was widely expected that they would be returning in 2009, and Armstrong was only coming back to ride the Tour.

'I didn't know what to think, and at first I was a bit worried when I heard what Lance wanted to do,' Bruyneel admits. 'It was unprecedented. This was Lance, but I wondered if even he could do it. But when I went to Austin and met him and saw him riding there, I knew he was serious and that he could ride at a good level again.'

When Bruyneel and Armstrong met in Texas the comeback was still a rumour to outsiders, but a growing one. Armstrong made the official announcement in a video message on his Livestrong cancer charity site, and the media frenzy began, with Armstrong looking to win hearts and minds. The reason he gave for his comeback was to increase cancer awareness in the countries where he would race, and he underlined this intention by announcing that he would take part in Australia's Tour Down Under stage race in January 2009. He had never raced in Australia before, and it would be his comeback race, so the publicity would be huge.

Before that, though, Armstrong had to meet the European media, and there was a lot to resolve. Why had he come back? Would he be competitive? How was it going to work out in Astana between him and Alberto Contador? And what about those urine samples from the 1999 Tour de France?

The first three questions were easy. Officially his comeback was the global cancer awareness campaign, but I believe that was a trade he'd done with himself. He missed racing, missed the competition and simply wanted the buzz back in his life. Armstrong told me at Astana's December 2008 training camp in Tenerife that he made his decision to try for the Tour during the Leadville 100 mountain bike race in the Rocky Mountains. 'It starts with the blast of a cannon, which is different, and from the moment that cannon went off I became totally immersed in racing and realised how much I had missed it. I had trained for Leadville, going away to concentrate on cycling by training at altitude, and I enjoyed the single-minded simplicity of that. By the end of Leadville I wanted to race at a high level again,' he said.

The question of whether he could be competitive had been resolved before his return was announced. Armstrong is a numbers man and he'd been in the lab to see if his numbers still added up. Cycling is physics, and if you can put out x watts per kilogram of body weight in a test then you will be able to keep up with the pro bunch, x+1 watts per kilo and you might place well, x+2 and you'll be further up the finish list. Armstrong was already at x + plenty; he doesn't guess. And the Alberto Contador question? Well, the races would decide who was strongest and would be team leader. The problem was the fourth question, those 1999 samples, and it wouldn't go away.

It all came about through an article that appeared in *L'Equipe* shortly after Armstrong stopped racing in 2005. A test for EPO was introduced at the 2000 Tour de France, which then evolved and became more sophisticated as the years went by. Then in 2005 a secret research project authorised by the World Anti-Doping Agency (WADA) tested urine samples that had been kept frozen from the 1999 Tour de France. The reason given was that this analysis would help WADA further refine its EPO test. However, someone at the Paris laboratory leaked the fact that some of the samples had tested positive for EPO to a journalist from *L'Equipe*, and they gave the journalist the unique code numbers that related to the riders concerned.

Testing labs never know whose sample they are testing. Each sample simply has a number, which is issued and held by the world cycling authority, the UCI. When the journalist took the numbers there he found that some of the positive samples belonged to Lance Armstrong.

L'Equipe wrote up their evidence under the headline 'Armstrong's Lie' in August 2005. They had the smoking gun they'd been looking for, proof that Armstrong had taken EPO, or had they? Argument raged with eminent scientists on both sides, some saying the evidence was good, and others doubting the validity of testing samples that had been frozen for so long on a number of levels. And, although some would say that this is a technicality, the evidence of those samples was not strong enough to bring a case against Armstrong for doping anyway.

The UCI condemned the *L'Equipe* piece and commissioned an independent investigation by the former head of the Netherlands anti-doping agency, Emile Vrijman. His conclusion was that the analysis results didn't constitute evidence of anything. He also stated, 'Representatives of the LNDD (the lab that carried out the research) concluded on their own that the right answer to whether the alleged "positive" urine samples constituted "adverse analytical findings" was an unqualified no.'

But as soon as Armstrong announced his comeback he was questioned repeatedly about the 1999 samples. All he did, and all he could do really in view of the possible legal ramifications of saying anything different, was refer to the Vrijman report. Given the detail of what was said in the report it was impossible to debate outside of that. Then it was suggested that if Armstrong had nothing to fear he should allow the Paris samples to be tested again, independently if he wanted that. A journalist suggested it at the Astana press conference Armstrong did in Tenerife, and Armstrong's reply was illuminating: 'Oh, come on. There isn't one person in this room that would sign up to that offer. Those samples have been open. Not one of you would do that.' But strangely, very few newspapers printed it.

He was being tested by WADA and the UCI almost weekly, but to appease his critics he announced that he would instigate an independent testing regime, which eventually he didn't do. He has been castigated for that in the press, but it could also be viewed that he was naive to suggest it in the first place. Given the amount of times he was being tested by the official bodies, what would it have proved? Some authorities, like the Italian coach Aldo Sassi, think independent testing actually undermines the official tests. 'I know many good teams do it nowadays, but what message does it give about the official testing procedure? They would be better to put money into improving and tightening that up,' Sassi reckons.

But at the end of all the hype and push and pull with the media, Armstrong was back as a pro athlete and was going to see if he could cut it at almost 38 years old in the most demanding race in the world, the Tour de France. He had kept in good shape since 2005, running marathons and riding his bike a lot, but the task he'd taken on was huge.

Armstrong had been working out like many 30-something fitness enthusiasts, albeit a slightly driven one, with a mix of running, swimming, bike and weights in the gym. Doing that had built some upper body muscle, which he had to lose before the Tour, but he wasn't the only one busy doing that in January 2009. In Britain Bradley Wiggins was about to get serious, and I mean really serious, about road racing for the first time in his life.

Wiggins was a hugely talented part of Great Britain's success story in track cycling. He has won multiple gold medals at world championships and the Olympic Games in the individual and team pursuit. He was a great track madison racer too, one of the best ever. But a lot of people who know what they are talking about thought Wiggins could do more. Barry Hoban was one of them. 'The old managers used to say give me a world pursuit champion and I'll give you back a world road champion in a couple of years, but sometimes it seems like Bradley can't be bothered,' he said in 2008.

Because the competition pool is bigger in pro road racing there is a feeling in cycling that road racing has more of a cachet than the track. Old racers like Hoban, a good pursuit rider himself by the way, and the millions of fans of road racing see the single-day Classics, the Grand Tours, and most of all the Tour de France as being the jewels in the crown of cycle sport, and far more prestigious than the track. To them it looked as if Wiggins was selling his talent short.

One of the men closest to the Wiggins story is British Cycling's head coach, Shane Sutton. This is his view of the pre-2009 Bradley Wiggins: 'I always maintained that he had a gift but never wrapped it very well. He had the ability to be one of the best road riders in the world, and he said he wanted to do that. From being a kid he said that he wanted to be one of the legends of the sport, but he had to go out there and do it. In 2009 he proved that he could.'

It had been evolving in his head over a number of years, but Wiggins really bought into the idea of having a proper go on the road over the winter of 2008–09. The easiest way to cycling fame in Britain had been through Olympic success, but that has bred an increased awareness of road racing in the general public. Mark Cavendish was also a factor, in that for a while Wiggins was in the same team and there he had used his gift of sustained speed to set the pace in the final kilometres for Cavendish's sprint to win in stages of the Tour de France and the Giro.

Sutton recalls that 'Bradley got consistently involved at the sharp end of races for the first time when he was leading out Mark in the sprints. He stuck out his elbows and fought hard, like you have to. With the track on a back burner in 2009, he had a good road training winter for the first time. He also began to look at losing weight and slowly bought into the ideas we had to make him a better road racer.'

Those ideas came from the coaches and staff of British Cycling, and not many people outside that circle knew how serious Wiggins was taking the road. And no one except them knew that the race he was taking seriously was the Tour de France.

In many respects Armstrong and Wiggins were in the same boat in the spring of 2009. Wiggins had to lose the upper body muscle that all track riders have because of the blistering starts they have to make, and Armstrong had to lose what he'd put on in the gym. Slowly but surely their weight dropped, while their power to weight ratio, the key to Tour success, began to increase.

But then Armstrong had a huge setback when he crashed and broke his collarbone in a Spanish race shortly before the Giro d'Italia. He had already raced much more in 2009 than during his previous Tour dominance, partly because of the cancer campaign but partly because he needed his race reflexes back, and he needed to feel comfortable in a big group again. For all the crucial moments in the Tour, all the searing attacks in the mountains and all the intense concentration of a time trial, there are many more hours of riding in the peloton, and those hours need to have zero cost. If a rider isn't comfortable in the swooping, flicking mass of riders just moving around in the Tour, then he will become exhausted quickly, mentally as much as physically. Riding in the peloton, sensing its moods and thoughts, must be second nature, and the only way of doing that is to race, a lot.

The collarbone was a tough break, literally. On the surface Armstrong was very matter of fact, as he would be, but beneath he had doubts. Sean Yates, who was a surrogate elder brother to Armstrong way back when the American was a new pro in the Motorola team, and in 2009 was a directeur sportif with Astana, reveals what was going on. 'Lance didn't think it was going to happen after he broke his collarbone. He didn't think he'd be ready for the Tour and I think he thought about stopping the project, but Johan spent a lot of time talking and e-mailing him and he got things back on course,' he says.

Armstrong returned to training as soon as possible. He started the Giro lacking condition but got stronger throughout the three weeks. The collarbone had cost him, but he knew he'd be competitive in the Tour. Now the overriding question was who would lead the Astana team.

Or at least it was in the minds of journalists. Armstrong had said all along that Contador was the best racer in the world, but that didn't stop him playing mind games. Right from the first training camp the Astana riders gravitated towards Armstrong and away from Contador. They probably didn't know it, but their body language betrayed it. Riding in groups, at the dinner table, having photographs taken, Armstrong was dead centre and Contador on the edge. It was subtle, and maybe Contador wasn't even aware of it, but Armstrong would have been. He's a Grand Master at this kind of stuff.

By Tour time Armstrong was still under-prepared. Not ideal, because the 2009 Tour had a very testing start. The usual short prologue time trial was replaced by a longer effort around the hilly terrain of Monaco. The old Armstrong would have liked to get a good punch in early, but this time he had to make do. The fast-cadence pedalling was still there, but the top-end power wasn't, and Armstrong lost 22 seconds to Contador.

And that was the story of the 2009 Tour really. Armstrong was cannier than his young team-mate. He didn't lose time on a difficult stage in crosswinds, which Contador did. He slowly took over the team, which he'd been working on doing all year, leaving Contador almost out in the cold. The thing was, though, that Contador was better, which is why he not only won the 2009 Tour but never once looked like losing it.

Armstrong finished third, an incredible performance for a 37-year-old on a comeback after three years out, and announced that he will return in 2010 with a new team, Radio Shack, that will be all about him; as if Astana wasn't. Andy Schleck, Frank's brother, finished second overall, the Luxembourg rider proving that he can almost match Contador in the mountains but is nowhere near him in a time trial. And the story of the 2009 Tour for British cycling fans was the fourth place of Bradley Wiggins.

It was an interesting result to what, if looked at coldly, wasn't an interesting Tour. The organisers liked the cliffhanger finish on L'Alpe d'Huez in 2008, so they contrived to create another in 2009. They gave the race a toughish start, but softened the middle bit, then made the last part just a run-in to Mont Ventoux, which was the finale just one day before the final stage into Paris.

It could have worked. The first four riders weren't separated by much time, so there could have been a battle royal on the infamous Ventoux, but instead a fierce headwind

backed the riders into each other. Even the best climber in
the world can't do much damage in that kind of headwind,
because it's too easy for the others to follow in those conditions. So even the Ventoux had its teeth pulled in 2009,
and the Tour de France hopefully learned that cliffhangers
either happen or they don't, but they can't be stage
managed.

The 2010 route is very different. It celebrates 100 years
of the Tour de France first climbing the big mountains with
a Pyrenean mountain-fest that looks extremely tough. The
Alps are no walkover either, so the climbers will be
rubbing their hands in anticipation. It's a Tour de France
for Alberto Contador or Andy Schleck, and if Schleck can't
improve on his time trialling, Contador will win.

That's quite a bold statement, but one that reflects their
known ability. There are unknowns in the 2010 Tour de
France, though. How good Lance Armstrong will be in his
second comeback year and whether Bradley Wiggins can
improve on fourth place are two of them.

The road will provide the answer, as it always does, but
that doesn't stop us having a good guess. Sean Yates knows
Armstrong, he knows cycling and he knows what it's like
to race when you are getting older. His pro career was a
long one, but when it was over he continued as an amateur
and even won a British open time trial title and a master's
world title. He still rides and competes as often as possible,
despite being 50 this year. 'I think Lance will be the same
as this year,' he told me recently. 'He'll be one year back,
which will see him improve, but he'll be one year older,
and that counts more. Every year you lose a bit of the top
end, the power you need for attacks in the mountains and
in the time trials. It showed as his weakness this year, and
Contador and Schleck know it now. They still need to

watch out, though, Lance will be dangerous, and if they let him dictate and ride his race they could be in trouble.'

The Wiggins question, though, is less easy to answer. His fourth place equals the best-ever Tour de France performance by a British racer, which was by Robert Millar in 1984. But Millar was a climber who was expected to do well in the Tour de France at some point in his career. Wiggins wasn't, until this year, but the climbing has always been there. 'If you can crank out 4,000 metres on the track in four and a quarter minutes, pedalling at 120 rpm … if you lose weight you are bound to go fast uphill. It's simple physics,' says Shane Sutton. Wiggins will also lead Team Sky, a British-based team whose mission statement is to provide a British winner of the Tour de France within five years from now. The team is backed by British Cycling, who it has to be said have achieved everything they've ever targeted. In that respect their Tour ambition looks good, but it will be a toughie. Will the British winner be Wiggins? I don't know, we'll be able to tell more in 2010. But if you are asking me for a name now, look out for a young rider called Peter Kennaugh.

So, while we are looking at the future, what does it hold for the Tour de France itself? Well, the immediate future looks good. The doping scandals from 1998 onwards threatened its very existence, and they went on until it was teetering on the very edge. A couple of years ago sponsors were pulling out and there was a general feeling within the sport that top-level pro road racing was in trouble. Now things might have changed. There wasn't a positive dope test during the 2009 Tour, and the ones that occurred in cycling that year were from the lower echelons of the sport; either young men impatient to get on, or old ones trying to hang on to a job.

In contrast to a couple of years ago sponsors seem happy and want to get involved with pro racing and the Tour because it represents good value for money. Cycling has done quite well in the current recession, so bike manufacturers are on the up, resulting in their being able to be the title sponsors of teams again, something that hasn't been possible since the fifties. As a green, low-cost means of transport, as well as a pastime, the future of cycling as a whole looks good. I expect more bike manufacturers to set up teams in the future.

For the rest of commerce the Tour is at a crossroads. Most team sponsors are European companies, but the Tour is increasingly a global event, and rumour has it that some world-renowned names are looking to get involved.

And the Tour itself? It will continue to adapt, develop and innovate, and it will continue to reflect the society in which we live. Foreign starts to the Tour are a regular feature, but for years there has been talk of starting the Tour on another continent. That will change the race slightly because recovery time will have to be built into the days after the start, but it will increase world interest, and the Tour likes world interest. Way back in the sixties it was said that Jacques Goddet never created a Tour that would help Raymond Poulidor because Jacques Anquetil was better known. And when Greg Lemond won the Tour they quickly dropped Perrier as the official race drink and signed with Coca-Cola.

But the Tour will guard against being packaged and too Americanised. At their heart the race directors have always been cyclists, or at least cycling fans. They know what cyclists and the fans want and have consistently delivered it. There will be problems and pressures in the future, but as long as the Tour gives its people what they want, spectacle, endeavour, courage and fighting spirit, the race should go on for at least another 100 extraordinary years. So long as it can find men mad enough to race it.

ACKNOWLEDGEMENTS

Thank you to Myles Archibald and everyone at HarperCollins who has worked on this book. To Steve Dobell for his sensitive but thorough editing. To my long-suffering wife Kath who has heard it all before but is still one of the two sounding boards I trust; the other is Luke Evans. And finally to everyone who has raced in the Tour de France, you provided the story.

INDEX